The Best 125 Vegetable Dishes

Susann Geiskopf-Hadler
and
Mindy Toomay

Prima Publishing
P.O. Box 1260BK
Rocklin, CA 95677
(916) 786-0426

Production by Tobi Giannone, Bookman Productions
Composition by Janet Hansen, Alphatype
Copyediting by Sandra Su
Interior design by Judith Levinson, Bookman Productions
Cover design by The Dunlavey Studio, Sacramento
Illustrations by Paul Page Design, Inc.
Cover illustration by Francis Livingston

Library of Congress Cataloging-in-Publication Data

Geiskopf-Hadler, Susann, 1950–
    The best 125 vegetable dishes / Susann Geiskopf-Hadler
and Mindy Toomay.
      p.   cm.
    Includes index.
    ISBN 1-55958-359-2
    1. Cookery (Vegetables)   I. Toomay, Mindy, 1951–
II. Title.   III. Title: Best one hundred twenty-five
vegetable dishes.
TX801.G43   1993
641.6'5—dc20   93-2504
                                   CIP

94 95 96 97 98 RRD 10 9 8 7 6 5 4 3 2 1

Printed in the United States of America

How to Order:
Single copies may be ordered from Prima Publishing, P.O. Box 1260BK, Rocklin, CA 95677; telephone (916) 786-0426. Quantity discounts are also available. On your letterhead, include information concerning the intended use of the books and the number of books you wish to purchase.

Contents

iii

Contents   *vii*

Almost Instant Recipes

Vegan Recipes

We dedicate this book, and all our food endeavors,
to our mothers
Jill Crampton Geiskopf (1919–1986)
Edith Cunningham Lackey (1918–1976)
whose cooking prowess made eating our vegetables
a real pleasure.

Acknowledgments

Thanks to our publishers, Ben and Nancy Dominitz, and to the capable Prima staff—particulary Jennifer Basye, Karen Blanco, Andi Reese Brady, and Jenn Nelson—for their enthusiastic support of our projects.

Lindy Dunlavey orchestrated another captivating cover using Francis Livingston's appetizing art. Thank you both.

The tried-and-true team at Bookman Productions, cheerfully led by Carol Dondrea and Tobi Giannone, made another tight production schedule work.

Even the children in our lives—notably, Cameron Davis and Lindsay and Natalie Geiskopf—gobbled up our vegetable experiments. Thanks, kids. And thanks to the long line of dependable grown-ups who feasted at our tables over the past few months and provided valuable feedback.

Thank you again, Guy and Tad, for being the best possible husbands for two busy cookbook authors.

Last, but certainly not least, thanks again to our faithful readers, who have made this cookbook series so successful.

Introduction

This book celebrates the flavors, colors, shapes, and textures of the delicious and diverse vegetable kingdom. We have enjoyed transforming these healthful gifts of nature into recipes that stimulate and satisfy the senses. And, as if sheer pleasure wasn't enough, vegetables are among the most nutritious of foods.

Today, fresh vegetables and fruits are considered essential for optimum health by such impressive organizations as the National Cancer Institute and the National Academy of Sciences. The Food Guide Pyramid, offered by the U.S. Department of Agriculture as the quintessential guide to a healthful diet tells us to eat plenty of vegetables—at least 3–5 servings a day.

So, the well-worn parental command to "eat your vegetables" is sound advice. Unfortunately, many insist their children eat the likes of canned peas and overcooked cauliflower. No wonder kids rebel and decide they don't like vegetables!

We invite you to discover for yourself the gastronomical pleasures of fresh produce. Sample our recipes with an open mind and we guarantee you will come to appreciate everything from artichokes to winter squash. Individual chapters showcase each vegetable's versatility. We encourage you to explore all the intriguing possibilities—from appetizers, soups, and side dishes to pizzas, pastas, and grilled dishes.

An ample selection of Almost Instant recipes will help even the busiest cooks fit fresh vegetables into every meal. In addition, the introductory material in each vegetable chapter offers historical highlights, nutritional and botanical data, a guide to selection and storage, as well as culinary tips.

Our advice is not simply to eat your vegetables, but to delight in them!

Stocking
the Pantry

Vegetables are versatile, lending themselves to many different types of preparation and combining well with a world of seasonings. Our recipes rely on distinctive ingredients and flavor enhancers—some commonplace, others more exotic—that we describe in this chapter. Keeping these items on hand in your pantry will make delicious vegetable cookery easy and convenient.

Grains and Pasta

Among the whole grains we most frequently use are bulgur wheat and various types of rice. Brown rice contains substantially more nutrients than polished white rice, and we usually prefer it. In addition to long-grain and short-grain brown rice, we often use an aromatic rice from India called basmati, which is sometimes sold as "aromatic rice." It is available for purchase virtually everywhere.

Another specialty rice we frequently use is the round-grain Italian type usually sold as "riso arborio." Its unique shape yields a superbly creamy cooked rice, making it suitable for risotto. Look for it at an Italian market or any gourmet food store.

Pasta is a grain derivative that appears on our tables frequently. It is a lowfat, high-fiber food that combines well with vegetables and many different kinds of seasoning. Most grocery stores now carry a wide variety of pasta shapes and flavors.

A cool pantry or cupboard is the best place to store grains and pasta. Heat and humidity can cause grains to rot or ferment. Stored in airtight containers away from light and heat sources, grains can be kept indefinitely. Check occasionally for signs of food pest infestation; discard any grains that are suspect, and wash containers and cupboard shelves with hot, soapy water.

Dried Beans and Peas

Dried beans and peas (also known as legumes) are wonderfully nutritious, delicious, and economical. With a little advance planning, it is easy to cook dried beans at home. Cook more than you need for a particular recipe and freeze the remainder for use at a later time.

When time is short, you may substitute canned beans for fresh-cooked ones. Be aware, however, that salt, sugar, and various preservatives are often present in canned beans, sometimes in large quantities. Be sure to read the labels, and choose beans without these added ingredients when possible. If they contain unwanted additives, drain and rinse canned beans thoroughly before using them in a recipe.

Tofu, Tempeh, and Miso

Tofu and tempeh, both derivatives of the soybean, are excellent sources of concentrated protein. Miso, another soybean derivative, is a rich, salty paste than can enhance meatless soups and sauces with its hearty flavor.

Tofu is made from soy milk curds and is available in a variety of textures, from silky smooth to coarse and firm. It tastes quite bland on its own and depends on creative seasoning. Because it soaks up flavors so well, however, it is a delicious addition to many types of dishes. Tofu can be sliced, diced, crumbled, mashed, or pureed. For most purposes, it is rinsed and blotted dry before using. Fresh tofu keeps for a week or so if stored in fresh water in the refrigerator. The water should be changed every day.

Tempeh is a unique fermented soybean product with a meaty texture and nutty flavor. The refrigerator life of fresh tempeh is only a few days, so buy it just before you intend to use it, or you may freeze it for long storage.

Miso is sold in tubs or airtight plastic wrappers. It will keep for months in your refrigerator in a tightly closed container. Different colors are available—generally speaking, the lighter the miso, the milder its flavor.

Tofu, tempeh, and miso may be purchased at any natural foods store or Asian specialty market. In many parts of the country, tofu is even available in standard supermarkets.

Fruits and Fruit Juices

Fresh fruits are packed with vitamins and minerals and are a good source of carbohydrates and dietary fiber. They are low in calories and sodium and are practically fat-free. Fruits can provide distinctive flavor notes, ranging from sweet to tart.

We use citrus juices frequently in our recipes, and we recommend fresh-squeezed juices in all cases. All citrus fruits are readily available; it takes only a moment to squeeze a small amount of fresh juice, and the flavors and nutritional benefits are far superior to those of frozen or bottled varieties.

Dairy Products

Whole milk derives almost half its calories from saturated fat, and most cheeses contain abundant fat and sodium. When we do use milk, yogurt, sour cream, or cheese, we prefer varieties that are lowfat, light, nonfat, or part-skim to satisfy our health concerns.

Goat and sheep milk cheeses, such as crumbly feta and soft chevre, have a unique piquant flavor that we enjoy in Mediterranean-inspired recipes. The French variety of feta is milder in flavor and lower in fat and sodium than its Greek counterpart. Specialty markets carry it, as do many supermarkets.

Sometimes we use butter, always in small amounts, when its flavor seems right for a particular dish. We prefer the unsalted variety for its purity and sweetness. We do not recommend substituting margarine for butter because of the health concerns associated with the hydrogenation process used to harden liquid oils into solid form.

Oils, Nuts, and Seeds

Olive oil and canola oil, both low in saturated fat and cholesterol-free, are our preferences for cooking when oil is called for. Extra virgin olive oil has a robust olive aroma and flavor. The flavor of canola oil is lighter, almost bland, so it won't overpower a delicately flavored dish. We also use both light and dark sesame oils occasionally, particularly in Asian-inspired dishes. The dark variety is pressed from toasted sesame seeds. Its smoky flavor is absolutely unique and quite delicious. Where it is called for in our recipes, there is no suitable substitute.

Nuts and seeds are high in fat, so we use them sparingly and we usually toast them to make the most of their rich flavor. We almost always call for fresh, raw, unsalted nuts and seeds, and nut butters made without additives like sugar or salt.

Seasonings

A cupboard well-stocked with dried herbs and spices and other lowfat flavor enhancers is a treasure trove for creative cooks. Seasonings add very little fat or calories but provide abundant flavor. The herbs and spices most frequently used in our recipes include: (1) dried basil, dill, oregano, rosemary, sage, tarragon, thyme, bay leaves, and saffron; (2) whole nutmeg, coriander, and anise, to be ground just before using; (3) commercially ground cinnamon, cumin, chili powder, paprika, curry blends, and peppers; and (4) whole mustard, celery, cumin, and dill seeds.

Dried herbs and spices do lose their potency, so buy them in small quantities. Natural food stores often sell them in bulk, enabling you to buy as much or as little as you like. Store dried herbs and spices in dated airtight containers, and discard and replace them after about a year.

Some of our recipes call for the brighter flavors of fresh herbs. Herbs are easy to grow in even a small garden space, or you can find a good selection at well-stocked produce markets. Though the results won't be quite the same, dried herbs can sometimes be substituted when fresh ones are called for in our recipes. Use half as much dried as you would fresh. Dried rosemary, oregano, tarragon, and dill are acceptable alternatives when fresh is not available. Parsley and cilantro should always be used fresh since the dried varieties tend to be flavorless.

Wines and Spirits

In moderation, fermented grape and grain beverages have a place in our diets. We find many culinary uses for dry sherry, vermouth, port, and brandy, as well as red and white wines and, occasionally, beer. The Japanese rice wine called sake, and mirin, its sweet wine counterpart, show up in a number of our Asian dishes. They are available at Asian specialty food shops and some well-stocked supermarkets.

Wines and spirits add interesting flavors without adding fat. In every case, the amounts used are small, so the quantity of alcohol in each serving is negligible. Because the flavors of these wines and spirits are essential to certain dishes, we suggest that those who object to their use simply bypass the recipes containing them.

Thickening Agents

Butter and flour are the classic thickeners for dairy-based sauces, and we occasionally use this type of white sauce in our vegetable dishes. However, to create sauces for sautés and stir-fried dishes, our preferred thickener is arrowroot powder, the ground dried root of a starchy tropical tuber. It is dissolved in a little cold water, then stirred or whisked into hot liquid. Cornstarch is interchangeable with arrowroot powder in our recipes. We prefer arrowroot because it is a less highly processed food. Arrowroot powder is available (sometimes sold as arrowroot flour) in natural food stores and well-stocked supermarkets.

Vegetables

Different selection and storage techniques apply to different vegetables; consult the individual vegetable chapters for detailed information.

Organic Produce

We recommend seeking out vegetables that are organically grown to avoid pesticide ingestion and to protect the environment. Organic foods are farmed without synthetic chemicals, so they work with, not against, nature. Until fifty years ago, farmers didn't depend on chemical fertilization and pest control. Today, widespread awareness about the negative health and environmental consequences of chemical use is bringing the world's farmers back to organic methods. When we buy organic foods, our dollars represent a vote for healthy and environmentally sound alternatives to chemically dependent farming methods.

When we consider the hidden price of chemically dependent farming in terms of potential medical care and chemical cleanup costs, organic produce seems a bargain, despite its sometimes higher cost at the market. Organic produce prices today reflect the cost of the government certification system, including the time-intensive documentatation farmers must provide.

In addition, producers, distributors, and retailers of organic products tend to be smaller, so high-volume price discounts are not yet available for most foods. As the organic industry comprises a greater and greater market share, cost will go down. Today, about 2 percent of the United States' food supply is grown using organic methods and the market for organic foods appears to be growing at a rate of about 35 percent a year.

On a personal health level, there are many reasons why organic produce is preferable. It probably provides more vitamins and minerals than conventionally grown produce, since you don't have to peel it to get rid of wax or chemical residues that may be present in the skin. Furthermore, organic produce in the market tends to be fresher and therefore more nutritious because it's grown mostly by local farmers close to the point of sale and doesn't require long storage or shipping. In addition, organic growers tend to choose varieties for cultivation based on good taste, color, and texture, rather than on how they respond to shipping and chemicals.

Vegetable Exotica

We discuss below some of the unusual vegetables that are used as ingredients in our recipes but that are not showcased in individual chapters.

Fennel   Fresh fennel looks similar to celery, with numerous stalks attached at their bases in overlapping layers to form a thick bulb. Its foliage, however, is feathery and the bulb is paler in color and more enlarged than that of a bunch of celery. Botanically, fennel is related to parsley, and it has a pronounced licorice flavor that is unique and delicious. It is prominently featured in traditional Italian cuisine. Though the leaves and stalks are edible, it is the bulb portion that is sliced and used as a vegetable in our recipes.

The fennel season peaks in fall and winter, but fennel is available year-round in some regions. Look for bulbs that have straight stalks protruding from a plump, tightly closed base. Wrap fennel in plastic and store in the vegetable crisper, where the bulb will stay fresh for a few days.

Jicama   Jicama is a round tuber with tan to brown skin and crisp, white flesh similar in texture to that of a water chestnut or crisp apple. In our recipes, it is peeled and added raw to dishes when a crunchy, slightly sweet counterpoint to other ingredients is desired. It is used extensively in Mexican cookery and com-bines well with Tex-Mex seasonings such as chili powder and lime juice.

Jicama tubers can range in weight from about a half pound to several pounds—the larger ones will have a thicker skin, but the flesh will be unaffected. Look for tubers that are unblemished and heavy, with no soft spots. Store jicama loosely wrapped in plastic in the vegetable crisper, where it will retain its freshness for several days.

Radicchio   A member of the chicory family, radicchio adds a unique, mildly bitter accent to salads and other dishes. Though different colors are cultivated worldwide, the most common variety in American markets is mottled purple and white.

Shop for small, crisp-looking leaves forming a loose, cabbagelike head. Color should be robust and glossy, with no brown spots. Wilted, tired-looking heads are too old. Wrap radicchio loosely in a plastic bag and store it in the refrigerator crisper. Wash the leaves and spin them dry just before using.

Shallots   Shallots—closely related to onions, garlic, leeks, and other alliums—are mild and aromatic. Their delicate, piquant taste is suitable for subtly flavored dishes and those combining fruits and vegetables.

The shallot has papery, brown skin similar to an onion's. However, its shape resembles that of a large clove of garlic or a tulip bulb. Choose shallots that are dry and firm and purchase them in small quantities. Store them in a well-ventilated, dry place and use them as soon as possible, as they tend to sprout and spoil more quickly than onions or garlic.

Tomatillos   Translated from Spanish, tomatillo means "little tomato." It is a variety of green husk tomato similar in size to a cherry tomato and wrapped in a loose, tan, papery covering which is removed before cooking. Tomatillos have a unique tart taste that provides an authentic accent in Latin-inspired dishes.

Choose fresh tomatillos that are hard when gently squeezed. The brown husk should be dry and unblemished. They store well, staying fresh for up to a few weeks when refrigerated in a paper bag. Look for fresh tomatillos in Mexican specialty food stores, or purchase them canned, packed in water, at well-stocked supermarkets.

Frequently Used Homemade Ingredients

When our recipes call for such ingredients as pesto or chutney, you may purchase commercial varieties. For optimum quality, however, make your own. It's easier than you think to keep homemade convenience foods on hand.

Bread Crumbs and Cubes

If you have a partial loaf of bread that has dried in the bin, simply whirl it in a food processor to either coarse or fine crumb consistency. It is sometimes useful to have seasoned bread crumbs on hand. Mix dried herbs and granulated garlic into the crumbs before storing.

You can also prepare dried bread crumbs from fresh bread. Preheat the oven to 350 degrees F. Use your hands to crumble bread onto a dry baking sheet. Place in the oven for 15 minutes, then turn off the heat and allow the crumbs to continue drying for about half an hour. Where recipes call for bread cubes, simply cut fresh bread into the desired size and proceed with baking as described above. Dried bread crumbs and cubes will keep for long periods in a dry place in an airtight container.

Salsa Fresca

Yield: 5 cups

Fresh tomatoes	2½	pounds
Canned whole green chilies	1	7-ounce can
Fresh-squeezed lemon juice	¼	cup
Onion	1	medium, finely diced
Fresh cilantro, minced	⅓	cup
Garlic	3	cloves, minced
Salt	⅛	teaspoon
Pepper		A few grinds

Blanch and peel the tomatoes. Coarsely chop them, drain off as much juice as possible, and set aside in a bowl. Drain the liquid from the canned green chilies. Finely chop them and add to the tomatoes. Add the lemon juice to the tomato mixture, along with the onion, cilantro, garlic, salt, and pepper.

Though its flavor improves over time, this salsa can also be enjoyed immediately. Store the portion you don't need right away in a tightly closed container in the refrigerator for several days, or freeze for longer periods. If you are accustomed to canning foods, this recipe may be made in larger quantities and put up for the pantry.

Each ¼ cup provides:

18	Calories	4 g	Carbohydrate
1 g	Protein	79 mg	Sodium
0 g	Fat	0 mg	Cholesterol
1 g	Dietary Fiber		

Homemade Vegetable Stock

Vegetable stock is quick and simple to prepare at home and far sur-
passes in richness the instant varieties, so please try this recipe and
always keep some on hand. (In a pinch, you may use vegetable broth
cubes as directed in our recipes that call for stock.) Every batch of
stock is different, because it's made from what you have on hand.
Here is a basic recipe—some more elaborate versions call for butter
and fresh herbs or other special seasonings, but we think this uncom-
plicated one may be the best and most versatile. Experiment and dis-
cover the variety of flavors that can be achieved with different
vegetable and herb combinations.

Include mushrooms among the chopped vegetables, if possible,
because they add richness to a stock. This is a great way to use the
shriveled ones that have been in your refrigerator too long. Use no
more than about a cup of cruciferous vegetables (the cabbage family,
including broccoli and cauliflower), as their strong flavors and aro-
mas may take over the stock. Good combinations of vegetables in-
clude asparagus stalks, carrots, green beans, summer squash, and
leafy greens. If you have leftover mushroom soaking liquid, vegetable
steaming liquid, or tomato juice from canned tomatoes, include it in
the stockpot in place of an equivalent amount of water.

Experiment with different combinations of herbs, but for the
most versatile stock, don't use more than ½ teaspoon of any single
herb, or its flavor may predominate. Good herbs to choose from are
basil, marjoram, dill, tarragon, chervil, rosemary, oregano, and
thyme.

Nutritional data not available due to wide range of possible
ingredients.

Yield: about 6 cups

Cold water	8	cups
Onion	1	medium, diced
Russet potato, unpeeled	1	medium, diced
Fresh vegetables, chopped	3	cups
Dried herbs	2	teaspoons
Bay leaves	1 or 2	
Salt	¼	teaspoon
Dried red chili flakes	⅛	teaspoon

Combine everything in a stockpot and bring to a boil over high heat. Reduce heat to low, cover, and simmer 30 minutes. Turn off the heat and allow to sit for 10 minutes before straining into glass jars. Store in the refrigerator for several days or freeze for longer periods.

Basil Pesto

Yield: 1 cup

Fresh basil leaves	**2**	**cups, firmly packed**
Olive oil	**⅓**	**cup**
Pine nuts	**¼**	**cup**
Garlic	**6**	**cloves, chopped**
Parmesan cheese, finely grated	**¾**	**cup**

Wash the basil, discard the stems, and dry thoroughly. In a food processor or blender, puree basil with ¼ cup of the olive oil, the pine nuts, garlic, and Parmesan until thick and homogenous. With the machine running, add the remaining olive oil in a thin stream to form a smooth paste.

Note: If you are harvesting basil from the garden at season's end, a few simple tips will facilitate cleaning the leaves. Use your clippers to snip off the main stems near the base of the plant, rather than pulling the plants up by the roots. Put a spray attachment on your hose and wash down the harvested branches of basil before bringing them into the kitchen.

Each tablespoon provides:

78	Calories	3 g	Carbohydrate
3 g	Protein	71 mg	Sodium
7 g	Fat	3 mg	Cholesterol
0 g	Dietary Fiber		

Rosemary Pesto

Yield: 1 cup

Fresh parsley	1½	**cups, firmly packed**
Fresh rosemary leaves*	½	**cup, loosely packed**
Garlic	6	**cloves, chopped**
Olive oil	½	**cup**
Parmesan cheese, finely grated	½	**cup**
Dried red chili flakes	¼	**teaspoon**
Raw unsalted walnuts, chopped	¼	**cup**

Wash the parsley and rosemary, discard the stems, and spin dry. In a food processor or blender, puree herbs, garlic, and ¼ cup of the olive oil until thick and homogenous. Add the Parmesan, chili flakes, and walnuts, and blend again. With the machine running, add the remaining olive oil in a thin stream. A thick, rich paste will result.

*We use a flat-leaf rosemary variety which has a more flowery taste and finer texture than the common needle-shaped type. Either will work, however.

Each tablespoon provides:

89	Calories	2 g	Carbohydrate
2 g	Protein	50 mg	Sodium
9 g	Fat	2 mg	Cholesterol
0 g	Dietary Fiber		

Pizza Crust

Yield: one 12-inch pizza

Lowfat milk	¼	cup plus 2 tablespoons
Active dry yeast	1¼	teaspoons
Granulated sugar		A scant pinch
Olive oil	1	tablespoon plus 2 teaspoons
Salt	¼	teaspoon
Fine cornmeal	2	tablespoons
Whole wheat pastry flour	¾	cup

Barely warm the lowfat milk—it should be body temperature or a little warmer. Combine the yeast and sugar with the warmed milk and stir to dissolve the yeast. Stir in 1 tablespoon of the olive oil and the salt, then the cornmeal. Add the pastry flour a few tablespoons at a time, stirring after each addition. The amount of flour stipulated is really only an estimate; the key is to add only enough flour to keep the dough from sticking to the bowl. It should be moist and soft. Turn it out onto a lightly floured surface and knead for 5 minutes.

Oil a large bowl with the remaining olive oil. Form the dough into a ball and place it in the bowl, turning once so its entire surface is coated with oil. Drape a tea towel over the bowl and set in a warm place to rise for about 40 minutes. The dough is ready when it has about doubled in size.

On a floured surface, roll the dough ball out, shaping it into a ⅛-inch-thick circle, slightly fatter at the edge. You may pull and stretch the dough with your hands to achieve the desired shape, but be gentle. Set the pizza on a baking pan—round ones are available for just this purpose. (If you get really serious about pizza baking, you will eventually want to invest in a pizza stone.) Top the crust and bake on the top rack in a preheated oven as specified in individual recipes.

Each crust provides:

622	Calories	85 g	Carbohydrate
19 g	Protein	594 mg	Sodium
26 g	Fat	4 mg	Cholesterol
14 g	Dietary Fiber		

Mango Chutney

Yield: 4 half-pints

Orange	1	medium
Apples	3	medium
Mangoes	2	medium
Lemon	1	medium
Onion	1	medium
Honey	1	cup
Cider vinegar	1	cup
Water	1	cup
Fresh ginger, finely chopped	2	tablespoons
Dried red chili flakes	1	teaspoon
Whole peppercorns	1	teaspoon
Ground allspice	1	teaspoon
Mustard seed	1	teaspoon
Whole cloves	1	teaspoon
Celery seed	1	teaspoon
Raisins	¾	cup

Chop the fruits and onion into small pieces. Combine with honey, vinegar, and water in a large saucepan or stockpot. Tie the ginger and dried spices in a square of cheesecloth and add to the pot. Bring to a boil over high heat, reduce heat to medium, and simmer 20 minutes, stirring occasionally. Add the raisins and continue to cook until thick, about 20 to 30 minutes longer, stirring frequently to prevent scorching. Remove spice bag. Spoon into half-pint jars, seal tightly, and store in the refrigerator for several weeks, or follow standard canning procedures and put up for the pantry.

Each tablespoon provides:

33	Calories	9 g	Carbohydrate
0 g	Protein	1 mg	Sodium
0 g	Fat	0 mg	Cholesterol
0 g	Dietary Fiber		

Fermented Black Bean Sauce

Yield: ¾ cup

Fermented black beans	½	**cup**
Low-sodium soy sauce	2	**tablespoons**
Water	2	**tablespoons**
Mirin	3	**tablespoons**
Canola oil	1	**tablespoon**
Brown sugar	1	**tablespoon**
Garlic	3	**cloves, minced**

Place all ingredients in a food processor or blender and puree until smooth. Place in a small jar and refrigerate until needed. It will stay fresh for several weeks.

Each tablespoon provides:

36	Calories	4 g	Carbohydrate
1 g	Protein	391 mg	Sodium
2 g	Fat	0 mg	Cholesterol
0 g	Dietary Fiber		

Nutrition Alert

People who are concerned about nutrition balance their food intake based on factors beyond the outmoded "five basic food groups" concept. In 1992, the U.S. Department of Agriculture (USDA) released the Food Guide Pyramid, presenting the food groups with a new and different emphasis. At the base of the pyramid are the foods from which we should get most of our calories. At the tip are the foods that should supply us with the fewest calories. (To order a brochure that depicts the Food Guide Pyramid and discusses the concept in detail, order Home and Garden Bulletin #252 from USDA, Human Nutrition Information Service, 6505 Belcrest Road, Hyattsville, MD 20782.)

The basic message of the pyramid is to cut down on fats and added sugars, as well as to eat a variety of foods from the different food groups. Our chief eating goals, says the USDA, should be variety, moderation, and balance. It is the overall picture that counts—what you eat over a period of days is more important than what you eat in a single meal. A diet primarily comprised of grains and cereal products (six to eleven servings per day), vegetables (three to five servings per day), and fruits (two to four servings per day), combined with lowfat protein sources (two to three servings per day) and lowfat dairy products (two to three servings per day) conforms to the Food Guide Pyramid, creating a well-balanced mix of proteins, carbohydrates, and fats.

For some people, three to five servings of vegetables will sound like a lot, but serving sizes stipulated by the Food Guide Pyramid are moderate. A cup of leafy raw vegetables (as in a salad), a half cup of chopped raw or cooked vegetables, three-quarters of a cup of vegetable juice, or a quarter cup of dried fruit equals one serving. There is no need to measure—the serving sizes are only a guideline. Furthermore, a single dish may supply servings in more than one category: for example, a sandwich may provide a grain serving (the bread), a dairy serving (the lowfat cheese), and a vegetable serving (the lettuce, sprouts, and tomato).

The nutritional experts who designed the Food Guide Pyramid recommend eating a variety of vegetables to be sure we are getting all the nutritional benefits this vast family of foods can provide. They also recommend making sure that at least one serving each day is high in vitamin A, at least one each day is high in vitamin C, at least one each day is high in fiber, and that we eat cruciferous vegetables several times each week.

Vitamins A, C, and E are particularly important because they function in the body as antioxidants. Antioxidants are a class of nutrients that can help to stabilize and neutralize free radicals. A free radical is an unstable oxygen molecule that can cause cell damage over time, increasing the body's vulnerability to serious illness, including cardiovascular disease and cancer.

Vitamin A is present in animal products or can be manufactured as needed by the body from the beta carotene in vegetables that are dark green (i.e., leafy greens and broccoli) or orange-yellow (i.e., sweet potatoes). Vitamin C is present in varying quantities in most fruits and vegetables—the best sources include citrus fruits, strawberries, tomatoes, broccoli, leafy greens, and sweet potatoes. Vitamin E occurs naturally in most vegetable oils, wheat germ, corn, nuts, olives, and many green vegetables.

Vegetables High in Vitamin A

Bok choy	Swiss chard
Carrots	Tomatoes
Spinach	Winter squash
Sweet potatoes	

Vegetables High in Vitamin C

Asparagus	Green onions
Bell peppers	Potatoes
Bok choy	Snow peas
Broccoli	Spinach
Brussels sprouts	Summer squash
Cabbage	Sweet potatoes
Cauliflower	Tomatoes
Chili peppers	

Studies have shown that antioxidants help protect us against the development of coronary heart disease and cancer, and may even slow down the aging process. Cruciferous vegetables contain considerable quantities of antioxidants, as well as beneficial nitrogen compounds called indoles, which have been shown in recent studies to be effective cancer preventers.

The Surgeon General and the American Heart Association are proponents of what is described as a "semi-vegetarian" approach to eating, which is based primarily on grains, vegetables, and fruits. The Food Guide Pyramid and other expert recommendations support semi-vegetarianism as an important aspect of a healthy lifestyle. The major shift for many Americans is to view meat, if it is to be consumed at all, as a side dish or condiment.

Many studies are being conducted to determine optimum levels of various food components in the human diet. Our intent here is to provide an introduction to basic nutrition. For further investigation, check with your local librarian or bookseller for thorough reference works.

The recipes in this book have been analyzed for calories, fat, dietary fiber, protein, carbohydrate, cholesterol, and sodium. We discuss below the importance of each of these components.

Calories

It is important to be aware of your total caloric intake in a day but most important to note is where the calories are coming from. Calories derive from three primary sources: protein, carbohydrates, and fats. Fats contain a greater concentration of calories than do carbohydrates or protein, and they are much harder for the body to metabolize. The U.S. Food and Drug Administration therefore suggests that the average American diet should be adjusted so that fewer calories come from fatty foods and more from carbohydrates. They specifically recommend that no more than 30 percent of the calories in our overall diets be derived from fat.

Fat

Our bodies need some fat, as it is an essential component in energy production, but it is estimated that most of us consume six to eight times more fat than we need. High-fat diets are implicated not only in heart disease, but also in the development of some cancers, most notably of the colon and breast. It is likely to contribute to a healthier—perhaps even longer—life to learn the basics about dietary fat.

There are nine calories in a gram of fat. A gram of protein or carbohydrate contains only four calories. Obviously, therefore, the less fat one consumes, the lower one's intake of calories and the lower one's ratio of calories from fat. Calories derived from dietary fats are more troublesome than calories from any other source, as the body is most efficient at converting fat calories into body fat.

Consider that the average tablespoon of oil contains fourteen grams of fat and 120 calories, while almost no fat is contained in a half cup of steamed brown rice (206 calories) or a cup of cooked broccoli (44 calories). This illustrates the volume of food that can be eaten without increasing one's fat-to-calories ratio.

One simple way of monitoring one's fat intake is by counting fat grams consumed. In the nutritional analyses provided with each of our recipes, fat is listed in total grams per serving to facilitate this. An easy way to calculate how much fat you should consume is to divide your body weight in half. This number is an estimate of the maximum fat in grams a moderately active person should ingest over the course of a day to maintain that weight.

Fats are divided into three categories: monounsaturated, polyunsaturated, and saturated. The term *saturation* refers to the number of hydrogen atoms present in the fat, with saturated fats containing the most.

The primary reason to pay attention to the saturation level of fats is because diets high in saturated fats increase levels of blood cholesterol in some people—a risk factor in heart disease. Not only do monounsaturated and polyunsaturated fats not harm our hearts, they actually appear to help reduce cholesterol levels in the blood when eaten in moderation as part of an overall lowfat diet.

Therefore, it is wise to choose foods higher in polyunsaturated or monounsaturated fats than in saturated fats. To assist in making this determination, remember that most saturated fats are from animal origin and are hard at room temperature (such as butter and cheese) and most unsaturated fats are of vegetable origin and are liquid at room temperature (such as olive and canola oils).

Fiber

Dietary fiber—also called roughage—is the material from plant foods that cannot be completely digested by humans. It provides the bulk necessary to keep the digestive and eliminative systems functioning properly. Foods high in fiber also tend to be high in beta-carotene, low in fat, and filling enough to reduce our dependence on higher-fat foods.

In recent years, evidence that dietary fiber promotes human health has mounted. Studies have linked high fiber intake with reduced risk of constipation; diverticulosis; colon, rectal, and breast cancer; heart disease; diabetes; and obesity. Because high-fiber diets tend to be low in fat and high in other health-promoting substances, it is difficult to prove the specific protective effects of fiber. However, the connection is compelling and studies are ongoing.

Many doctors now recommend adding fiber to the diet for optimum health. Even such slow-to-change organizations as the USDA and the National Cancer Institute (NCI) have recently made increased fiber consumption part of their standard recommendations for a healthy diet.

NCI recommends that we eat between twenty and thirty grams of fiber daily, but that our consumption not exceed thirty-five grams per day. Experts estimate that most Americans now eat only about half of the recommended amount. A recent national food survey showed that diets including five servings of fruits and vegetables daily—as recommended in the Food Guide Pyramid—provided about seventeen grams of fiber.

When whole grains and legumes are included in the daily diet, it's easy to reach the recommended level.

Experts agree that fiber should come from foods rather than supplements that provide no nutrients. Ways to consume more fiber—along with valuable vitamins, minerals, and amino acids—include choosing whole-grain rather than refined-flour products, not peeling fruits and vegetables, and eating dried peas and beans.

It is especially important for people on high-fiber diets to drink plenty of water, or the fiber can slow down or block healthy bowel functioning. Eating too much fiber can cause gastrointestinal distress in people unaccustomed to it, so fiber content should be increased gradually.

The term *dietary fiber* encompasses both soluble and insoluble types. The dietary fiber value included in our nutritional analyses includes both types.

Vegetables High in Fiber

Artichokes	Corn
Broccoli	Green beans
Brussels sprouts	Onions
Cabbage	Peas
Carrots	Potatoes
Cauliflower	Spinach

Protein

Since our bodies store only small amounts of protein, it needs to be replenished on a daily basis. However, though protein is needed for growth and tissue repair, it is not needed in great abundance. The National Academy of Science's Food and Nutrition Board recommends forty-five grams of protein per day for the average 120-pound woman and fifty-five grams for the average 154-pound man. Some nutritionists think this is more protein than needed on average, however. Recent nutritional studies suggest, in fact, that the detrimental effects of excessive protein consumption should be of greater concern to most Americans than the threat of protein deficiency. While this debate continues, it makes sense to choose protein sources that are low in fat and, thus, calories.

Most people associate protein consumption with eating meat; however, the protein in our recipes derives from combining grains with legumes and dairy products and is quite sufficient to meet the body's protein needs.

Carbohydrates

There is a common misconception that carbohydrates such as pasta, grains, and potatoes are high in calories and low in nutritive value. However, starchy complex carbohydrates do not present a calorie problem; the problem is typically with the fats that are added to them. Complex carbohydrates are actually low in fat and are a good source of fiber.

Nutritional experts now suggest that more of our daily calories come from carbohydrates than from fats or protein, since the body provides energy more economically from carbohydrates. Carbohydrates are quickly converted into glucose, the body's main fuel.

Cholesterol

Many volumes have been written on cholesterol in recent years, and much is being discovered about its role in overall health and nutrition. Cholesterol is essential for cell wall construction, the transmission of nerve impulses, and the synthesis of important hormones. It plays a vital role in the healthy functioning of the body and poses no problem when present in the correct amount. However, in excess, cholesterol is a major risk factor in the development of heart disease. The U.S. Senate Select Committee on Nutrition and Human Needs recommends that the average person consume no more than 300 milligrams of cholesterol per day. Have your cholesterol level checked by your doctor and follow his or her specific guidelines.

Recent studies have shown that the total amount of fat a person eats—especially saturated fat—may be more responsible for the cholesterol level in the body than the actual cholesterol count found in food.

Current evidence suggests that a high-fiber diet low in overall fat can improve cholesterol levels, particularly the harmful type called LDL. Vegetables are certainly major players in such a diet.

Sodium

The American Heart Association recommends that sodium intake be limited to 3,000 milligrams per day (a teaspoon of salt contains 2,200 milligrams of sodium). However, the actual physiological requirement is only about 220 milligrams a day.

Sodium, like other food components that we ingest, plays an important role in the functioning of the body. It is essential for good health, since each cell of the body must be bathed continually in a saline solution. High sodium intake, however, disrupts this balance and is associated with high blood pressure and such life-threatening conditions as heart and kidney disease and strokes.

Many foods naturally contain some sodium, so you do not need to add much when cooking to achieve good flavor. Particularly if you have salt-related health concerns, dishes that taste a little bland unsalted can be seasoned with herbs or other salt-free alternatives. When our recipes call for salt, you may add less than the recommended amount, or none at all, if your doctor has drastically reduced your sodium intake.

Monitoring your intake of the preceding food components is important; however, unless you're under a doctor's instructions, you needn't be overly rigid. It is preferable to balance your intake over the course of a day, or even several days, rather than attempt to make each meal fit the pattern recommended by nutritional experts. This rule of thumb allows you to enjoy a recipe that may be higher in fat or salt, for instance, than you would normally choose, knowing that at your next meal you can eliminate that component altogether to achieve a healthy daily balance.

The information given here is not set in stone; the science of nutrition is constantly evolving. The analyses for our recipes is provided for people on normal diets who want to plan healthier meals. If your physician has prescribed a special diet, check with a registered dietician to see how these recipes fit into your guidelines.

We encourage you to spend some time learning about how foods break down and are used by the body as fuel. A basic understanding of the process and application of a few simple rules can contribute to a longer and—more important—a healthier life.

Seven Simple Guidelines for a Healthy Diet

(from National Cancer Institute, U.S. Department of Health and Human Services)

1. Eat a variety of foods
2. Maintain a desirable weight
3. Avoid too much fat, saturated fat, and cholesterol
4. Eat foods with adequate starch and fiber
5. Avoid excessive sugar
6. Avoid excessive sodium
7. If you drink alcoholic beverages, do so in moderation

Artichokes

The exotic-looking globe artichoke is the unopened flower bud of a thistlelike plant called *Cynara scolymus*, a relative of the common daisy. Overlapping leaves appear on the outside, encasing the sought-after tender center. This fleshy center portion is commonly called the heart; more accurately, it is the bottom or base of the artichoke flower. As if Mother Nature were protecting her favorite morsel, this base is covered with *choke*, fuzzy fibers that must be removed to get at the delicious prize. The tidbits sold as "marinated artichoke hearts" are actually made from tiny whole artichokes in which the choke has not yet developed.

The artichoke is mentioned in early Roman works, and historians tell us it was cultivated widely in fifteenth-century Florence. The Italians still love this succulent thistle—Italy,

France, and Spain continue to be the leading growers and consumers of artichokes. The plant came to the Americas with European immigrants who settled in Louisiana in the nineteenth century. Today, most of the domestic crop is grown in the cool, moist climate of the Central Coast region of California.

A few dozen varieties of artichoke exist, but Green Globe is the most common commercial cultivar in the United States. Many European artichoke varieties have a purplish or reddish hue, and are more conical in shape, but these are a rare find in American markets.

Small specimens often sold as baby artichokes are not less mature, they are simply the smaller buds that develop near the base of the plant. Large buds form on the main stalk and medium ones on the side branches.

By the way, Jerusalem artichokes (*Helianthus tuberosus*)—also called sunchokes—are not artichokes at all, but a nutritious edible tuber related to the sunflower. They are particularly notable for their iron content, delivering nearly as much as animal products.

The Nutrition Picture

Artichokes are a rich vegetable source of vitamin C, fiber, calcium, magnesium, niacin, phosphorus, and potassium. Though fat-free, artichokes are higher in calories and sodium than most vegetables—still, a medium artichoke contains only fifty calories and eighty milligrams of sodium.

Selection and Storage

The peak season for artichokes, during which price and quality will be most attractive, is March through May. A secondary crop appears in the markets in October.

The type of dish you are preparing will determine the size of artichoke you should select—large ones are best for stuffing, medium ones for eating with dips, and small ones for marinating or stewing. Plan on one medium artichoke per person as a side dish, or one large one stuffed as a main dish.

Whatever their size, artichokes should feel fleshy and heavy. They should have a compact appearance with leaves tightly closed. Though bronzing or a whitish outer surface is normal in the fall crop (a condition known as *winter kissed*), a uniform green surface is a sign of good quality in the spring and summer seasons. Purplish streaks are not a problem.

Avoid dry or woody artichokes and those with leaves that appear loose or open. Pass over artichokes with dark, bruised spots, or with tiny holes in the stem or base—these usually indicate worm damage that may have penetrated the edible parts. Plump and succulent artichokes will squeak slightly when gently squeezed—this is another good test of freshness. Also, when artichokes are at their freshest, the bottom outer leaves will break off with a crisp snap.

Sprinkle whole, fresh artichokes lightly with water and store them in the refrigerator in a closed plastic bag. Don't rinse or trim artichokes before refrigerating. Cooked artichokes may be stored wrapped in plastic or in a covered glass dish in the refrigerator for a few days.

If you don't enjoy the ceremony of eating whole artichokes (see "Culinary Tips" below), you may purchase artichoke bottoms and hearts in cans. Water-packed varieties are available, in addition to the ones packed in jars with marinade. Because preparing a quantity of artichoke bottoms from fresh globe artichokes is rather laborious, we keep the canned, water-packed variety on hand. They are suitable for many raw and cooked uses. Frozen artichoke hearts are also sometimes available.

Culinary Tips

- Use stainless steel or enameled cast-iron vessels and stainless steel utensils when cooking artichokes since metals such as aluminum, iron, and carbon steel will cause blackening and affect the flavor.

- To cook whole artichokes, use a sharp knife to trim off most of the stem and about ½ inch of the pointy end of the leaves. If there are small, tough leaves around the base of the artichoke, remove and discard them. Vigorously swirl the artichokes in a basin of water or rinse thoroughly before cooking, to flush out any earwigs that may be present (this is especially important with home-grown artichokes). Bring a few inches of water to a boil in a stockpot over high heat. Seasonings may be added to the water, if you wish (see page 38 for our basic recipe). Put a steaming tray in the pan and place the artichokes on the tray, leaves pointing down, so they sit securely. Cover the pan tightly, reduce heat to medium, and steam 25 to 45 minutes, depending on the size of the artichoke. When leaves pull off easily and the base is tender when pierced with a sharp knife, the artichoke is done. Drain well before serving.

- Eating a whole artichoke is a ritual, to be lingered over and savored, leaf by leaf. Pluck off a leaf and place it in your mouth with the curved side down, bite into it gently, and pull the leaf out, scraping with your teeth to remove the tender bite at the bottom. The translucent, pale leaves beneath the edible outer ones are actually the flower's petals. Pluck them off in a bunch, and bite off the fleshy bottom portion. Use a spoon to scrape out the choke, then slice and eat the artichoke bottom. Place an empty bowl on the table as a receptacle for the inedible parts of the artichokes.

- Trimmed artichokes oxidize and darken rapidly. If you are trimming a large number of artichokes or will not be cooking them immediately, set the trimmed ones aside in a large bowl of cold water to which 1 tablespoon of lemon juice or vinegar has been added.

- We sometimes cook fresh artichokes when we need artichoke bottoms for a recipe. When they are done, simply remove the leaves and scrape out the choke, then proceed with the recipe.
- Water-packed canned artichoke hearts or bottoms should be rinsed and drained before using to remove as much of the added sodium as possible. Canned or frozen artichokes should be cooked only long enough to heat through or they will lose their succulent consistency.

Layered Artichoke and Dried Tomato Torta

This torta makes a delicious do-ahead appetizer that will dazzle your guests. The flavors meld together so that no single ingredient predominates. If you do not have a mold pan, use a bowl or ramekin. Any leftovers will be a treat for you to enjoy over the course of a few days.

Yield: 16 appetizer servings

Dried tomatoes, minced	3	tablespoons
Artichoke bottoms, water-packed	1	13¾-ounce can
Fresh-squeezed lemon juice	1	tablespoon
Fresh chives, minced	2	tablespoons
Garlic	2	cloves, minced
Olive oil	¼	cup
Parmesan cheese, finely grated	¼	cup
Pepper	⅛	teaspoon
Salt	⅛	teaspoon
Firm-style silken tofu	8	ounces
Light cream cheese	8	ounces

Reconstitute the tomatoes if they are too dry to mince by soaking for 15 to 30 minutes in hot water. Drain them well and mince them. Set aside. Drain the artichoke bottoms and pat them dry. Place them in a food processor and chop finely. Add the lemon juice, chives, and garlic and pulse to combine. With the motor running, add the olive oil in a slow, steady stream until homogenous. Add the Parmesan, pepper, and salt and pulse to combine. Remove to a bowl and set aside.

The Best 125 Vegetable Dishes

Drain the tofu and pat dry with a tea towel. Place it, along with the cream cheese, in a food processor and combine until smooth. Drape a damp piece of cheesecloth over a 3-cup mold, allowing about 2 inches of overhang. Place ⅓ of the cream cheese mixture over the bottom of the mold, spreading to create an even layer. Add ½ of the artichoke mixture, spreading evenly over the cheese layer. Repeat the layers, ending with the cream cheese mixture on top. Cover with the overhanging cheesecloth. Refrigerate at least 2 hours, or overnight.

To unmold the torta, fold open the cheesecloth, place a serving plate on top of the mold, and gently invert to release the torta onto the plate. Carefully peel away the cloth and garnish with fresh chopped chives, if desired. Serve with baguette slices or crisp crackers.

Each serving provides:

96	Calories	4 g	Carbohydrate
5 g	Protein	131 mg	Sodium
8 g	Fat	8 mg	Cholesterol
1 g	Dietary Fiber		

Herb Steamed Artichokes

VEGAN

*These herb and vinegar infused artichokes are delicious without
condiments, though you may serve them with a dipping sauce if you
don't mind the added fat and calories. Dill Dijon Sauce (page 358)
would be an excellent choice for a dip.*

Yield: 4 side-dish servings

Bay leaves	2	
Garlic	3	cloves, chopped
Dried red chili flakes	¼	teaspoon
Salt	¼	teaspoon
Cider vinegar	2	tablespoons
Mixed dried herbs*	1	to 2 teaspoons
Artichokes	4	large

Bring a few inches of water to a boil in a stockpot over high
heat and add the bay leaves, garlic, chili flakes, salt, vinegar,
and herbs.

Meanwhile, use a sharp knife to trim off most of the stem of
the artichokes and about ½ inch of the pointy ends of their
leaves. If there are small, tough leaves around the base, remove
and discard them. Vigorously swirl artichokes in a basin of
water or rinse thoroughly before cooking, to flush out any earwigs that may be present (this is especially crucial with home-
grown artichokes). Put a steaming tray in the pan and place the
artichokes on the tray, leaves pointing down, so they sit securely.
Cover the pan tightly, reduce heat to medium, and steam 25
to 45 minutes, depending on the size of the artichokes. When

*Herbs could include one or all of the following: basil, dill, marjoram, oregano,
rosemary, tarragon, thyme.

leaves pull off easily and the base is tender when pierced with a sharp knife, the artichoke is done.

Remove the artichokes from the water with tongs, squeezing gently to drain well. Serve hot, cold, or at room temperature on individual plates. Place an empty bowl on the table as a receptacle for the inedible parts of the artichokes. (Refer to instructions on page 34 if you want to learn how to eat a whole artichoke.)

Each serving provides:

39	Calories	9 g	Carbohydrate
3 g	Protein	93 mg	Sodium
0 g	Fat	0 mg	Cholesterol
4 g	Dietary Fiber		

Artichoke, Squash, and Red Pepper Sauté with Garlic, Rosemary, and Dill

ALMOST INSTANT, VEGAN

This is among the simplest and most succulent of Mediterranean-inspired side dishes. It is convenient to prepare from canned, quartered artichoke hearts.

Yield: 4 side-dish servings

Red bell pepper	1	medium
Dry sherry	3	tablespoons
Garlic	2	cloves, minced
Crookneck squash, diced	1	cup
Dried rosemary	1	teaspoon, crushed
Dill seed	½	teaspoon
Salt		A pinch
Pepper		A few grinds
Quartered artichoke hearts, water-packed	1	8½-ounce can (drained weight)
Fresh-squeezed lemon juice	2	tablespoons
Fresh lemon wedges	1	per serving

Cut the pepper in half lengthwise and remove the stem, seeds, and membranes. Chop the pulp into 1-inch pieces. Heat the sherry with 3 tablespoons of water in a heavy-bottomed skillet that has a tight-fitting lid. When it begins to simmer, stir in the garlic, then add the peppers, squash, rosemary, dill seed, salt, and pepper. Cover, reduce heat to medium-low, and cook 5 minutes. Remove the lid and cook, stirring frequently, until peppers are tender and there is still a little liquid remaining in the pan, about 2 to 3 minutes.

Meanwhile, drain the artichoke hearts and remove any choke material you find. When peppers are ready, add the artichokes and lemon juice and stir gently as you cook for about 2 minutes longer. You want the artichokes to just heat through. Serve hot or at room temperature, garnished with lemon wedges.

Each serving provides:

70	Calories	15 g	Carbohydrate
3 g	Protein	65 mg	Sodium
1 g	Fat	0 mg	Cholesterol
3 g	Dietary Fiber		

Artichoke Coddled Egg with Corn and Mozzarella

The artichoke becomes the edible vessel for a perfectly poached egg. The sauce is spicy and delicious when spooned inside the artichoke to enjoy with the filling. The leaves may also be dipped into the sauce as you eat them.

Yield: 4 main-dish servings

Artichokes	4	large
Low-sodium tomato sauce	$\frac{1}{4}$	cup
Garlic	2	cloves, minced
Fresh cilantro, minced	$\frac{1}{4}$	cup
Salt	$\frac{1}{8}$	teaspoon
Pepper		Several grinds
Firm-style silken tofu	5	ounces
Corn kernels, fresh or frozen	1	cup
Fine bread crumbs	$\frac{1}{4}$	cup
Part-skim mozzarella cheese, grated	4	ounces (1 cup)
Eggs	4	medium

The sauce

Plain nonfat yogurt	4	tablespoons
Light sour cream	3	tablespoons
Cider vinegar	1	tablespoon
Fresh cilantro, minced	2	tablespoons
Granulated garlic	$\frac{1}{2}$	teaspoon
Ground cumin	$\frac{1}{8}$	teaspoon
Chili powder	$\frac{1}{8}$	teaspoon

Wash the artichokes. Trim the stem ends of the artichokes so they will sit flat on their bases. Remove any tough outer leaves around the base of each artichoke and trim away about ½ inch of the pointy leaf tips. Place the artichokes on a steamer rack in a large pan, leaves pointing down, and add water to just cover the rack. Cover, bring to a boil over high heat, reduce heat to medium-high, and cook for 25 to 35 minutes, depending on their size, until they are barely fork tender (they will finish cooking in the oven). Remove the artichokes from the water with tongs, squeezing gently to drain well, and set aside to cool a little. When they are cool enough to handle, gently spread the leaves open and use a spoon to scrape out the choke from the center of each artichoke. Preheat the oven to 350 degrees F.

Meanwhile, mix the tomato sauce, garlic, cilantro, salt, and pepper together in a bowl. Rinse the tofu and pat it dry with a tea towel. Crumble the tofu and add it to the bowl along with corn and bread crumbs. Stir to combine thoroughly. Spoon equal amounts into the cavity of each artichoke. Place ⅛ of the cheese on top of the tofu mixture in each artichoke. Gently crack one egg over the cheese in each artichoke, being careful not to break the yolk. Top with the remaining cheese. Place the artichokes in a shallow baking dish and add 1 inch of hot water. Bake, uncovered, 25 minutes.

While the artichokes are in the oven, whisk the sauce ingredients together in a bowl. Set aside in the refrigerator. Remove the artichokes from the oven and turn on the broiler. When broiler is preheated, place the pan of artichokes under the broiler for 1 minute to crisp the cheese and finish cooking the egg. Serve immediately, passing the sauce.

Each serving provides:

361	Calories	36 g	Carbohydrate
27 g	Protein	494 mg	Sodium
15 g	Fat	207 mg	Cholesterol
10 g	Dietary Fiber		

Artichoke and Rice Casserole with Fresh Basil, Feta, and Tomatoes

Earthy and satisfying, yet light and refreshing in flavor, this dish evokes the mood of the Mediterranean. Cook the rice ahead of time and you will find this dish wonderfully quick and simple to prepare. You may use whatever kind of rice you have on hand, though we prefer the nutty flavor of the short-grain brown variety here.

Yield: 4 main-dish servings

Low-sodium whole tomatoes	1	28-ounce can
Dried oregano	1	teaspoon
Granulated garlic	½	teaspoon
Dried red chili flakes	¼	teaspoon
Salt	⅛	teaspoon
Quartered artichoke hearts, water-packed	1	8½-ounce can (drained weight)
Cooked brown rice	2	cups
Fresh basil leaves	1	cup, tightly packed, chopped
Feta cheese, crumbled	2	ounces (½ cup)
Olive oil	2	teaspoons
Parmesan cheese, finely grated	2	tablespoons

Drain the juice from the can of tomatoes; save it in the refrigerator for another use, such as soup stock. Place the whole tomatoes, oregano, granulated garlic, chili flakes, and salt in a skillet over medium heat. Bring to a simmer and cook for 10 minutes, stirring frequently and breaking the tomatoes up with a wooden spoon as they cook. Preheat the oven to 375 degrees F.

Meanwhile, drain the artichokes, removing any choke material you find, and chop them. Toss the artichokes with the rice, basil, and feta in a soufflé dish or small casserole until well distributed. Toss again with the olive oil. When tomato sauce is ready, pour the sauce over the contents of the casserole, shaking the dish a little so the tomato sauce settles. Sprinkle the Parmesan evenly over the top, cover, and bake for 20 minutes. Remove the cover and bake an additional 15 minutes. Serve very hot.

Each serving provides:

253	Calories	40 g	Carbohydrate
10 g	Protein	335 mg	Sodium
8 g	Fat	15 mg	Cholesterol
6 g	Dietary Fiber		

Asparagus

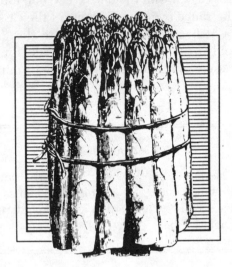

Asparagus spears, appreciated by discriminating gourmands the world over, are the succulent fresh shoots of a plant called *Asparagus officinalis*. It is a member of the lily family, and is thus related to onions, leeks, and garlic. If you have only eaten this vegetable canned and have decided you don't like it based on that experience, give fresh asparagus a try. When properly prepared, its crisp texture and nutty sweetness are delightful.

Asparagus was prized for medicinal purposes in ancient Greece and Rome, and references date back even farther, to ancient Egyptian times. The wild form, from which today's commercial variety was cultivated, still grows abundantly in sandy places, woods, and riverbanks in parts of Europe, Asia, and northern Africa.

Though green asparagus is the only variety cultivated on a commercial scale in the United States, white and purple asparagus are more common in other parts of the world. The white spears require special cultivation techniques and are considered quite a delicacy. Though rarely available in this country, white asparagus is a common sight in the vegetable markets of France and Italy.

California is this country's largest producer of asparagus.

The Nutrition Picture

Asparagus is rich in three nutrients reputed to be important cancer preventers: beta carotene, vitamin C, and selenium. It also provides good quantities of vitamins B_1 and B_2. It is low in calories, contains no fat or cholesterol, and has only a trace of sodium.

A perhaps indelicate but important note: A sulfur compound in asparagus taints some people's urine with a distinctive odor. This is a common reaction and is nothing to worry about.

Selection and Storage

Asparagus may seem high in price relative to other vegetables. However, its price tag is probably justified—the spears must be harvested by hand.

The asparagus season is quite short—peak months are April and May in warmer regions of the United States, though you may begin to see it in grocery stores as early as February in some places. In the midwest and east, the season extends from May through July. Winter asparagus is sometimes available, usually imported from South America, but its quality tends to suffer during shipping.

Enjoy fresh asparagus when it's in season—the texture and flavor of just-picked and quickly steamed spears is superlative.

Fresh asparagus loses about half its total weight when trimmed and cooked, so shop accordingly. A pound of trimmed asparagus yields about four side-dish servings.

Choose bundles of uniform-size spears, if possible, to ensure even cooking. Pencil-thin spears are a treat when you can find truly fresh ones, and they require only a moment to cook. Whatever their thickness, asparagus spears should be firm, plump, and straight—not flaccid, flat, or twisted. They should be deep green for most of their length, though the cut ends normally appear whitish. Look for purplish tips that are tightly closed and pointy. Partially open, wilted, or mushy tips are signs of spoilage.

Asparagus deteriorates rapidly unless it is kept cold, so it should be displayed for purchase in the green grocer's refrigerated case, or on ice at farm stands. At home, store it loosely wrapped in a plastic or paper bag in the coldest part of the refrigerator. Eat fresh asparagus the same day you purchase it, if possible, though it will keep fairly well for a few days.

If you can't get fresh asparagus, the next best choice is frozen spears, if they are available. They retain most of their nutrients and flavor, and have a fairly good texture, if not overcooked. Canned varieties, on the other hand, leach most of their nutrients into the canning liquid and their texture tends to be mushy. We recommend avoiding canned asparagus and enjoying this delicate vegetable as a fleeting spring pleasure.

Culinary Tips

- Rinse asparagus under cool running water. If the tips appear sandy, dunk them in water and swirl vigorously. Snap off the tough, whitish ends (you may wish to save them, as they make a wonderful addition to Homemade Vegetable Stock; see page 12). Some cooks prefer to peel the stems with a vegetable parer to within two to three inches of the tip to remove any trace of stringiness; however, if you are buying truly fresh asparagus in season, this really isn't necessary.

- Cook asparagus briefly—overcooking produces bitterness. The spears should remain firm and bright green. When you can barely pierce the thick end all the way through with a fork, it's done.

- Though not essential, a tall, cylindrical steamer made especially for asparagus is ideal. It immerses the thicker bottom end in water so it cooks more rapidly. This way, both ends are perfectly cooked at the same moment. This vessel is also wonderful for cooking whole leeks and corn on the cob.

Asparagus and Roasted Red Peppers with Apples, Jicama, and Lime

ALMOST INSTANT, VEGAN

Simple to prepare and beautiful on the table, this unusual salad combination of fruit and vegetables would be welcome at any Southwestern feast. If you cannot find an apple that is perfectly crisp, sweet, and delicious, simply leave it out.

Yield: 6 side-dish servings

Red bell pepper	1	large
Asparagus	1½	pounds
Fresh-squeezed lime juice	2	tablespoons
Fresh-squeezed lemon juice	2	tablespoons
Apple, red or golden delicious	1	medium, very crisp
Jicama	½	pound
Chili powder	1	teaspoon
Salt	¼	teaspoon
Pepper		Several grinds

Roast the pepper over a gas burner, under a broiler, or on a hot grill until the skin is charred black all over and the pepper has begun to collapse. Place immediately in a paper bag and fold closed. The steam in the bag will finish cooking the pepper. When cool enough to handle, remove the skin, discard the stem and seeds, and cut into thin 1-inch strips. Set aside.

Rinse the asparagus spears and snap off the tough stem ends. Cut into 2-inch pieces and place on a steamer rack in a saucepan that has a tight-fitting lid. Add about an inch of water, cover, and cook over medium-high heat about 6 minutes, until asparagus is barely fork tender. Rinse immediately with cold water to stop the cooking and drain well; toss with the red pepper strips and set aside.

Combine the lime and lemon juices in a medium bowl. Wash the apple, remove the core, and slice into thin wedges. Place the apple in the bowl and toss to coat with the citrus juices. Peel the jicama and cut into thin bite-size strips. Add to the apple and toss again. Transfer the apple and jicama to a pretty platter, retaining the juices in the bowl and arranging the slices around the edge of the platter. Add the asparagus and pepper mixture to the citrus juices and toss to combine, then spoon into the center of the platter. In a small bowl, combine the chili powder, salt, and pepper. Use your fingers to sprinkle this mixture evenly over everything on the platter and garnish with lemon and lime wedges, if desired. Serve at room temperature.

Each serving provides:

50	Calories	11 g	Carbohydrate
3 g	Protein	98 mg	Sodium
0 g	Fat	0 mg	Cholesterol
2 g	Dietary Fiber		

Cream of Asparagus Soup with Dried Tomato and Mustard Croutons

A wonderful celebration of spring, this lovely soup with its crispy garnish sets the tone for a very special dinner party.

Yield: 6 first-course servings

Dried tomato, minced	¼	cup
Olive oil	1	tablespoon
Dijon mustard	2	teaspoons
Paprika	1½	teaspoons
Sourdough French bread	4	½-inch slices
Asparagus	1¾	pounds
Red onion	1	small, diced
Garlic	4	cloves, minced
Dry sherry	⅔	cup
Dried rosemary	1	teaspoon
Salt	½	teaspoon
Pepper		Several grinds
Unsalted butter	1	tablespoon
Unbleached flour	1	tablespoon
Lowfat milk	¾	cup
Parmesan cheese, finely grated	¼	cup

Reconstitute the dried tomatoes if they are too dry to mince by soaking for 15 to 30 minutes in hot water. Drain them well and mince them. Set aside. Meanwhile, preheat the oven to 350 degrees F. Stir together the olive oil, mustard, and 1 teaspoon of the paprika until well combined. Spread this mixture evenly over both sides of the bread slices and cut them into ½-inch cubes. Spread the cubes out on a cookie sheet and bake for about 25 minutes, turning occasionally so cubes crisp evenly. When the bread cubes are crisp and lightly browned, they are done. Remove from the oven and set aside. (The croutons can be made a day or more ahead of time, if you wish. Store them in a closed paper bag at room temperature until needed.)

To make the soup, discard the tough stem ends of the asparagus. Chop the asparagus and combine it in a stockpot with the onion, 3 cloves of the garlic, sherry, rosemary, salt, a few grinds of pepper, and 2 cups of water. Bring this mixture to a simmer over high heat, then cover, reduce heat to medium-low, and simmer 15 minutes. Asparagus should be very soft.

While asparagus is cooking, make a white sauce by melting the butter in a heavy-bottomed saucepan over medium-low heat. Add remaining ½ teaspoon paprika and remaining 1 clove garlic and stir for a moment, then stir in the flour. Cook, stirring constantly, for 1 minute, then whisk in the milk and Parmesan. Cook, whisking frequently, 7 to 10 minutes, until the sauce has thickened. Stir in a pinch of salt and the pepper.

Transfer the asparagus mixture in small batches to a blender or food processor and puree to a smooth consistency (make sure the blender lid is firmly closed to prevent splattering). Return the pureed asparagus to the pot, stir in the white sauce and dried tomatoes, and cook over medium-low heat another 5 minutes. Transfer to warmed bowls and top each serving with croutons.

Each serving provides:

222	Calories	27 g	Carbohydrate
8 g	Protein	464 mg	Sodium
7 g	Fat	10 mg	Cholesterol
3 g	Dietary Fiber		

Asparagus Risotto with Oyster Mushrooms and Ginger

VEGAN

A true comfort food, risotto is a good choice for evenings when appetites are strong. This stunning asparagus and mushroom version would be the perfect meal after a day of working in the spring garden.

Yield: 6 main-dish servings

Homemade Vegetable Stock*	5½	**cups**
Low-sodium soy sauce	1	**tablespoon**
Fresh ginger, grated	1	**tablespoon**
Asparagus	¾	**pound**
Fresh oyster mushrooms	6	**ounces**
Dark sesame oil	½	**tablespoon**
Garlic	4	**cloves, minced**
Dried red chili flakes	¼	**teaspoon**
Red bell pepper	½	**medium, diced**
Salt	⅛	**teaspoon**
Dry sherry	¼	**cup**
Olive oil	½	**tablespoon**
Arborio rice, uncooked	1½	**cups**
Green onion	1,	**minced**

Heat the stock, soy sauce, and ginger in a saucepan until just steaming, and keep this broth handy near the stove. Rinse the asparagus, break off the tough stem ends, and cut at a slant into 1-inch pieces. Rinse the mushrooms, pat dry, and chop coarsely.

*If you do not have Homemade Vegetable Stock on hand, make some according to the directions on page 12, or dissolve ½ of a large, low-sodium vegetable broth cube in 5½ cups of hot water.

In a large heavy-bottomed saucepan, heat the sesame oil over medium heat. Add 2 cloves of the garlic and the red chili flakes and sauté a minute or two. Add the bell pepper, asparagus, and salt. Sauté for 5 minutes, stirring frequently. Stir in the mushrooms, add the sherry, and immediately cover the pan tightly. Cook an additional 2 minutes, then remove from the heat and set aside with the lid on.

In a large, heavy-bottomed saucepan, heat the olive oil over medium heat. Sauté the remaining 2 cloves of garlic for a minute, then add the rice and stir to coat with the oil and garlic. Add 1 cup of broth to the rice, and stir gently until the liquid is absorbed. Add the remaining broth ½ cup at a time, stirring almost constantly and waiting until liquid is absorbed before each addition. When the last addition of broth has been absorbed and the rice is tender, stir in the asparagus and mushrooms, along with any pan juices. Heat through for 1 minute. Transfer to a warmed serving bowl or tureen and sprinkle with the green onions. Serve very hot.

Each serving provides:

244	Calories	46 g	Carbohydrate
6 g	Protein	168 mg	Sodium
3 g	Fat	0 mg	Cholesterol
1 g	Dietary Fiber		

Asparagus and Mushroom Pizza with Mustard, Dill, Mozzarella, and Feta

Even six-year-old Cameron loves this unusual springtime pizza. The flavors are in perfect balance, and it's as pretty as it is delicious. A hot outdoor grill is a good option for cooking pizza, particularly on a warm day when you don't want to heat up the kitchen.

Yield: 6 main-dish servings

Pizza crust	1	12-inch crust
Asparagus	1	pound
Mushrooms	½	pound, sliced
Garlic	3	cloves, minced
Salt	⅛	teaspoon
Pepper		Several grinds
Prepared whole-grain mustard	2	tablespoons
Red onion, thinly sliced	⅓	cup
Part-skim mozzarella cheese, grated	4	ounces (1 cup)
Fresh dill, minced	1	tablespoon
Feta cheese, crumbled	1	ounce (¼ cup)
Paprika	¼	teaspoon

Prepare pizza crust from the recipe on page 16, or use a commercial crust for an Almost Instant pizza.

Preheat the oven to 450 degrees F. Rinse the asparagus and break off the tough ends. Slice the spears at a slant into 1-inch pieces. Place the asparagus in a skillet with the mushrooms, garlic, salt, pepper, and 2 tablespoons of water. Cover and cook over medium heat 5 minutes, then remove the lid and cook an additional 5 minutes, stirring frequently. Most of the liquid should have evaporated.

Meanwhile, use a rubber spatula to spread the mustard over the pizza crust, leaving a 1-inch rim around the outside. Use a slotted spoon to transfer the asparagus mixture to the pizza, spreading it out evenly and leaving the 1-inch rim around the outside with no topping. Distribute the onion slices evenly over the asparagus mixture, then top with the mozzarella. Sprinkle the dill, feta, and paprika evenly over the top and bake about 12 minutes, until cheese has melted and browned just a little. Serve very hot.

Each serving provides:

195	Calories	18 g	Carbohydrate
12 g	Protein	350 mg	Sodium
8 g	Fat	17 mg	Cholesterol
1 g	Dietary Fiber		

Linguine with Asparagus, Toasted Walnuts, and Fresh Herbs

ALMOST INSTANT

In the tradition of primavera-style pasta, this dish makes the most of spring asparagus. It is a satisfying main dish for four hearty appetites. You may use just about whatever fresh herbs are available—our favorite blend includes oregano, tarragon, and thyme. The Parmesan adds a rich note, but those on a vegan diet may simply omit it.

Yield: 4 main-dish servings

Raw, unsalted walnut pieces	⅓	cup
Asparagus	1	pound
Yellow bell pepper	1	medium
Olive oil	1	tablespoon
Yellow onion	1	medium, diced
Garlic	8	cloves, minced
Carrot	1	large, thinly sliced
Salt	¼	teaspoon
Pepper		Several grinds
Dry sherry	½	cup
Fresh herbs	3	tablespoons
Dried linguine	12	ounces
Parmesan cheese, finely grated	¼	cup

Place the walnuts in a single layer in a dry, heavy-bottomed skillet over medium-high heat. Shake the pan or stir frequently until the nuts are golden brown and emit a wonderful roasted aroma. Immediately remove from the pan. When slightly cooled, chop them and set aside.

Put several quarts of water on to boil for the pasta. Rinse the asparagus and break off the tough stem ends. Cut the spears at a slant into 1-inch pieces. Cut the bell pepper in half lengthwise, remove the stem and seeds, and slice the halves into long, thin strips. Set the asparagus and bell pepper strips aside.

Heat the oil in a heavy-bottomed skillet over medium heat and sauté the onion and garlic for 2 minutes. Add the carrot, ⅛ teaspoon of the salt, and the pepper and stir and sauté for 3 minutes. Stir in the asparagus and bell peppers, then pour in the sherry and immediately tightly cover the pan. Cook for 6 minutes, then remove the lid and stir in the herbs.

Meanwhile, cook the linguine in the boiling water until al dente. Drain well and toss with the asparagus mixture, then with the walnuts and cheese. Serve very hot, passing the pepper grinder.

Each serving provides:

537	Calories	81 g	Carbohydrate
18 g	Protein	254 mg	Sodium
13 g	Fat	4 mg	Cholesterol
5 g	Dietary Fiber		

Beets

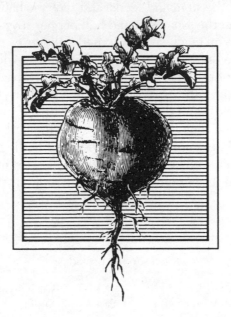

Red, rounded beets are the most common commercially grown variety in modern times, but historians suggest edible beet roots were originally oblong and yellow in color. In ancient times, only the greens of the beet were eaten, while the roots were reserved primarily for making medicines.

The round beet was probably first developed in sixteenth-century Europe, but was not common as a food for another 200 years. Today, elongated beets as well as golden or white ones are available only rarely, in specialty markets or for home cultivation.

Today's common beet, *Beta vulgaris*, is related to Swiss chard and is widely cultivated in the cooler regions of the United States or during the cool season in warmer regions. A full 95 percent of the domestic crop is canned, but we think freshly cooked beets are far superior in flavor and texture and prefer them in our recipes.

The Nutrition Picture

Beet roots have the highest sugar content of any vegetable, and are somewhat higher in calories than most. In fact, one type of beet—appropriately called the sugar beet—is actually processed into sugar, with 100 pounds of beets yielding 5 pounds of sugar. Fully one-third of the world's sugar supply is derived from sugar beets.

Beet roots supply good quantities of vitamin C and dietary fiber. However, to get the most nutritional benefit from this vegetable, buy beets with the green tops still attached whenever possible—the greens are an excellent source of beta carotene, calcium, and iron.

A word of warning: Urine or feces can turn pinkish or even bright red for a couple of days in people who cannot metabolize the pigments that make beets red. This is no cause for alarm, and is no reason to avoid eating beets.

Selection and Storage

Fresh beets are in good supply year-round, though their peak season is June through October. When shopping for beets, plan on one medium beet per person as a side-dish serving.

Select beets with greens attached if possible—crisp, fresh greens pack a wonderful supply of nutrients and are an indication that the beets are freshly harvested. Wilted or yellowing greens should be twisted off and discarded, but the beets themselves may still be good if they meet the other tests of freshness.

Look for deep red, hard, smooth roots that are free of cuts. Soft or shriveled beets are past their prime. Small beets will be more tender than the larger specimens—as the season wears on, roots get larger and tougher. If buying beets in a bunch, try to choose roots of equal size so they will cook in the same amount of time.

To minimize moisture loss from the root, remove the beet greens before storing, leaving a half inch of the stems attached. Store the greens in a separate plastic bag in the refrigerator. Tiny beets can be stored with greens attached for a day or so. Don't wash the beets or the greens before storage. Wrapped in plastic in the refrigerator, the greens will stay crisp for a day or two, the roots will keep for up to three weeks.

When fresh beets are not available, the canned, unpickled variety may be substituted in most recipes. They retain their sweetness, but lose some of their vitamin C. As always, we recommend the fresh vegetable for optimum flavor, texture, and nutrition.

Culinary Tips

- Use raw, grated beets on salads or sandwiches.
- Beet greens can be steamed or substituted for other greens in your favorite recipes. Rinse the greens carefully and chop them coarsely. Small, tender, raw beet greens are good in salads.
- Wash loose dirt off beet roots before cooking, but do not peel them and leave ½ inch of stem and the entire taproot intact so nutrients and colored juices stay sealed inside the beet. Cooked beets are easy to peel by hand once

they have cooled off a bit. Do this in the sink, as it is a messy procedure.

- Beets are done when easily pierced all the way through with a sharp knife.
- Rinse unpickled canned beets well to remove as much of the additives as possible.
- As a rule of thumb; one medium beet, without greens, weighs ¼ pound.

Beet Puree with Celery Seed and Chevre

This deliciously intriguing and visually stunning vegetable side dish would be very much at home at an elegant summer dinner party. Combine it with dishes that have crisp or chewy textures to balance the creaminess of the puree. For this dish, purchase small beets, if possible, which are less fibrous than the larger ones and will yield the smoothest consistency.

Yield: 4 side-dish servings

Small beets, without greens	¾	pound
Red potatoes	½	pound, peeled and diced
Dry white wine	¼	cup
Soft chevre	2	ounces
Fresh-squeezed lemon juice	2	teaspoons
Salt	⅛	teaspoon
Pepper		Several grinds
Celery seed	½	teaspoon
Celery leaves, minced	2	tablespoons

Rinse the beets and place them on a steamer rack in a saucepan that has a tight-fitting lid. Add about 2 inches of water, cover the pan, and cook over medium-high heat about 15 minutes, until each beet can be easily pierced all the way through with a sharp knife (cooking time will be longer if you use larger beets). Remove the lid to check the water level midway through the cooking time and add additional hot water, if necessary. Set the cooked beets aside to cool in a colander. When beets are cool enough to handle, peel and cut the beets into small chunks. Set aside in a bowl.

Meanwhile, boil the potatoes in enough water to cover them until quite tender—about 10 minutes. Drain the potatoes and transfer them to a food processor. Add the chopped beets, wine, chevre, lemon juice, salt, pepper, and celery seed, and puree until a thick, smooth consistency is achieved. Mound into a bowl or onto a platter, smoothing the surface a little with a rubber spatula. Sprinkle evenly with the chopped celery leaves and serve at room temperature. You may serve the puree in individual ramekins, if you wish.

Each serving provides:

118	Calories	16 g	Carbohydrate
5 g	Protein	171 mg	Sodium
3 g	Fat	7 mg	Cholesterol
2 g	Dietary Fiber		

Beets in Yogurt Sauce with Mustard, Caraway, and Fresh Mint

This is an unusual, but quite successful, marriage of flavors. You may serve the beets cold or at room temperature, depending on the season and the rest of the menu. Cook the beets and mix up the sauce ahead of time, if you wish, to simplify the dinner hour. In any case, the sauce comes together quick as a wink.

Yield: 4 side-dish servings

Beets	1	**pound (4 medium)**
Caraway seed	½	**teaspoon**
Plain nonfat yogurt	½	**cup**
Dijon mustard	2	**teaspoons**
Granulated sugar	1	**teaspoon**
Salt		**A pinch**
Fresh mint leaves, minced	2	**tablespoons**

Rinse the beets and place them on a steamer rack in a saucepan that has a tight-fitting lid. Add about 2 inches of water, cover the pan, and cook over medium-high heat about 25 minutes, until each beet can be easily pierced all the way through with a sharp knife (cooking time will vary, depending on the size of the beet). Remove the lid to check the water level midway through the cooking time and add additional hot water, if necessary. Set the cooked beets aside to cool in a colander. When beets are cool enough to handle, peel and cut into thin strips.

Meanwhile, toast the caraway seeds in a dry, heavy-bottomed skillet—stirring or shaking the pan frequently—until they begin to pop and emit a nutty aroma. Crush the seeds lightly with a mortar and pestle or in a spice grinder. In a bowl, stir together the yogurt, mustard, sugar, salt, and caraway seeds until well combined. Stir in the mint. Cover and set aside in the refrigerator for up to several hours, but bring to room temperature before tossing with the beets. Serve immediately or chill. Garnish with mint leaves, if desired.

Each serving provides:

59	Calories	12 g	Carbohydrate
3 g	Protein	187 mg	Sodium
0 g	Fat	1 mg	Cholesterol
1 g	Dietary Fiber		

Beets with Fresh Mozzarella and Roasted Peppers

This recipe calls for fresh mozzarella cheese, which is common in the cheese shops of Italy, and is now available in many specialty food shops. It is usually sold water-packed, sometimes called buffalo mozzarella. Seek it out—the flavor and texture is delicious! Chilled salad plates are recommended for this dish.

Yield: 6 side-dish servings

The salad

Red bell peppers	2	large
Beets, with greens	4	medium (about 1¾ pounds)
Fresh mozzarella cheese	6	ounces
Freshly grated nutmeg		Several grinds
Fresh tarragon	6	sprigs

The marinade

Olive oil	3	tablespoons
Tarragon white wine vinegar	2	tablespoons
Fresh-squeezed lemon juice	2	tablespoons
Granulated garlic	⅛	teaspoon
Salt		Scant ⅛ teaspoon
Pepper		Several grinds

Roast the peppers over a gas burner, under a broiler, or on a hot grill until the skin is charred black all over and the peppers have begun to collapse. Place immediately in a paper bag and fold closed. The steam in the bag will finish cooking the pepper. When cool enough to handle, remove the skin, discard the stem and seeds, and cut into thin strips. Whisk together the marinade ingredients. Toss with the peppers and set aside to marinate while you prepare the rest of the salad.

Trim the greens from the beets, leaving about ½ inch of stems attached to the roots. Set the greens aside. Rinse the beets and place them on a steamer rack in a pan that has a tight-fitting lid. Add about 2 inches of water, cover the pan, and cook over medium-high heat about 25 minutes, until each beet can be easily pierced all the way through with a sharp knife (cooking time will vary, depending on the size of the beet). Remove the lid to check the water level midway through the cooking time and add additional hot water, if necessary.

Wash the beet greens, removing the tough stems. Arrange the greens on top of the beets during the last 5 minutes of cooking to steam them lightly until they wilt. Remove the greens from the pan and plunge into ice water to set the color. Drain well and set aside. Drain the beets and cover with cold water. When cool enough to handle, peel and cut into ¼-inch slices.

Cut the mozzarella into ¼-inch slices. Coarsely chop the beet greens and arrange equal portions to cover half of each plate. Arrange equal portions of the beet and cheese slices on each bed of greens, then spoon the peppers onto the other half of the plate. Drizzle each portion of beets and cheese with about 1 tablespoon of the marinade and add several grinds of fresh nutmeg. Garnish with the tarragon sprigs and serve immediately.

Each serving provides:

188	Calories	12 g	Carbohydrate
7 g	Protein	217 mg	Sodium
13 g	Fat	20 mg	Cholesterol
1 g	Dietary Fiber		

Borscht with Fresh Lemon and Dill

ALMOST INSTANT

We have eaten many versions of borscht over the years and especially enjoy this light, fresh-flavored one. It is easy to prepare and as nutritious as it is delicious.

Yield: 4 main-dish servings

Beets	¾	pound (3 medium)
Carrots	2	medium
Russet potato	1	large
Homemade Vegetable Stock*	6	cups
Yellow onion	1	medium, chopped
Green cabbage, chopped	1	cup
Fresh-squeezed lemon juice	¼	cup
Dried dill weed	1	teaspoon
Salt	⅛	teaspoon
Pepper		Several grinds
Plain nonfat yogurt	½	cup

Peel the beets and grate them. Grate the carrots and dice the potato. In a large stockpot combine the stock, beets, carrot,

---

*If you do not have Homemade Vegetable Stock on hand, make some according to the directions on page 12, or dissolve 1 large, low-sodium vegetable broth cube in 6 cups of hot water.

potato, and onion. Bring to a boil over high heat, reduce heat to medium, and cook 10 minutes. Add the cabbage, lemon juice, dill, salt, and pepper and cook an additional 10 minutes. Serve hot or cold, passing the yogurt.

Each serving provides:

146	Calories	29 g	Carbohydrate
6 g	Protein	212 mg	Sodium
1 g	Fat	1 mg	Cholesterol
4 g	Dietary Fiber		

Beets and Greens with Miso Tahini Sauce and Bulgur

VEGAN

This dish is scrumptious and wholesome and pairs wonderfully on a menu with Curried Cauliflower and Garbanzo Bean Salad with Cherry Tomatoes (page 132). The preparation has several steps, but once you make it, you will realize how simple a meal it is. If you wish, you may serve the beets without the bulgur as a side dish. In that case, you will need less of the sauce, but the remainder will keep well in the refrigerator.

Yield: 4 main-dish servings

Beets, with greens	2	**pounds (8 medium)**
Bulgur wheat, uncooked	1¼	**cups**
Salt		**A pinch**
Pepper		**Several grinds**
Green onions	3,	**minced**
Toasted sesame tahini	3	**tablespoons**
White miso	1	**tablespoon**
Lemon juice	2	**tablespoons**
Garlic	1	**clove, minced**
Cayenne		**A pinch**

Trim the greens from the beets, leaving about ½ inch of stems attached to the roots. Set the greens aside. Rinse the beets and place them on a steamer rack in a saucepan that has a tight-fitting lid. Add about 2 inches of water, cover the pan, and cook over medium-high heat about 25 minutes, until each beet can be easily pierced all the way through with a sharp knife (cooking time will vary, depending on the size of the beet). Remove the lid to check the water level midway through the cooking time and add additional hot water, if necessary. Set the cooked beets aside to cool in a colander.

Meanwhile, place the bulgur in a medium saucepan over high heat and stir and roast about 2 minutes. Stir in 2½ cups of water, the salt, pepper, and 2 of the green onions. Bring to a boil over high heat, reduce heat to very low, cover the pan, and cook 15 minutes. Allow to sit 5 minutes before removing the lid.

Meanwhile, in a small bowl, mash the tahini and miso together with a fork until well combined. Add the lemon juice and mash some more until incorporated. Add ⅓ cup hot water a little at a time, stirring to incorporate after each addition. When all the water has been added, whisk to create a smooth, thick consistency. Stir in the garlic and cayenne and set aside in a warm place.

Wash the beet greens, removing the tough stems. Tear the greens into bite-size pieces. Do not dry them—the water that clings to the leaves will provide the liquid for steaming. Pile into a saucepan, cover, and cook over medium heat 5 minutes, until greens are wilted. Drain in a colander, using the back of a wooden spoon to press out as much water as possible. Keep warm.

When the beets are cool enough to handle, slip the skins off. Slice the beets into ¼-inch rounds.

To serve, mound the hot bulgur in the center of a platter. Arrange the sliced beets and their greens around the outside in a pretty pattern. Drizzle the sauce slowly over everything to distribute it evenly, sprinkle with the remaining green onions, and serve hot or at room temperature.

Each serving provides:

290	Calories	51 g	Carbohydrate
11 g	Protein	468 mg	Sodium
7 g	Fat	0 mg	Cholesterol
10 g	Dietary Fiber		

Broccoli

Broccoli—botanically classified as *Brassica oleracea botrytis cymosa,* family Cruciferae—has grown wild in Mediterranean areas for hundreds of years and has been cultivated in Europe since the late seventeenth century. Domestic cultivation didn't start in earnest in the United States until the 1920s, although broccoli was reputedly first introduced to American soil long before by Thomas Jefferson.

Green umbrella head broccoli, the most common form grown in this country, thrives in cool coastal areas and during the cool season in warmer regions. Under the right climatic conditions, broccoli is an easy crop for home gardeners and will provide food for the table over a long period as you gradually harvest from the side branches after you eat the main head. Tender young broccoli fresh from the garden is a treat not to be missed. Left too long on the plant or stored too long after harvesting, broccoli becomes tough, fibrous, and unappetizing.

The Nutrition Picture

Broccoli is considered by many health experts to be one of the most nutritious vegetables. There are many good reasons for its super-food reputation.

Broccoli's membership in the cruciferous family (along with cabbage, cauliflower, Brussels sprouts, and bok choy, among others) explains a good deal of its nutritional appeal. These vegetables are excellent sources of fiber and antioxidants like carotenoids and vitamin C. Studies have shown that antioxidants help rid the body of free radicals—unstable oxygen molecules associated with the development of cancer and other major diseases. In addition, the cruciferous cousins contain beneficial nitrogen compounds called indoles that have been shown in recent studies to be effective cancer preventers. Indeed, evidence that cruciferous vegetables protect us against cancer has become so convincing that the National Cancer Institute, part of the U.S. Department of Health and Human Services, now recommends eating these vegetables several times each week. Studies have specifically linked broccoli consumption with a lower risk of colon cancer.

By weight, cooked fresh broccoli contains more vitamin C than an orange and as much calcium as milk. Some nutritional researchers suspect that high-protein foods leach calcium from the body during metabolism, so low-protein calcium sources like broccoli are especially important. To top things off, broccoli is low in fat and sodium and high in potassium. Broccoli leaves are edible, and contain more beta carotene than the florets.

Selection and Storage

Broccoli is widely available all year, but is most abundant and least expensive from October through May. You may expect to get about four side-dish servings from one and a half to two pounds of untrimmed broccoli (about one pound trimmed).

Look for heads that are uniformly green and tightly closed; if yellow flowers are beginning to open, the broccoli is well past its prime. Color is indicative of nutritional value—florets that are dark green, purplish, or bluish green contain the most beta carotene and vitamin C. The stems should be crisp and, ideally, slender where they connect with the florets. Leaves should not be yellowed or wilted and stems should not be brown. Slimy spots are a sign of spoilage, as is a strong cabbage-like smell. The aroma of fresh broccoli is clean and mild.

Store uncut, unwashed broccoli in an open plastic bag in the refrigerator crisper. Make certain the surface is dry; moisture encourages the formation of mold. Use broccoli within a day or two of purchase, if possible. Four days is about the maximum time it will stay crisp and fresh in the refrigerator. Cooked broccoli will keep well in a tightly closed container in the refrigerator for a few days.

Since fresh broccoli is almost always available, why settle for frozen, which is nutritionally inferior?

Culinary Tips

- If the cut end of the broccoli stalk is especially thick or fibrous, trim off and discard a few inches of it. Cut the florets and their stems off the stalk. Use a sharp knife to peel the edible stalk if it is particularly thick-skinned. It makes a delicious crispy addition to salads when sliced and added raw, or cook it for a few minutes before adding the florets. Washed broccoli leaves may also be eaten raw in salads, or steam them for a minute or two.

- The broccoli odor some people find unpleasant results from overcooking, which causes strong-smelling sulfur compounds to be released. Texture and color also become unappetizing when broccoli is cooked too long. Be careful to cook it only until it is fork tender.

Sherry Sautéed Broccoli with Fresh Herbs and Toasted Walnuts

ALMOST INSTANT, VEGAN

Quick and simple to prepare, and absolutely delectable, this side dish makes a fine accompaniment to almost any entrée. You may use a combination of the herbs rather than a single one if you wish.

Yield: 4 side-dish servings

Raw, unsalted walnuts, chopped	2	**tablespoons**
Broccoli	1	**pound**
Dry sherry	2	**tablespoons**
Olive oil	1	**tablespoon**
Garlic	1	**clove, minced**
Salt	⅛	**teaspoon**
Fresh marjoram, oregano, or thyme leaves, minced	2	**teaspoons**
Pepper		**A few grinds**
Lemon wedges	1	**per person**

Place the walnut pieces in a single layer in a dry, heavy-bottomed skillet over medium-high heat. Cook for several minutes, stirring or shaking the pan frequently, until nuts are golden brown and emit a roasted aroma. Remove from the pan and set aside.

Cut off and discard the tough stem ends of the broccoli and peel the remaining stalks if they are particularly thick-skinned. Cut off the heads and chop into uniform bite-size pieces. Thinly slice the stem portion. Combine the sherry in a small bowl with 2 tablespoons of water and set aside.

Heat the olive oil over medium heat in a skillet that has a tight-fitting lid and sauté the garlic and broccoli stems for 2 to 3 minutes, stirring frequently, until they begin to brown a bit. Add the broccoli florets and the salt and stir. Holding the lid to the pan in one hand, pour in the sherry mixture and immediately cover the pan tightly. Cook for 4 to 6 minutes. Remove the lid after 4 minutes to make sure there is still a little liquid in the pan; you want the broccoli to brown slightly, but not to scorch. If the liquid is gone but the broccoli is not yet tender, add one or two tablespoons of water and replace the lid. If the broccoli is tender and there is still liquid in the pan, stir and cook, uncovered, for a minute or two longer, until it has evaporated. Toss the broccoli in a warmed serving bowl with the herbs, pepper, and toasted walnuts. Serve immediately, garnished with lemon wedges.

Each serving provides:

101	Calories	9 g	Carbohydrate
4 g	Protein	101 mg	Sodium
6 g	Fat	0 mg	Cholesterol
3 g	Dietary Fiber		

Broccoli Braised in Black Bean Sauce

ALMOST INSTANT, VEGAN

This uniquely seasoned side dish is delicious with steamed basmati rice and grilled fish or as part of an Oriental meal. Our homemade Fermented Black Bean Sauce is easy to prepare and keeps well in the refrigerator. Commercially prepared black bean sauces are also available in Asian markets.

Yield: 6 side-dish servings

Raw sesame seeds	2	teaspoons
Broccoli	1½	pounds
Dark sesame oil	1	teaspoon
Mirin	2	tablespoons
Garlic	2	cloves, minced
Fermented Black Bean Sauce (see page 20)	3	tablespoons
Arrowroot powder or cornstarch	1	teaspoon

Place the sesame seeds in a small, dry, cast-iron skillet over medium-high heat. Shake the pan frequently and soon they will begin to brown and emit a roasted aroma. Remove immediately from the pan and set aside until needed.

Cut off and discard the tough stem ends of the broccoli and peel the remaining stalks if they are particularly thick-skinned. Cut the broccoli lengthwise into even-size spears. Put the sesame oil and mirin in a large skillet over medium-high heat and stir in the garlic. Cook for about a minute, then add the Fermented Black Bean Sauce and ½ cup of water. Add the broccoli, stir to coat, and cover. Cook 10 to 12 minutes, stirring occasionally, until fork tender.

Meanwhile, place 1 tablespoon of water and the arrowroot powder in a small jar with a tight-fitting lid and shake to dissolve. Reduce the heat to medium, stir in the arrowroot mixture, and stir for a minute or two until thickened. Transfer to a serving bowl and sprinkle with the sesame seeds.

Each serving provides:

66	Calories	8 g	Carbohydrate
3 g	Protein	215 mg	Sodium
2 g	Fat	0 mg	Cholesterol
2 g	Dietary Fiber		

Broccoli with Cumin and Coriander

ALMOST INSTANT, VEGAN

This broccoli side dish comes together very quickly. Serve it as an accompaniment to any Tex-Mex or Middle Eastern main dish.

Yield: 6 side-dish servings

Broccoli	1¼ pounds
Red onion, minced	2 tablespoons
Dry sherry	2 tablespoons
Olive oil	2 tablespoons
Ground cumin	⅛ teaspoon
Granulated garlic	⅛ teaspoon
Ground coriander	⅛ teaspoon
Salt	Scant ⅛ teaspoon
Pepper	Several grinds

Cut off and discard the tough stem ends of the broccoli and peel the remaining stalks if they are particularly thick-skinned. Cut the broccoli lengthwise into even-size spears. Place them on a steamer rack in a saucepan with a tight-fitting lid. Add about an inch of water, cover, and cook over medium-high heat 10 to 12 minutes, until just fork tender.

Meanwhile, place the onion, sherry, oil, cumin, garlic, coriander, salt, and pepper in a blender or food processor and puree. Drain the broccoli thoroughly and place on a serving platter. Drizzle with the oil mixture and serve immediately.

Each serving provides:

65	Calories	4 g	Carbohydrate
2 g	Protein	60 mg	Sodium
5 g	Fat	0 mg	Cholesterol
2 g	Dietary Fiber		

Broccoli and Mushrooms en Papillote with Paprika, Feta, and Dill Seed

ALMOST INSTANT

This delectable dish features the distinctive flavors of Eastern Europe. The packets can be prepared and wrapped ahead of time and kept in the refrigerator until just before cooking. If the packets are going directly from the refrigerator to the oven, add two minutes to their baking time.

Yield: 4 side-dish servings

Paprika	1	**teaspoon**
Dill seed, crushed	½	**teaspoon**
Salt		**A pinch**
Pepper		**Several grinds**
Broccoli	1¼	**pounds**
Mushrooms	¼	**pound**
Red onion		**Several paper-thin slices**
Dark beer or ale	4	**tablespoons**
Feta cheese, crumbled	3	**ounces (¾ cup)**
Fresh lemon wedges	1	**per person**
Parchment paper for baking	4	**12 × 16-inch pieces**

Preheat the oven to 425 degrees F. In a small dish, combine the paprika, dill seed, salt, and pepper. Cut off and discard the tough stem ends of the broccoli and peel the remaining stalks if they are particularly thick-skinned. Cut the broccoli lengthwise into even-size spears. Brush or wipe loose dirt particles from the mushrooms and quarter them.

Fold each piece of parchment in half and crease to create 8 × 12-inch rectangles. Use scissors to cut each rectangle into a half-heart shape. Open out the hearts and distribute the broccoli spears, positioning them near the center of each crease. Add ¼ of the mushrooms and onion slices to each packet, arranging loosely on top of the broccoli. Sprinkle everything evenly with the spice mixture. Pour 1 tablespoon of beer over each portion, and top each with ¼ of the feta. Close the heart so that the edges of the paper meet. Beginning at the round end, fold over about ½ inch of the paper and crease sharply. Work your way around the shape of the heart, folding in the edges and creasing sharply in overlapping pleats. Twist the pointy end to seal everything tightly in the paper packet. Repeat this process with the remaining packets.

Place the packets in a single layer on a baking sheet and bake for 12 minutes. Place each packet on a warmed serving plate and instruct your guests to pinch and tear the paper to release the aromatic steam. The contents can then be lifted out onto the plate and the paper removed from the table and discarded. Serve very hot, with lemon wedges.

Each serving provides:

116	Calories	12 g	Carbohydrate
8 g	Protein	311 mg	Sodium
5 g	Fat	19 mg	Cholesterol
4 g	Dietary Fiber		

Marinated Broccoli Salad with Jarlsberg and Mandarin Oranges

The colors of this composed salad are beautiful—a great way to bring a bit of spring into a winter day.

Yield: 6 side-dish servings

Broccoli	1½	pounds
Mandarin oranges	1	11-ounce can
Olive oil	⅓	cup
Raspberry vinegar	¼	cup
Garlic	1	clove, minced
Dried tarragon	½	teaspoon
Dried chervil	½	teaspoon
Butter lettuce	6	large leaves
Reduced-fat Jarlsberg cheese, shredded	2	ounces (1 cup)

Cut off and discard the tough stem ends of the broccoli and peel the remaining stalks if they are particularly thick-skinned. Cut the broccoli lengthwise into even-size spears. Place the spears on a steamer rack in a saucepan that has a tight-fitting lid. Add about 1 inch of water, cover, and cook over medium-high heat about 6 minutes, until bright green and barely tender-crisp. Plunge briefly into a bowl of ice water to stop the cooking and to cool the broccoli. Drain well. Drain the oranges, retaining their liquid.

Whisk together the oil, vinegar, garlic, tarragon, and chervil. Add 3 tablespoons of the reserved orange liquid and whisk to incorporate. Place the broccoli and orange segments in a shallow bowl and pour the marinade over them. Cover and refrigerate for about 1 hour, or as long as overnight.

Line six chilled salad bowls with the lettuce leaves and place the broccoli and oranges on top. Spoon about 1 tablespoon of the marinade over each serving. Discard the remaining marinade, or save it to use as a salad dressing over the course of a week. Top with the Jarlsberg and serve.

Each serving provides:

134	Calories	13 g	Carbohydrate
5 g	Protein	56 mg	Sodium
8 g	Fat	5 mg	Cholesterol
2 g	Dietary Fiber		

Creamy Broccoli Soup with Dill, Mustard, and Paprika

ALMOST INSTANT

This lovely green soup is a wonderful way to begin an elegant dinner party. You can also serve it as a main course for four, with plenty of crusty bread and a tart and hearty salad on the side.

Yield: 6 first-course servings

Broccoli	1	**pound**
Garlic	4	**cloves, minced**
Bay leaf	1	
Dried dill	1	**teaspoon**
Dill seed	¼	**teaspoon**
Salt	¼	**teaspoon plus ⅛ teaspoon**
Nonfat milk	1½	**cups**
Unsalted butter	1	**tablespoon**
Paprika	1½	**teaspoons**
Unbleached flour	1	**tablespoon**
Pepper		**Several grinds**
Parmesan cheese, finely grated	2	**tablespoons**
Dijon mustard	1	**teaspoon**

Trim off and discard the tough stem ends of the broccoli. Peel the remaining stalks if they are particularly thick-skinned. Coarsely chop the stalk and heads. Combine the broccoli, garlic, bay leaf, dill, dill seed, and ¼ teaspoon salt in a large saucepan with 2 cups of water. Bring to a simmer over high heat, reduce heat to medium, cover and cook 10 minutes. Broccoli should be very tender.

The Best 125 Vegetable Dishes

Meanwhile, place the milk in a small saucepan and heat over very low heat until it is steaming. Do not bring to a boil. Melt the butter in a medium saucepan over medium-low heat and add the paprika. Stir around for a moment, then stir in the flour. Stir constantly for about a minute to slightly cook the flour, then pour in the heated milk in a thin, steady stream, whisking constantly. Bring the sauce to a simmer over medium heat, reduce heat to medium-low, and cook for 10 minutes, whisking frequently, until thickened. Stir in the remaining ⅛ teaspoon salt, pepper, Parmesan cheese, and mustard.

Meanwhile, remove the bay leaf and puree the broccoli and its cooking liquid in a blender in small batches. Return the broccoli puree to the saucepan and stir in the white sauce. Cook another minute or two, until heated through. Serve very hot with a dusting of paprika.

Each serving provides:

79	Calories	9 g	Carbohydrate
5 g	Protein	248 mg	Sodium
3 g	Fat	8 mg	Cholesterol
2 g	Dietary Fiber		

Pasta and Broccoli with Creamy Spiced Tomato Sauce

ALMOST INSTANT

Prepare this quick and delicious standby whenever you are in a rush to get a meal on the table. Put the pasta water on to boil, and twenty minutes later you'll be serving a great feast.

Yield: 6 main-course servings

Tomatoes	¾	pound, chopped
Light sour cream	¾	cup
Plain nonfat yogurt	¾	cup
Chopped black olives	1	4¼-ounce can
Fresh cilantro, minced	¼	cup
Chili powder	1	tablespoon
Dried oregano	2	teaspoons
Garlic	3	cloves, minced
Salt	¼	teaspoon
Pepper		Several grinds
Broccoli	1	pound
Dried pasta spirals	12	ounces
Parmesan cheese, finely grated	¼	cup

Put several quarts of water on to boil for the pasta. In a medium saucepan, combine the tomatoes, sour cream, yogurt, olives, cilantro, chili powder, oregano, garlic, salt, and pepper. Cook over medium heat for 15 minutes, stirring frequently.

Meanwhile, trim off and discard the tough stem ends of the broccoli. Peel the remaining stalks if they are particularly thick-skinned. Chop the stalks and heads into small, uniform pieces. Cook the pasta in the boiling water until al dente, adding the broccoli for the last 4 minutes. Drain well and toss with the hot sauce and Parmesan. Serve immediately in warmed bowls.

Each serving provides:

355	Calories	56 g	Carbohydrate
15 g	Protein	391 mg	Sodium
9 g	Fat	13 mg	Cholesterol
5 g	Dietary Fiber		

Cabbage

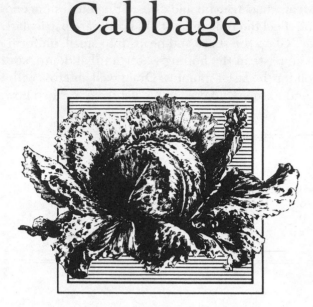

According to historians, cabbage has been cultivated for at least 2,500 years, originally in the eastern Mediterranean region. It played an important role in the cuisines of the ancient Greeks and Romans, though the cabbage they enjoyed was probably a nonheaded, loose-leaf variety. More cold-resistant, heading varieties—now classified as *Brassica oleracea capitata* (family Cruciferae)—were developed during the Middle Ages in northern Europe and became a mainstay in the diets of peasants there. Other cabbage family members included in this chapter are Brussels sprouts, napa cabbage, and bok choy.

Brussels sprouts were named after the capital of Belgium, where it is believed they were first cultivated. Declared the official vegetable of Belgium in 1820, Brussels sprouts look and taste much like tiny heads of cabbage, though their flavor and texture are more delicate. The growth habit of Brussels sprouts is unique—many tiny heads sprout from its tall, thick stem. The sprouts nearest the bottom of the stalk are the most mature at any given time.

Many varieties of cabbage have been cultivated for ornamental purposes, and indeed even the culinary type is a handsome plant in the cool-season garden. Napa cabbage has crinkly leaves and the head is elongated rather than round in shape. Sometimes sold as Chinese cabbage, napa is more delicate in texture and flavor than standard head cabbage. Its pale-green and ivory leaves are thin, crisp, and juicy and contribute a pleasant piquant crunch when added raw to salads.

Bok choy, also called Chinese cabbage, is a staple of Asian cooking. It is comprised of dark-green leaves attached to thick, smooth, white stems. The leaves have a delicious peppery taste; the stems are somewhat sweeter and quite succulent.

The Nutrition Picture

Cabbage is the grandmother of the cruciferous family of vegetables and shares with its relatives many nutritional benefits. These superfoods are good sources of fiber and antioxidants like carotenoids and vitamin C. Studies have shown that antioxidants help rid the body of free radicals, unstable oxygen molecules associated with the development of cancer and other major diseases. In addition, the cruciferous cousins contain beneficial nitrogen compounds called indoles that have been shown in recent studies to be effective cancer preventers. Indeed, evidence that cruciferous vegetables protect us against cancer has become so convincing that the National Cancer Institute, part of the U.S. Department of Health and Human Services, now recommends eating cruciferous vegetables several times each week.

Cabbage is very low in calories and contains no fat to speak of, no cholesterol, and very little sodium. In addition, it is high in potassium. The purple variety has a slightly higher vitamin C and fiber content.

Brussels sprouts have the same cancer-inhibiting properties as cabbage and other cruciferous vegetables. In addition, protein comprises 31 percent of their calories.

Bok choy and napa cabbage have some nutritional advantages over the round-heading varieties. They are both higher in calcium, and bok choy provides more beta carotene. In vitamin C, folacin, potassium, and fiber content, they are roughly equivalent to head cabbage.

Selection and Storage

It is easy to enjoy the nutritional advantages of cabbage, since head varieties are readily available and inexpensive year-round. Winter cabbages tend to be slightly sweeter due to their cold growing conditions. A two-pound head of cabbage will feed six as a side dish when cooked.

Select solid, heavy heads with only a few loose leaves wrapping a dense and compact core. Check for worm holes in the outer leaves, which may penetrate to the edible interior. The stem end should not be dry or split and the leaves should be tightly attached.

Head cabbage stores well for long periods and retains most of its vitamin C when kept cold. Store whole cabbages in an open plastic bag in the refrigerator—they will stay crisp and fresh for two weeks or so. Cover a cut cabbage tightly with plastic wrap and use within a few days. Don't buy partial heads, even if tightly wrapped in the green grocer's refrigerated case. Nutrient loss in cut heads begins immediately and progresses rapidly.

The peak season for Brussels sprouts is autumn through early spring. California is their primary producer, as they thrive in the moist coastal climate. Choose sprouts of even size that are small, compact, and unblemished. They should not appear puffy or feel soft. Their color should be bright green, without yellow or wilted leaves. Freshly harvested sprouts have a mild, clean aroma, not a strong cabbage smell. Avoid sprouts with tiny worm holes, which may penetrate to the center.

Don't wash or trim Brussels sprouts before storing, except to remove yellowed outer leaves. Outer green leaves contain most of the nutrients, so don't peel them off, even if they are somewhat loose. Store sprouts in an open plastic bag in the refrigerator for up to a few days. Frozen Brussels sprouts are available year-round, but they tend to be bitter and mushy, so enjoy these miniature cabbages only when available fresh and in season.

Napa cabbage and other crinkly-leaf varieties known as savoy cabbages tend to be looser and lighter in weight than smooth-surfaced heads. Select those with a fresh, crisp, glossy appearance and store them as you would other types of head cabbage.

Signs of freshness in bok choy include unwilted leaves and crisp, glossy stems. The leaves should be a deep, spinach green, the stems pearly white. The leaves begin to deteriorate rapidly, so plan to eat bok choy the same day you purchase it. Baby bok choy, harvested at about six inches in length, is a wonderful delicacy when available.

Culinary Tips

- Remove any damaged or wilted outer leaves from head cabbages and cut as directed in recipes.
- Head cabbages are delicious both raw and cooked. Don't discard the core portion; it can be grated into salads or chopped and cooked along with the leaves.

- Cabbages of all varieties smell strong and unappetizing when overcooked. Their textures and flavors also suffer with overcooking, so be sure to cook cabbage until just fork tender.

- Keep in mind that the color of purple cabbage will bleed out during cooking, tinting your other ingredients a bright pink.

- Trim off the stem ends of Brussels sprouts below where the leaves are attached so they remain connected. Make an X incision in the bottom of each stem to help heat penetrate for even cooking. Insert a fork into the stem end to test for doneness—sprouts are done when barely tender.

- Wash bok choy carefully, as dirt and insects may be hiding in the center of the bunch. Bok choy is usually chopped before cooking, but the baby variety is wonderful when cooked and served as a whole bunch.

Braised Cabbage with Red Onion and Paprika

ALMOST INSTANT

This braised dish is very easy to prepare, and it is delicious, without a hint of bitterness.

Yield: 6 side-dish servings

Green cabbage	**1½**	**pounds (1 small)**
Red onion	**1**	**medium**
Unsalted butter	**1**	**tablespoon**
Dry sherry	**2**	**tablespoons**
Dried tarragon	**½**	**teaspoon**
Salt	**¼**	**teaspoon**
Pepper		**Several grinds**
Paprika	**1**	**teaspoon**

Cut the cabbage in half and remove the center core. Dice the core and thinly slice the remaining cabbage. Cut the onion in half, then cut each half into thin slices. Place the butter and sherry in a skillet over medium-high heat, along with ⅓ cup water. Add the cabbage, onion, tarragon, salt, and pepper. Cover, reduce heat to medium, and cook for 10 minutes until the cabbage wilts and is just fork tender. Add the paprika, toss, and serve.

Each serving provides:

69	Calories	10 g	Carbohydrate
2 g	Protein	115 mg	Sodium
2 g	Fat	5 mg	Cholesterol
3 g	Dietary Fiber		

Brussels Sprouts with Fresh Dill and Pimientos

ALMOST INSTANT, VEGAN

This has become a traditional Thanksgiving side dish at our tables. It pairs well with all of the savory flavors enjoyed that day. Make it, however, any time during Brussels sprout season, as only fresh ones will do. Dried dill weed may be used if fresh is not available; use half the amount called for in the recipe and add it to the stock along with the Brussels sprouts.

Yield: 6 side-dish servings

Brussels sprouts	1	pound
Low-sodium vegetable broth cube	½	large
Olive oil	1	tablespoon
Granulated sugar	½	teaspoon
Dried red chili flakes	⅛	teaspoon
Fresh-squeezed lemon juice	2	teaspoons
Fresh dill, minced	2	tablespoons
Sliced pimientos, undrained	1	2-ounce jar
Salt		Scant ⅛ teaspoon
Pepper		Several grinds

Trim the stem ends and remove any wilted or discolored outer leaves from the Brussels sprouts. Cut each one in half, if large, or if small, make an X incision in the bottom. This ensures more even cooking. Make a stock by dissolving the vegetable broth cube in ¾ cup hot water. Place the stock, oil, sugar, chili flakes, and lemon juice in a large skillet over medium-high heat. Bring to a simmer, add the Brussels sprouts, reduce heat to medium, cover, and simmer 12 to 15 minutes, until just fork tender.

Remove the lid after 12 minutes to make sure there is still a little liquid in the pan; you want the Brussels sprouts to brown slightly, but not to scorch. If the liquid is gone but the Brussels sprouts are not yet tender, add a tablespoon or two of water and replace the lid. If they are tender and there is still liquid in the pan, stir and cook, uncovered, for a minute or two longer, until it has evaporated. Stir in the dill, pimientos, salt, and pepper. Serve immediately.

Each serving provides:

59	Calories	7 g	Carbohydrate
3 g	Protein	83 mg	Sodium
3 g	Fat	0 mg	Cholesterol
4 g	Dietary Fiber		

Baby Bok Choy with Lemon Miso Sauce

This member of the cabbage family is frequently showing up in supermarkets, especially on the West Coast. It has a sweetness about it not usually associated with cabbage. If baby bok choy is not available, you may substitute a pound of regular bok choy.

Yield: 6 side-dish servings

Baby bok choy	1	**pound**
Fresh-squeezed lemon juice	¼	**cup**
White miso	2	**tablespoons**
Garlic	2	**cloves, minced**
Arrowroot powder or cornstarch	1	**tablespoon**

Slice each bunch of bok choy in half lengthwise and place on a steamer rack in a saucepan that has a tight-fitting lid. Add about 1 inch of water, cover, and bring to a boil over high heat. Reduce heat to medium-high and cook for about 10 minutes, until fork tender.

Meanwhile, in a small pan, whisk together the lemon juice, miso, garlic, and ¼ cup water. Heat over low heat until steaming. Place 2 tablespoons of water in a small jar with a tight-fitting lid and add the arrowroot or cornstarch. Shake to dissolve. Whisk the arrowroot mixture into the lemon juice mixture and cook until thickened, about 1 minute. Do not overcook, as it will get gummy. Drain the bok choy and fan it out on a large serving platter, leaf end out. Drizzle with the sauce and serve immediately.

Each serving provides:

30	Calories	6 g	Carbohydrate
2 g	Protein	258 mg	Sodium
0 g	Fat	0 mg	Cholesterol
0 g	Dietary Fiber		

Overnight Cabbage Slaw
with Pimiento-Stuffed Olives

VEGAN

We frequently prepare this at Easter. The night before, after you have finished coloring the eggs and hidden the Easter baskets, you can quickly prepare this slaw and have it ready for an early-afternoon buffet lunch.

Yield: 12 side-dish servings

Rice wine vinegar	½	**cup**
Honey	2	**tablespoons**
Olive oil	2	**tablespoons**
Dijon mustard	2	**teaspoons**
Celery seed	1	**teaspoon**
Pepper		**Several grinds**
Green cabbage	2½	**pounds (1 medium)**
Red onion	1	**medium**
Green bell peppers	2	**medium, diced**
Pimiento-stuffed olives, drained	1	**cup, sliced**

Combine the vinegar, honey, oil, mustard, celery seed, and pepper in small saucepan. Bring to a boil over medium-high heat, stirring frequently, and cook for 1 minute. Set aside.

Finely shred the cabbage and put it in a large bowl. Cut the onion in half and finely slice each half. Separate the rings and combine with the cabbage. Add the bell pepper and olives. Toss to combine. Pour on the dressing and toss again to evenly distribute it. Cover and chill for 8 to 24 hours.

Each serving provides:

81	Calories	11 g	Carbohydrate
2 g	Protein	318 mg	Sodium
4 g	Fat	0 mg	Cholesterol
3 g	Dietary Fiber		

Cabbage and Potatoes
Baked with Tomatoes,
Oregano, and Smoked Cheese

Simple and humble, this casserole is nevertheless delicious and soul-satisfying. Because it is hearty, we usually serve it as a main dish, but you could also prepare it as a side dish for a crowd.

Yield: 4 main-dish servings

Red potatoes	1	**pound**
		(4 medium)
Green cabbage, finely		
chopped	4	**cups**
Tomatoes	1½	**pounds**
		(3 medium)
Olive oil	1	**tablespoon plus**
		½ teaspoon
Garlic	3	**cloves, minced**
Dried oregano	2	**teaspoons**
Dried rosemary	½	**teaspoon,**
		crushed
Dill seed	½	**teaspoon**
Salt	¼	**teaspoon**
Pepper		**Several grinds**
Smoked cheddar cheese,		
grated	4	**ounces (1 cup)**

Put several quarts of water in a stockpot and bring to a boil. Scrub the potatoes and drop them into the boiling water. Bring back to a boil over high heat, reduce heat to medium-high, and cook 15 to 20 minutes, depending on their size. The potatoes should be easy to pierce all the way through with a sharp knife, but not on the verge of falling apart. Transfer them to a colander, rinse with cold water, and set aside to cool.

Meanwhile, place the cabbage in a saucepan or skillet with 2 tablespoons of water. Cover and cook over low heat for 5 minutes, to barely wilt the cabbage. The liquid should all evaporate; if it doesn't, pour off the liquid in the bottom of the pan before proceeding. Cut the tomatoes in half crosswise and squeeze out and discard the seed pockets. Chop the tomatoes and combine them in a large bowl with 1 tablespoon of the olive oil, the garlic, oregano, rosemary, dill seed, salt, and pepper. Add the cabbage and toss again.

Preheat the oven to 375 degrees F. When potatoes are cool enough to handle, dice them. There is no need to peel them. Toss the potatoes with the cabbage mixture and cheese. Rub a large casserole dish with the remaining ½ teaspoon oil. Place the cabbage mixture in the dish, cover, and bake for 25 to 30 minutes, until the cheese has melted and everything is piping hot. Serve immediately.

Each serving provides:

200	Calories	23 g	Carbohydrate
8 g	Protein	232 mg	Sodium
10 g	Fat	20 mg	Cholesterol
4 g	Dietary Fiber		

Curried Cabbage and Couscous en Papillote

This unusual but delicious vegetable main dish is colorful and aromatic, a wonderful surprise when the packets are opened at the table. Accompany it with falafel patties and cucumber yogurt salad for an exotic Middle Eastern meal.

Yield: 4 main-dish servings

Dry sherry	½	cup
Olive oil	1	tablespoon
Ground turmeric	½	teaspoon
Cayenne	¼	teaspoon
Anise seed	½	teaspoon, crushed
Garlic	2	cloves, minced
Salt	⅛	teaspoon
Pepper		Several grinds
Green cabbage	½	pound
Carrots	2	medium
Red bell pepper	1	medium
Couscous, uncooked	¾	cup
Light sour cream	½	cup
Parchment paper for baking	4	12 × 16-inch pieces

Preheat the oven to 450 degrees F. Whisk together the sherry, olive oil, turmeric, cayenne, anise, garlic, salt, and pepper with ¾ cup water. Finely slice the cabbage and set aside. Peel the carrots and cut into matchsticks. Cut the bell pepper into ¼-inch slices.

Fold each piece of parchment in half and crease to create 8 × 12-inch rectangles. Use scissors to cut each rectangle into a half-heart shape. Open out the hearts and place 3 tablespoons of couscous near the center of each crease. Layer the cabbage, carrots, and bell pepper on top of the couscous. Distribute the sherry sauce equally between the packets as you seal each one, being careful that the sauce does not run out. Close the heart so that the edges of the paper meet. Beginning at the round end, fold over about ½ inch of the paper and crease sharply. Work your way around the shape of the heart, folding in the edges and creasing sharply in overlapping pleats. Twist the pointy end to seal everything tightly in the paper packet. Repeat this process with the remaining packets.

Place the packets in a single layer on a baking sheet and bake for 18 minutes. Transfer each packet to a warmed serving plate and instruct your guests to pinch and tear the paper to release the aromatic steam. The contents may then be lifted out onto the plate and the paper removed from the table and discarded. Pass the sour cream.

Each serving provides:

300	Calories	42 g	Carbohydrate
8 g	Protein	104 mg	Sodium
8 g	Fat	10 mg	Cholesterol
3 g	Dietary Fiber		

Spicy Napa Cabbage Sauté over Buckwheat Noodles in a Miso Broth

VEGAN

Earthy, delicious, and supremely nourishing, this meal in a bowl is the perfect choice for a cool evening in early autumn. It has quite a few steps, but none of them are difficult or terribly time-consuming. Any unfamiliar ingredients can be located at an Asian specialty market.

Yield: 4 main-dish servings

Dried shiitake mushrooms	1	**ounce**
Raw sesame seeds	1	**tablespoon**
Dried soba noodles (Japanese buckwheat)	8	**ounces**
Dark sesame oil	2	**teaspoons**
Low-sodium vegetable broth cube	½	**large**
Low-sodium soy sauce	1	**tablespoon plus 1 teaspoon**
Mirin	1	**tablespoon**
Sake	1	**tablespoon**
Fresh ginger, grated	1	**tablespoon**
Peanut oil	2	**teaspoons**
Garlic	3	**cloves, minced**
Dried red chili flakes	¼	**teaspoon, crushed**
Mustard seed	¼	**teaspoon, crushed**

The Best 125 Vegetable Dishes

Yellow onion	1	medium
Red bell pepper	1	medium, slivered
Napa cabbage, shredded	3	cups
White miso	1	tablespoon

Place the mushrooms in 2 cups of warm water and set aside to soak for 30 minutes, then lift the mushrooms from the liquid and set aside. Strain the soaking liquid through a paper coffee filter and place in a saucepan. Rinse the mushrooms under a small stream of cold water to remove any grit lodged in the membranes under the caps. Trim off the stems and sliver the mushrooms. Set aside. Place the sesame seeds in a heavy, dry skillet and cook over medium heat, stirring or shaking the pan frequently, until the seeds are lightly browned and emit a roasted aroma. Grind them coarsely in a spice grinder or with a mortar and pestle. Set aside.

In a stockpot, bring a few quarts of water to a boil over high heat. When boiling rapidly, add the noodles and cook for 10 minutes after the water returns to a boil. Noodles should be cooked past the al dente stage, but should not be mushy. Drain well, toss with 1 teaspoon dark sesame oil, and return to the pan in which they were cooked. Put a lid on the pan and set aside.

Meanwhile, add 1½ cups of water to the mushroom soaking liquid and bring to a boil. Add the vegetable broth cube and stir to dissolve, then add 1 teaspoon of the soy sauce, the mirin, sake, ginger, and ground sesame seeds. Remove the resulting broth from the heat, but keep warm.

In a wok or heavy-bottomed skillet, heat the peanut oil with the remaining 1 teaspoon sesame oil over medium-high heat. Add the garlic, chili flakes, and mustard seed and stir and sauté for 1 minute. Add the onion and bell pepper and stir and sauté for 5 minutes. Add the cabbage and mushrooms and stir, then stir in the remaining 1 tablespoon soy sauce. Sauté, stirring frequently, 10 to 12 minutes, until the vegetables are limp and browned.

Meanwhile, reheat the broth, if necessary. When it is hot, dissolve the miso in 3 tablespoons of the broth in a small bowl, then stir this mixture into the broth pot. Ladle equal portions of the broth into four deep, warmed serving bowls. Divide the noodles evenly among the bowls and top with the stir-fried vegetables. Serve very hot.

Each serving provides:

336	Calories	60 g	Carbohydrate
12 g	Protein	841 mg	Sodium
7 g	Fat	0 mg	Cholesterol
2 g	Dietary Fiber		

Carrots

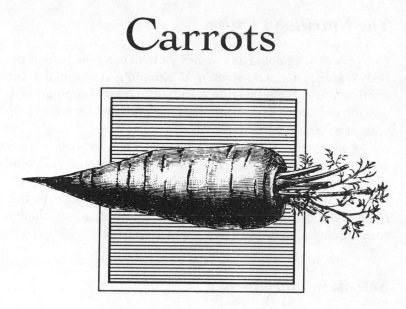

The carrot is native to the the warmer parts of Europe and western Asia. Like many of today's favorite vegetables, it was prized by Greeks and Romans, but mostly for medicinal purposes. Carrots were grown as a food crop in China, India, and Japan as early as the thirteenth century. An elongated orange carrot similar to the one enjoyed today was probably developed in the seventeenth century.

Known botanically as *Daucus carota sativa,* the common carrot is the most popular member of the Umbelliferae family, which includes parsley, dill, fennel, caraway, and celery. Deadly hemlock is also a distant relative.

The Nutrition Picture

Carrots are most noted as a source of beta carotene, which the body converts to usable vitamin A. Vitamin A is essential to the good health of the retina, but despite the carrot's reputation as a vision enhancer, its consumption has not been shown to help with most vision problems.

Among vegetables, carrots are second only to beets in sugar content. They are also high in soluble fiber, potassium, calcium, phosphorus, vitamin B$_1$, vitamin C (when raw), and vitamin E.

Carrots have an excellent nutrition profile, practically free of fat and sodium, so do include them in your diet even though they are higher in calories than many vegetables.

Selection and Storage

Carrots are available year-round, so there is never a need to resort to canned or frozen varieties, which have inferior levels of vitamins C and A, and potassium. When buying fresh carrots, plan on about ¾ of a pound to yield 4 side-dish servings.

Carrot tops are an excellent indicator of freshness—if they are crisp and bright green, you can be sure the carrots are fresh from the harvest. Often, however, clip-top carrots are the only available kind. Try to find ones that are sold loose, rather than in plastic bags, so you can inspect them for freshness.

Select well-shaped carrots that are firm, not flaccid. Younger carrots tend to be more tender, though more mature ones can be sweeter, since they have converted more of their starch to sugar while in the ground. The best quality carrots are ruddy orange in color, not pale or yellowish; the darker their color, the more beta carotene they contain. A green tint around the top is acceptable, but trim off and discard any green portions, as they will have a bitter taste.

Store carrots in a loosely closed plastic bag in the refrigerator. Tops should be twisted off before storage, or they will draw moisture from the roots. Don't store carrots with apples, which produce ethylene gas that can turn carrots bitter.

The nubbins sold as baby carrots are often trimmed-down remnants of larger carrots which are past their prime. Avoid these. True baby carrots are the ones sold unpeeled and with greens attached, looking exactly like miniature carrots.

Culinary Tips

- Scrub carrots with a brush under running water to remove surface dirt and bacteria, even if they look clean. This is preferable to peeling, since many of the carrot's nutrients reside in or just under the skin.
- Though raw carrots are delicious and nutritious, it is advisable to also eat them cooked because slight cooking makes their beta carotene more accessible. Eating tomatoes with carrots will also help maximize the body's utilization of beta carotene.
- As a rule of thumb, 1 large carrot weighs ⅓ pound.

Carrots with Fresh Fennel and Anise Seed

This recipe is a delightful way to present carrots. Their sweetness is enhanced by the subtle flavors of anise and fennel.

Yield: 4 side-dish servings

Carrots	1	pound (3 large)
Fresh fennel bulb	1	medium
Yellow onion	1	small
Anise seed	1	teaspoon
Unsalted butter	1	tablespoon
Garlic	2	cloves, minced
Fresh-squeezed lemon juice	3	tablespoons

Scrub the carrots and cut them at a slant into ½-inch slices. Remove the outer layer of the fennel bulb and any green, feathery leaves and shoots. Thinly slice the fennel. Cut the onion in half, then thinly slice each half. Crush the anise seed with a mortar and pestle or in a small food processor. Melt the butter in a large skillet over medium-high heat and stir in the garlic and anise seed. Cook for a minute, then stir in the lemon juice, carrots, fennel, and onion. Add ½ cup water, cover, and cook for 5 minutes. Reduce the heat to medium and cook 15 to 20 minutes, stirring occasionally. Remove the lid after 15 minutes to make sure there is still some liquid in the pan; you want the carrots to brown slightly, but not to scorch. If the liquid is gone but the carrots are not yet tender, add a tablespoon or two of water and replace the lid. If the carrots are tender and there is still liquid in the pan, stir and cook, uncovered, for a minute or two longer, until it has evaporated. Serve immediately.

Each serving provides:

99	Calories	17 g	Carbohydrate
3 g	Protein	114 mg	Sodium
3 g	Fat	8 mg	Cholesterol
4 g	Dietary Fiber		

Carrots Sautéed with Pineapple and Rum

ALMOST INSTANT

This dish is a simple and delicious way to eat your fill of nutritious carrots. It would combine well with a Tex-Mex, Caribbean, or Middle Eastern entrée. Mint leaves make a pretty garnish if you have some growing in the garden.

Yield: 4 side-dish serving

Carrots	¾	pound (4 small)
Unsalted butter	1	tablespoon
Shallots	2,	slivered
Salt		A pinch
Pepper		A few grinds
Unsweetened pineapple chunks	1	8-ounce can
Dark rum	2	tablespoons

Scrub the carrots and cut them at a slant into ¼-inch slices. Melt the butter in a heavy-bottomed skillet over medium-high heat and sauté the shallots for a minute, then add the carrots, salt, and pepper and stir and sauté 5 minutes. The carrots will begin to brown. Measure ⅓ cup of the juice from the canned pineapple. Pour this into the skillet, along with the rum, and stir. Immediately cover and cook for 5 minutes. Remove the lid, stir in the pineapple chunks, and cook for 2 minutes longer to just heat through. Transfer to a warmed serving bowl. Serve hot or at room temperature.

Each serving provides:

116	Calories	18 g	Carbohydrate
1 g	Protein	64 mg	Sodium
3 g	Fat	8 mg	Cholesterol
3 g	Dietary Fiber		

Creamy Spiced Carrots and Currants with Mint

ALMOST INSTANT

The sweetness of the carrots is accentuated by the currants, but the jalapeños provide plenty of heat to balance things out. A delicious, exotic-tasting dish, we like to serve this with polenta or steamed couscous and grilled fish, or as part of a curry feast.

Yield: 4 side-dish servings

Carrots	¾ pound (4 small)
Currants	2 tablespoons
Garlic	4 cloves, minced
Ground cumin	½ teaspoon
Ground cinnamon	¼ teaspoon
Salt	⅛ teaspoon
Plain nonfat yogurt	¾ cup
Fresh mint leaves, minced	¼ cup
Pickled jalapeño, seeded and minced	2 teaspoons

Scrub the carrots and dice them uniformly. Combine the carrots, currants, garlic, cumin, cinnamon, and salt in a skillet with ⅔ cup water. Cover and cook over medium-high heat 8 to 10 minutes, until fork tender. Remove the lid after 8 minutes to make sure there is still a little liquid left in the pan. You want the carrots to brown a bit, but not to scorch. If the liquid is gone but the carrots are not yet tender, add a tablespoon of water, cover, and cook another minute or two. If the carrots are tender, but the liquid is not yet gone, stir and cook a minute or two longer with the lid off, until the liquid evaporates. Turn off the heat and stir in the yogurt, then the mint and jalapeño. Allow to sit in the hot pan for a minute or so to warm the yogurt, then serve.

Each serving provides:

80	Calories	17 g	Carbohydrate
4 g	Protein	153 mg	Sodium
0 g	Fat	1 mg	Cholesterol
3 g	Dietary Fiber		

Asian-Style Carrot Salad

VEGAN

This dish uses the squiggly dried Chinese noodles often sold as "ramen." They are added to this salad uncooked, which lends a delightful crunch. The flavors marry well, producing a salad you will want to prepare frequently for family gatherings. You may hold it over in the refrigerator for several hours; however, if left too long, the noodles lose their crispness.

Yield: 8 side-dish servings

The dressing

Dark sesame oil	2	tablespoons
Rice wine vinegar	6	tablespoons
Low-sodium soy sauce	3	tablespoons
Fresh-squeezed orange juice	1	cup
Garlic	3	cloves, minced
Fresh ginger, grated	½	teaspoon

The salad

Carrots	1	pound (3 large)
Napa cabbage	1	pound
Green onions	6,	minced
Dried Oriental-style noodles	4	ounces

Whisk together the dressing ingredients and set aside at room temperature. Wash, peel, and grate the carrots and place in a large bowl. Wash the cabbage leaves, spin them dry, and cut into ¼-inch crosswise strips. Add them to the grated carrots, along with the minced green onions, and toss well to combine. Break the noodles into about 1-inch sections and add to the salad. Pour on the dressing, toss well to combine, and allow to sit for at least 20 minutes before serving.

Each serving provides:

133	Calories	23 g	Carbohydrate
4 g	Protein	362 mg	Sodium
4 g	Fat	0 mg	Cholesterol
3 g	Dietary Fiber		

Spicy Carrot and Cilantro Soup

This spicy soup will warm you on a cold winter day. Serve it with hearty whole wheat or rye bread. If you want a milder soup, use less cayenne pepper.

Yield: 4 main-course servings

Carrots	2	**pounds (6 large)**
Homemade Vegetable Stock*	4	**cups**
Fresh-squeezed lemon juice	¼	**cup**
Curry powder	1	**teaspoon**
Cayenne		**Scant ⅛ teaspoon**
Fresh cilantro, minced	½	**cup**
Lowfat milk	1	**cup**

*If you do not have Homemade Vegetable Stock on hand, make some according to the directions on page 12, or dissolve 1 large, low-sodium vegetable broth cube in 4 cups of hot water.

The Best 125 Vegetable Dishes

Scrub the carrots and slice them into ½-inch rounds. Combine the stock and carrots in a large saucepan and bring to a boil over high heat. Reduce heat to medium-high, cover, and simmer until fork tender, about 25 minutes. Transfer to a blender or food processor in small batches and puree until smooth. Return to the pot over medium-high heat and add the lemon juice, curry, cayenne, and cilantro. Stir in the milk. Heat through, but do not boil, and serve immediately.

Each serving provides:

138	Calories	26 g	Carbohydrate
5 g	Protein	155 mg	Sodium
2 g	Fat	5 mg	Cholesterol
7 g	Dietary Fiber		

Carrots Braised in Wine with Dill and Parsley

ALMOST INSTANT, VEGAN

Carrots cooked this way maintain a firm texture that is infused with flavor. The braising medium is wine and a slightly sweet one like Riesling is a perfect choice.

Yield: 4 side-dish servings

Carrots	¾	**pound (4 small)**
Olive oil	1	**tablespoon**
Garlic	2	**cloves, minced**
White wine	½	**cup**
Dried dill weed	½	**teaspoon**
Fresh parsley, minced	2	**tablespoons**

Scrub the carrots and cut them at a slant into thick slices. Heat the oil in a large skillet over medium heat and sauté the garlic for a minute. Add the wine, dill weed, and carrots. Stir, cover, and cook for 10 minutes until fork tender. Stir in the parsley and continue to cook for a minute or two, until remaining liquid evaporates. Transfer to a bowl and serve immediately.

Each serving provides:

86	Calories	9 g	Carbohydrate
1 g	Protein	29 mg	Sodium
4 g	Fat	0 mg	Cholesterol
3 g	Dietary Fiber		

Cauliflower

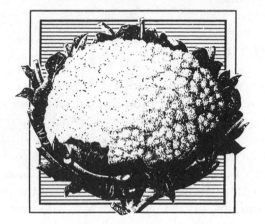

It is widely agreed that cauliflower was first cultivated for the table during Babylonian times, in the Tigris-Euphrates valley. These dense-headed edible flowers were brought to Europe during the Moorish invasion of Spain, but were originally assumed by Europeans to be ornamental, rather than culinary.

Cauliflower is so closely related to broccoli that they share the same botanical name: *Brassica oleracea botrytis*. In this country, white flower heads are most prized, but elsewhere in the world green or purple heads are preferred.

Cauliflower develops its characteristic shape, texture, and white color by virtue of a special cultivation technique. When the flower of the plant begins to form, the grower wraps and ties the plant's leaves around it for shade. The resulting head (also called the curd) is wonderfully succulent and pale in color because it has been protected from the heat and light of the sun. As with other cruciferous vegetables, cauliflower grows best in cool weather. Coastal California and New York are its major domestic producers.

The Nutrition Picture

Cauliflower is a great lowfat, low-sodium, and low-calorie source of important nutrients. It provides considerable amounts of potassium, phosphorus, and dietary fiber, and is a primary vegetable source of folic acid, one of the important B vitamins.

Like the rest of the cruciferous family, cauliflower is a good source of fiber and antioxidants like carotenoids and vitamin C. Studies have shown that antioxidants help rid the body of free radicals—unstable oxygen molecules associated with the development of cancer and other major diseases. In addition, the cruciferous cousins contain beneficial nitrogen compounds called indoles, which have been shown in recent studies to be effective cancer preventers. Indeed, evidence that cruciferous vegetables protect us against cancer has become so convincing that the National Cancer Institute, part of the U.S. Department of Health and Human Services, now recommends eating these vegetables several times each week.

Selection and Storage

Cauliflower is in good supply almost year-round, but it is most abundant and least expensive in autumn. When shopping for cauliflower, purchase a two-pound head for a yield of four to six servings.

Select firm, heavy, dense heads without brownish bruises or discoloration. The size of the head does not affect quality. Foliage should be crisp and vibrant green in color, not wilted or yellowish. Don't be concerned if you see small leaves growing between the florets—this will not affect the cauliflower's quality.

Fresh heads should have a mild cabbage scent, not a strong smell. There is also a tactile freshness test: Heads that crumble when scraped with a fingernail have been too long off the plant.

Stored in an open plastic bag in the refrigerator, cauliflower will keep for several days. Position it curd side down to prevent the collection of moisture, which will encourage the growth of mold.

Frozen cauliflower tends to be mushy and much lower in vitamin C and potassium than its fresh counterpart. As always, we recommend eating fresh vegetables in season for the best taste and texture and the highest nutrient values.

Culinary Tips

- Discard any wilted or yellowing leaves and rinse the cauliflower well before using.
- The leaves and core of a cauliflower can be eaten, raw or cooked, along with the curd.
- Cook cauliflower in stainless steel or enameled cast iron, as its color will be altered by contact with aluminum or iron.
- As with broccoli, quick cooking over high heat keeps cauliflower's color bright and its texture crisp and reduces the release of the sulfur compounds that cause an unpleasant odor.
- As a rule of thumb, one medium head of cauliflower weighs 1½ pounds untrimmed.

Cauliflower with Mustard Cheddar Glaze

ALMOST INSTANT

This recipe stems from a childhood favorite. Although then it was made with yellow "baseball mustard," today our preference is Dijon. This version is also decidedly lower in fat than the original. The pound weight for the cauliflower is before the leaves and core are removed, just as you find it in the supermarket.

Yield: 4 side-dish servings

Cauliflower	1	medium (1½ pounds)
Reduced-calorie mayonnaise	2	tablespoons
Plain nonfat yogurt	2	tablespoons
Dijon mustard	1	tablespoon
Dried tarragon	¼	teaspoon
Granulated garlic	⅛	teaspoon
Sharp Cheddar cheese, grated	1	ounce (½ cup)

Trim the outer leaves and core from the cauliflower, but leave it whole. Place it on a steamer rack in a saucepan that has a tight-fitting lid. Add about 2 inches of water, cover, and cook over medium-high heat 10 to 12 minutes, until almost fork tender. Remove from the pan and transfer to an ungreased glass pie pan.

Meanwhile, preheat the oven to 350 degrees F. Whisk together the mayonnaise, yogurt, mustard, tarragon, and garlic. Pour this over the partially cooked cauliflower and top with the grated cheese. Bake, uncovered, for 6 to 8 minutes to melt the cheese. Serve immediately.

Each serving provides:

74	Calories	5 g	Carbohydrate
4 g	Protein	212 mg	Sodium
5 g	Fat	10 mg	Cholesterol
2 g	Dietary Fiber		

Cauliflower Sautéed with Peaches and Cardamom

ALMOST INSTANT, VEGAN

This subtle interplay of flavors is stupendous, but to be enjoyed only in the summertime, when peaches are at their peak of sweetness.

Yield: 4 side-dish servings

Cauliflower, chopped	4	**cups**
Shallots, peeled and slivered	2	**medium**
Salt	¼	**teaspoon**
Peaches	¾	**pound**
Ground cardamom	½	**teaspoon**
Pepper		**Several grinds**
Fresh parsley, minced	2	**tablespoons**

Combine the cauliflower, shallots, and salt with ⅓ cup water in a heavy-bottomed skillet. Cover and cook over medium-low heat 7 minutes, until cauliflower is barely fork tender.

The Best 125 Vegetable Dishes

Meanwhile, peel the peaches and slice the flesh from the pits into bite-size chunks. When cauliflower is tender, add the peaches, cardamom, and pepper to the skillet and cook, stirring gently but frequently, for 3 minutes or so, until peaches are heated through. Toss with the parsley in a bowl and serve hot or at room temperature.

Each serving provides:

56	Calories	13 g	Carbohydrate
3 g	Protein	151 mg	Sodium
0 g	Fat	0 mg	Cholesterol
4 g	Dietary Fiber		

Curried Cauliflower and Garbanzo Bean Salad with Cherry Tomatoes

ALMOST INSTANT, VEGAN

This quite filling and nourishing cold dish makes a wonderful potluck contribution or summer buffet offering. Store leftovers in the refrigerator in a tightly closed container and enjoy them over the course of a few days—the flavor actually improves with time.

Yield: 6 side-dish servings

Cumin seed	½	teaspoon
Fresh-squeezed lemon juice	2	tablespoons
Fresh-squeezed orange juice	2	tablespoons
Olive oil	2	tablespoons
Curry powder	1	teaspoon
Low-sodium soy sauce	2	teaspoons
Salt	¼	teaspoon
Cherry tomatoes	½	pound
Cauliflower, chopped	1	pound
Red onion, minced	⅓	cup
Fresh cilantro, minced	⅓	cup
Cooked garbanzo beans (chickpeas)	1½ cups	
Pepper	Several grinds	
Butter lettuce	1	head

Toast the cumin seed in a dry, heavy-bottomed skillet, stirring or shaking the pan frequently until the seeds begin to pop and emit a nutty aroma. Crush to a coarse meal consistency with a mortar and pestle or in a spice grinder. Combine with the lemon juice, orange juice, olive oil, curry powder, soy sauce, and salt in a small bowl. Remove the stems from the cherry tomatoes and halve or quarter them lengthwise, depending on their size.

Toss with the dressing in a pretty serving bowl, cover with a clean tea towel, and set aside at room temperature.

Place the cauliflower on a steamer rack in a saucepan that has a tight-fitting lid. Add about an inch of water, cover, and cook over medium heat 7 minutes, until fork tender. Immediately plunge it into ice water to stop the cooking. Drain very thoroughly. Combine with the tomato mixture, red onion, cilantro, garbanzo beans, and pepper. You may serve the salad immediately, or chill for several hours. When you are ready to serve it, wash and dry the butter lettuce. Tear it into bite-size pieces and toss with the cauliflower mixture. Garnish with cilantro sprigs, if desired.

Each serving provides:

147	Calories	20 g	Carbohydrate
6 g	Protein	178 mg	Sodium
6 g	Fat	0 mg	Cholesterol
4 g	Dietary Fiber		

Cauliflower Soup with Tomatoes, Rosemary, Chard, and Ricotta Cheese

Hearty and delicious, this is a perfect cold weather soup. Serve it with a crusty bread, a tart salad, and fruity red wine.

Yield: 6 main-dish servings

Unsalted butter	1	tablespoon
Yellow onion	1	medium
Garlic	4	cloves, minced
Dried rosemary	1½	teaspoons
Dried red chili flakes	¼	teaspoon
Cauliflower, finely chopped	4	cups
Dry sherry	½	cup
Salt	¾	teaspoon
Homemade Vegetable Stock°	5	cups
Low-sodium whole tomatoes, canned	2	cups, with juice
Swiss chard	½	pound
Dried oregano	1	teaspoon
Pepper		A few grinds
Part-skim ricotta cheese	1	cup
Nutmeg, freshly grated		A few grinds per serving

°If you do not have Homemade Vegetable Stock on hand, make some according to the directions on page 12, or dissolve 1 large, low-sodium vegetable broth cube in 5 cups of hot water.

Heat the butter in a stockpot over medium heat and sauté the onion, garlic, rosemary, and chili flakes for 3 minutes. Add the cauliflower, sherry, ½ teaspoon of the salt, and the stock. Bring to a boil over high heat, then reduce heat to medium and simmer 20 minutes.

Meanwhile, put the whole tomatoes in a bowl and use a spoon to break them up. Wash the chard, sliver the stems, and coarsely chop the leaves. Put the tomatoes in a large, stainless steel skillet with the chard stems, remaining ¼ teaspoon salt, oregano, and pepper. Bring to a simmer over medium-high heat and cook 5 minutes. Add the chard leaves to the simmering tomatoes, cover, reduce heat to low, and cook 5 minutes.

When cauliflower mixture is done, transfer it in small batches to a blender, adding some of the ricotta cheese to each batch. Puree until fairly smooth and collect in a large bowl. Return the puree to the stockpot and stir in the tomato mixture. Heat through for a few minutes and serve very hot, passing the nutmeg grinder.

Each serving provides:

169	Calories	17 g	Carbohydrate
8 g	Protein	485 mg	Sodium
6 g	Fat	18 mg	Cholesterol
3 g	Dietary Fiber		

Risotto with Cauliflower, Tarragon, Anise Liqueur, and Feta

Tarragon is the flavor that unifies this delectable dish. Serve it with a light red wine and a salad with balsamic vinaigrette for a delightful meal.

Yield: 4 main-dish servings

Dried tomatoes, minced	2	tablespoons
Cauliflower, chopped	3	cups
Olive oil	1	tablespoon
Green onions	3,	minced
Garlic	3	cloves, minced
Arborio rice, uncooked	1	cup
Dried tarragon, crumbled	1	tablespoon plus 1 teaspoon
Anise liqueur	¼	cup
Capers, drained and minced	3	tablespoons
Feta cheese, crumbled	2	ounces (½ cup)
Pepper		Several grinds

Reconstitute the tomatoes if they are too dry to mince by soaking for 15 to 30 minutes in hot water. Drain them well and mince them. Set aside.

Place the cauliflower on a steamer rack in a saucepan that has a tight-fitting lid. Add about two inches of water, cover the pan, and cook over medium-high heat about 7 minutes, until barely fork tender. Immediately plunge the cauliflower into ice water to stop the cooking, drain well, and set aside in a colander.

Heat the oil in a heavy-bottomed saucepan over medium heat and sauté the onions, garlic, and dried tomato for 1 minute. Add the rice and tarragon, stirring to coat with the oil and seasonings. Add the anise liqueur and stir gently until the liquid is absorbed. Add 4 cups of hot water, ½ cup at a time, stirring almost constantly and waiting until liquid is absorbed before each addition. Add the capers and the cauliflower with the last ½ cup water. When the last addition of water has been absorbed and risotto is tender, transfer to warmed individual bowls, top each serving with a quarter of the feta, and grind on some black pepper. Serve immediately.

Each serving provides:

332	Calories	53 g	Carbohydrate
8 g	Protein	372 mg	Sodium
8 g	Fat	15 mg	Cholesterol
3 g	Dietary Fiber		

Stir-Fry of Cauliflower, Tomatoes, Orange, and Fresh Basil

ALMOST INSTANT, VEGAN

This fresh, light dish highlights a vegetable from the cruciferous family that is often overlooked as the center of a meal. The rich, smoky flavor of the sesame oil and the peppery character of the fresh basil complement the sweetness of the orange juice perfectly.

Yield: 4 main-dish servings

Basmati rice, uncooked	1	cup
Olive oil	1	teaspoon
Granulated garlic	½	teaspoon
Canola oil	1	tablespoon
Dark sesame oil	1	tablespoon
Yellow onion	1	medium, diced
Cauliflower, chopped	4	cups
Fresh-squeezed orange juice	½	cup
Fresh pear tomatoes	½	pound, diced
Tomatillos, water-packed, drained	1	12-ounce can, chopped
Fresh basil leaves, minced	½	cup
Arrowroot powder or cornstarch	1	tablespoon

Place 2¼ cups of water in a medium saucepan over high heat and bring to a boil. Add the rice, olive oil, and garlic. Cover, reduce heat to very low, and cook 20 minutes. Allow to sit 5 minutes, then fluff with a fork before serving.

Meanwhile, heat the remaining oils in a wok over medium-high heat and add the onion. Sauté 2 to 3 minutes until it becomes opaque. Add the cauliflower and stir. Stir in the orange juice, cover, and cook 5 minutes, stirring occasionally. Add the tomatoes, tomatillos, and basil. Stir to combine, lower the heat to medium-low, cover, and cook 5 to 7 minutes, stirring occasionally, until cauliflower is fork tender. Combine 2 tablespoons of water with the arrowroot powder in a jar with a tight-fitting lid. Shake to dissolve, then stir into the cauliflower mixture, cooking for a moment or two to thicken the sauce. Place equal portions of the cooked rice on warmed serving plates and spoon the cauliflower mixture over the top.

Each serving provides:

312	Calories	55 g	Carbohydrate
9 g	Protein	43 mg	Sodium
9 g	Fat	0 mg	Cholesterol
4 g	Dietary Fiber		

Pasta with Cauliflower, Mint, Raisins, and Pine Nuts

ALMOST INSTANT

This pasta dish is delectably hot, sweet, and tart. It calls for simple ingredients that you may not be used to combining; however, the result is outstanding. Serve at a casual dinner party with a fruity Merlot, salad, and bread.

Yield: 6 main-dish servings

Pine nuts	¼	cup
Dry sherry	2	tablespoons
Garlic	3	cloves, minced
Yellow onion	1	medium, minced
Cauliflower, chopped	7	cups
Golden raisins	1	cup
No-Yolks egg noodles	12	ounces
Unsalted butter	2	tablespoons
Unbleached flour	2	tablespoons
Ground cumin	½	teaspoon
Cayenne	⅛	teaspoon
Lowfat milk	1	cup
Fresh mint leaves, minced	½	cup
Plain nonfat yogurt	½	cup

Put several quarts of water on to boil for the pasta. Place the pine nuts in a single layer in a dry, heavy-bottomed skillet over medium-high heat. Shake the pan or stir frequently until the nuts are golden brown and emit a wonderful roasted aroma. Remove immediately from the pan and set aside until needed.

Put the sherry, garlic, and onion in a large skillet over medium-high heat, stir to combine, and cook 3 minutes. Stir in the cauliflower, then pour in ¾ cup of hot water. Cover, reduce heat to medium, and cook 6 minutes. Remove the lid, stir in the raisins, reduce heat to low, and continue to cook 1 to 2 minutes, until the cauliflower is fork tender. The cooking liquid will evaporate, so stir frequently to prevent scorching. Turn off the heat, stir, cover, and set aside while you cook the pasta and complete the sauce.

Cook the pasta in the boiling water until al dente. Meanwhile, melt the butter in a small skillet over medium heat. Stir in the flour, cumin, and cayenne and cook for about a minute. Gradually whisk in the milk and continue to cook, stirring frequently, about 5 minutes, or until the sauce thickens. Stir in the mint and turn off the heat. Drain the pasta well and place it in a large, warmed serving bowl. Add the cauliflower mixture and yogurt and toss to combine. Pour the mint cream sauce over the pasta and cauliflower, toss to combine, and top with the pine nuts. Serve immediately.

Each serving provides:

420	Calories	76 g	Carbohydrate
16 g	Protein	81 mg	Sodium
8 g	Fat	14 mg	Cholesterol
5 g	Dietary Fiber		

Corn

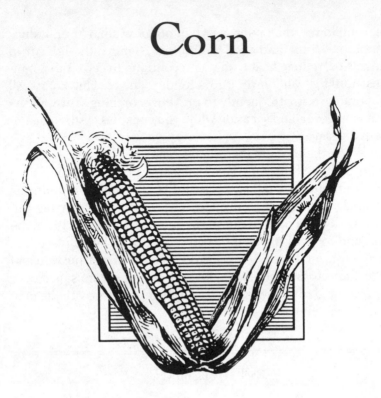

Corn was a staple food of the Mayans, Aztecs, and Incas, as well as the Indians of North America, and was revered by them as sacred. Columbus is thought to have brought corn to Spain from what is now Cuba in 1496.

Corn is botanically classified as *Zea mays*. *Maize* is still the name used for corn by native Americans, and by people in many other cultures around the world. The word *corn* to the British, for example, is applied to any popular cereal grain. What we call corn is maize to them.

The edible kernels of the corn plant are considered a grain, but the plant is technically a grass. Sweet corn for eating fresh was not widely cultivated until the mid 1800s. Today there are more than two hundred varieties, most with yellow or white kernels.

Sweet corn is harvested when it is immature, when the kernels are most tender and juicy. Florida is the leading domestic producer of fresh sweet corn for winter markets, and New York and Ohio are among the leading growers of summer corn, though many other states produce an impressive corn crop.

Corn now figures prominently in the cuisines of many cultures—polenta in Italy, and masa for tortillas in Mexico, for example—but sweet corn on the cob is primarily enjoyed in the United States.

Field corn denotes those varieties that are allowed to mature on the plant to a starchier stage before being fed to cattle or processed into starch, sweeteners, whiskey, papers, and plastics. Popcorn is made from a particularly thick-walled strain of field corn. It makes a nutritious high-fiber snack when not drenched in butter and salt.

The Nutrition Picture

Corn is high in carbohydrates and is a good vegetable source of protein. In addition, yellow-kerneled varieties provide some beta carotene. Corn is fairly low in calories, has only a trace of sodium, and provides respectable quantities of iron, zinc, potassium, calcium, and phosphorus.

Selection and Storage

Corn is primarily a hot weather vegetable; in most parts of the country, harvest time is late summer and early fall. Florida-grown sweet corn, however, is available in markets December through May. Plan on one ear per person. One ear of corn yields about ½ cup of kernels.

After harvest, warm temperatures quickly convert corn's sugar into starch; therefore, it should be displayed in a refrigerated bin or on ice and in the shade at outdoor markets. Take along a small cooler if you are traveling outside the city to buy corn from a farm stand. Purchase ears with the husks still on, as the sugar conversion process accelerates once the husks have been removed.

Select corn with grassy green and damp husks and pale, moist, and soft silk. Dried out husks and dark brown silk indicate the ears are past their prime. Husks on fresh corn should be loose around the tip but snug around the rest of the ear.

With corn, in particular, we recommend careful inspection at the market to avoid disappointment later in the kitchen. If no kernels are showing, gently pull back a strip of husk to examine the top rows, but replace the husk immediately after your inspection to protect the sweetness of the corn. Exposed kernels should be plump and smooth looking, not shriveled. Rows should be full, tightly packed, and fairly even, exuding milky liquid when pricked. Kernels at the tip will be small but should still be juicy. The cut stem ends rust over time—pass over any rusty looking ears.

Corn on the cob should be stored at cold temperatures with husks intact to retain moisture until cooking. Husked corn should be refrigerated in an open plastic bag. Cook corn as soon as possible after purchase—preferably within a few hours—as it is sweetest when cooked directly after picking. Corn not used immediately can be stored for a day or two, or you may parboil it for a minute, wrap tightly, and refrigerate for an additional two or three days.

Corn freezes well, though its vitamin C content diminishes, so frozen corn is a reasonable choice when good quality fresh corn isn't available. Canned corn, on the other hand, often includes extra salt and sugar and is not suitable as a substitute for fresh in our recipes.

Culinary Tips

- Strip off the husks and carefully remove the strands of corn silk clinging to the ears. If necessary, use a dry brush to gently dislodge any silk stuck between the rows of kernels.

- If a recipe calls for fresh corn kernels, cut them from the cob with a sharp knife, being careful not to cut through to the cob itself. One medium ear of corn will yield about ½ cup of kernels.

- If it's necessary to substitute frozen corn kernels for fresh, cooking times may need to be reduced.

- Do not salt corn while it's cooking, as this may toughen the kernels.

- Corn on the cob only needs to heat through—2 to 5 minutes of steaming will be long enough. Overcooked corn will be tough and pulpy rather than juicy.

- For grilling, cut off the tassel end of each ear, leave ears wrapped in their husks, and soak them in ice water for 5 minutes before placing on the grill. Corn is done when husks are blackened.

- To freeze whole ears at home, remove husks and silk, blanch for 3 minutes, cool in ice water, drain, and seal in plastic bags.

Steamed Corn with Pimiento and Horseradish

ALMOST INSTANT, VEGAN

Fresh, sweet corn is essential for this dish, so wait until it is at the peak of the season. The horseradish adds a subtle, not hot, flavor; however, you may increase the amount if you like the heat.

Yield: 6 side-dish servings

Corn kernels, fresh	3	cups (6 ears)
Prepared horseradish	1	teaspoon
Salt	⅛	teaspoon
Pepper		Several grinds
Minced pimientos	1	4-ounce jar
Fresh parsley, minced	¼	cup

Place the corn kernels on a steamer rack in a saucepan that has a tight-fitting lid. Add about 2 inches of water, cover, and cook over medium-high heat for 10 to 12 minutes (cooking time will depend on the variety and sugar content of the corn; it should be tender-crisp).

Meanwhile, mix together the horseradish, salt, pepper, and undrained pimientos in a medium bowl. Drain the corn and add to the pimiento mixture. Toss to combine, then add the parsley, toss again, and serve immediately.

Each serving provides:

83	Calories	18 g	Carbohydrate
3 g	Protein	64 mg	Sodium
1 g	Fat	0 mg	Cholesterol
3 g	Dietary Fiber		

Corn, Chard, and Tomato Sauté with Rosemary and Garlic

ALMOST INSTANT

These three summer treasures are delicious cooked together with Mediterranean seasonings. This dish is especially wonderful if the vegetables are home-grown.

Yield: 6 side-dish servings

Swiss chard	½	pound
Tomato	1	large (about ¾ pound)
Dried rosemary	½	teaspoon, crushed
Dried red chili flakes	⅛	teaspoon
Garlic	2	cloves, minced
Corn kernels, fresh	2	cups (4 ears)
Salt	¼	teaspoon
Half-and-half	2	tablespoons
Parmesan cheese, finely grated	2	tablespoons

Wash the chard carefully, but do not dry it. Cut the stems crosswise into ¼-inch slices. Coarsely chop the leaves. Set aside separately. Cut the tomato in half crosswise and squeeze out and discard the juicy seed pockets. Remove the core and dice the tomato. Set aside.

Heat 3 tablespoons of water in a skillet over medium heat with the rosemary, chili flakes, and garlic. When it begins to simmer, add the corn and chard stems. Sauté, stirring frequently, 3 minutes. Add the tomato and salt to the pan, then pile in the chard greens. Cover and cook for 7 minutes. Remove the lid and stir gently until everything is well distributed. If there is still watery liquid in the pan, continue to cook, uncovered, stirring constantly, until it has evaporated. Turn off the heat and stir in the cream and Parmesan until well distributed. Transfer to a platter and serve piping hot or warm.

Each serving provides:

122	Calories	21 g	Carbohydrate
5 g	Protein	324 mg	Sodium
3 g	Fat	7 mg	Cholesterol
3 g	Dietary Fiber		

Corn on the Cob with Chili Cheese Spread

ALMOST INSTANT

We often enjoy fresh corn on the cob simply steamed or grilled to perfection. As a change of pace, this tangy spread—not recommended for dieters—elevates corn on the cob from the good to the sublime. It would make a wonderful side dish with any lowfat Tex-Mex entrée. The spread can be made days ahead of time, if you wish. Store it tightly covered in the refrigerator, and bring it to room temperature before serving so it is soft and spreadable.

Yield: 6 side-dish servings

Unsalted butter	3	tablespoons
Parmesan cheese, finely grated	2	tablespoons
Chili powder	2	teaspoons
Granulated garlic	¼	teaspoon
Salt		A pinch
Corn on the cob	6	medium ears

For ease of preparation, leave the butter out to soften at room temperature for an hour or so before making the spread.

Bring 3 quarts of water to a boil in a stockpot over high heat. Meanwhile, add the cheese, chili powder, granulated garlic, and salt to the butter in a small bowl and mash and whip with a fork until well incorporated. Transfer to a small serving crock or bowl and set aside at room temperature (or prepare well ahead of time and store tightly covered in the refrigerator, but return to room temperature before serving).

Remove and discard the corn husks and silk. Place the corn in the boiling water and cook 5 minutes. Drain well and serve piping hot, with the spread in the center of the table and a small knife for spreading at each plate.

Each serving provides:

139	Calories	18 g	Carbohydrate
4 g	Protein	76 mg	Sodium
7 g	Fat	17 mg	Cholesterol
3 g	Dietary Fiber		

Corn, Pineapple, and Jicama Salad with Tomatillos and Rum

VEGAN

Delicious, refreshing, and easy to make, this salad is the perfect accompaniment for blackened grilled fish. It is also an unusual summer potluck offering. Fresh pineapple makes it a real treat, but canned, unsweetened pineapple, well drained, could be substituted, if necessary.

Yield: 8 side-dish servings

Jicama, peeled and diced	1	cup
Fresh-squeezed lemon juice	1	tablespoon
Pineapple, minced	1	cup
Corn kernels, fresh	2	cups (4 ears)
Tomatillos, water-packed	1	12-ounce can
Red onion, minced	¼	cup
Fresh-squeezed lime juice	3	tablespoons
Olive oil	1	tablespoon
Mirin	1	tablespoon
Dark rum	1	tablespoon
Fresh cilantro, minced	1	tablespoon
Salt	⅛	teaspoon
Cayenne		A pinch

Toss the jicama in a bowl with the lemon juice. Slice the peel off half a fresh pineapple, cut the pineapple into lengthwise quarters, and remove and discard the tough core portion. Mince the pineapple and drain well in a strainer positioned over a bowl to catch the juice. Save the pineapple juice and the remaining half pineapple for another use. Toss the minced pineapple with the jicama.

Bring 4 cups of water to a boil in a large saucepan and add the corn kernels. As soon as the water comes back to a rolling boil, rinse the corn under cold water and drain very well. Combine with the jicama and pineapple. Drain the tomatillos well and chop them coarsely. Add the tomatillos and onion to the corn mixture and toss to distribute everything evenly. Whisk together the lime juice, olive oil, mirin, rum, cilantro, salt, and cayenne and toss with the salad ingredients until well combined. Chill for at least ½ hour, or up to several hours, before serving.

Each serving provides:

85	Calories	14 g	Carbohydrate
2 g	Protein	42 mg	Sodium
2 g	Fat	0 mg	Cholesterol
2 g	Dietary Fiber		

Curried Corn Chowder
with Cumin-Seared Tofu

The seared tofu adds a delicious flavor to this curry soup, and is also wonderful eaten all by itself. The variety of colors, flavors, and textures makes this a picture-perfect soup. Granny Smith is our preferred apple variety for this dish, but another green apple could be used.

Yield: 4 main-course servings

Apple, green	1	medium (½ pound)
Homemade Vegetable Stock*	3	cups
Red onion, diced	1	cup
Garlic	2	cloves, minced
Curry powder	1	teaspoon
Firm-style tofu	6	ounces
Canola oil	2	teaspoons
Worcestershire sauce	1	tablespoon
Ground cumin	¼	teaspoon
Cayenne		A pinch
Granulated garlic	¼	teaspoon
Corn kernels, fresh or frozen	1½	cups (3 ears)
Red bell pepper	1	medium, diced
Fresh cilantro, minced	¼	cup
Lowfat buttermilk	3	cups
Salt	¼	teaspoon
Pepper		Several grinds

*If you do not have Homemade Vegetable Stock on hand, make some according to the directions on page 12, or dissolve 1 large, low-sodium vegetable broth cube in 3 cups of hot water.

The Best 125 Vegetable Dishes

Peel, core, and dice the apple. Combine it with the stock, along with the onion, garlic, and curry powder, in a stockpot. Bring to a boil, then reduce heat to medium and simmer 20 minutes, until the apple and onion are tender. Transfer to a blender or food processor in small batches and puree until smooth.

Meanwhile, rinse the tofu and pat dry with a tea towel. Cut into ½-inch cubes. Heat the canola oil in a small skillet over medium-high heat and add the Worcestershire sauce, cumin, cayenne, and granulated garlic. Gently fold in the tofu, tossing to coat every side with oil and seasonings. Continue to cook 3 to 4 minutes, stirring occasionally. Remove the pan from the heat and set aside in a warm spot.

Return the pureed soup to the stockpot and add the corn, red bell pepper, and cilantro. Bring to a simmer over medium-high heat, reduce heat to medium, and cook 5 to 7 minutes, until the corn is tender. Stir in the buttermilk and heat through, but do not boil. Season with salt and pepper. Serve in warmed soup bowls topped with the seared tofu.

Each serving provides:

301	Calories	37 g	Carbohydrate
17 g	Protein	441 mg	Sodium
11 g	Fat	11 mg	Cholesterol
4 g	Dietary Fiber		

Buttermilk Corn Cakes
with Green Chilies

These corn cakes may be served in many different ways. Serve them as a side dish at a Cajun dinner or as an appetizer topped with guacamole to begin a Southwestern feast. They also make a wonderful brunch entrée for 10 to 12 people when served with salsa, guacamole, and black beans. Any leftovers can be stored tightly wrapped in the refrigerator to be enjoyed reheated, cold, or at room temperature over the next day or two. No oil will be needed to cook the cakes if you use a well-tempered cast-iron skillet. If you don't have one, lightly oil the pan.

Yield: 16 side-dish servings (about 48 cakes)

Fine yellow cornmeal	1¼	cups
Unbleached flour	½	cup
Baking soda	1	teaspoon
Salt	½	teaspoon
Granulated sugar	1	teaspoon
Mild chili powder	2	teaspoons
Ground cumin	1	teaspoon
Lowfat buttermilk	1	cup
Canola oil	1	tablespoon
Whole egg	1	large
Egg white	1	large
Corn kernels, fresh or frozen	3	cups (6 ears)
Diced green chilies	1	4-ounce can

Combine the cornmeal, flour, baking soda, salt, sugar, chili powder, and cumin in a large bowl. Add the buttermilk and oil, stirring until well combined. Separate the whole egg. Lightly beat the yolk and stir it into the batter. Beat the egg whites until stiff and gently fold them in. Let stand 10 minutes.

Fold in the corn and green chilies until just incorporated. Thoroughly preheat a well-tempered cast-iron skillet or griddle over medium-high heat until a few drops of water sizzle and jump when flicked into the pan. Spoon in the batter to form 2-inch cakes. Cook until bubbles form, about 3 to 4 minutes, then turn and cook about 3 minutes longer to brown the other side. If the cakes brown too fast, reduce the temperature a little. Hold the finished cakes in a warm oven while you cook the remaining batches. Serve hot or at room temperature.

Each serving provides:

104	Calories	19 g	Carbohydrate
3 g	Protein	222 mg	Sodium
2 g	Fat	14 mg	Cholesterol
2 g	Dietary Fiber		

Corn, Sweet Pepper, and Cumin Risotto

Depending on the weather and how hungry we are, this recipe makes a wonderful starter, main dish, or side dish in the summer. For a vegan version of this dish, omit the Parmesan cheese.

Yield: 6 side-dish servings

Olive oil	1 tablespoon
Dry sherry	¼ cup
Garlic	2 cloves, minced
Ground cumin	⅛ teaspoon
Chili powder	½ teaspoon
Red bell pepper	1 medium, diced
Green bell pepper	1 medium, diced
Corn kernels, fresh	2 cups (4 ears)
Homemade Vegetable Stock*	3½ cups
Unsalted butter	1 tablespoon
Arborio rice, uncooked	1 cup
Fresh basil leaves, chopped	¼ cup
Pepper	Several grinds
Parmesan cheese, finely grated	¼ cup

*If you do not have Homemade Vegetable Stock on hand, make some according to the directions on page 12, or dissolve 1 large, low-sodium vegetable broth cube in 3½ cups of hot water.

Heat the olive oil and 2 tablespoons of the sherry in a skillet over medium-high heat. Add the garlic, cumin, and chili powder and cook for about a minute. Stir in the bell peppers and corn, cover, and cook 10 minutes, stirring occasionally. Remove from the heat and set aside.

Meanwhile, heat the stock in a saucepan until steaming, and keep it handy near the stove. Melt the butter in a heavy-bottomed saucepan and add the remaining 2 tablespoons of sherry. Add the rice and stir to coat with the butter and sherry. Add the stock, ½ cup at a time, stirring almost constantly and waiting until the liquid is absorbed before each addition. Add the sautéed corn mixture with the last ½ cup of stock. When the last addition of stock has been absorbed and the rice is tender, add the basil, pepper, and Parmesan. Stir to incorporate and serve immediately.

Each serving provides:

252	Calories	40 g	Carbohydrate
6 g	Protein	110 mg	Sodium
7 g	Fat	8 mg	Cholesterol
2 g	Dietary Fiber		

Eggplant

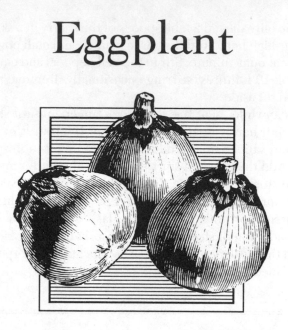

Third-century Chinese texts contain references to eggplant, though it is considered a native of India. It is still widely used in Asian and Middle Eastern cooking. Arab traders introduced the plant to Spain in the twelfth century, and it eventually became a favored ingredient in Mediterranean cuisines. The first eggplant variety the English-speaking world encountered was probably a small, white variety, hence its name.

Eggplant is a member of the nightshade family, which includes tomatoes, potatoes, and pimientos, as well as the deadly nightshade. Indeed, in early times eggplant was used as a decorative plant—eating it was thought to induce madness. Its botanical name reflects this early suspicion—*Solanum melongena,* which translates to "soothing mad fruit."

Today, eggplant is widely grown in most warm regions of the world. In addition to the large oval type most common in American kitchens, narrow, elongated varieties are available— typically sold as Japanese or Asian eggplants. These have fewer seeds and thinner skins and are therefore preferred for some uses. White and variegated eggplant varieties are occasionally available and can be substituted for the purple variety in our recipes.

The eggplant is self-pollinating and needs a long, hot growing season and well-drained soil. It is well adapted to tropical and semitropical climates. In this country, Florida and other Gulf Coast states are the leading producers. Winter supplies are supplemented by crops from California and Mexico.

The Nutrition Picture

Eggplant is not a particularly good source of any single vitamin or mineral, but it does deliver fair quantities of potassium, phosphorus, calcium, and magnesium, as well as some amino acids, the building blocks of protein. In addition, its meaty texture makes it a good low-calorie, lowfat choice for a main dish.

Selection and Storage

Eggplant is generally available all year, though availability and quality peak from July through October. It is difficult to estimate an average serving size of eggplant, as its versatility makes it suitable for many different types of preparation. An average globe eggplant weighs about a pound.

Look for eggplants that are well-shaped and symmetrical, with shiny, taut skin. Brown or withered patches on the skin indicate spoilage. Wrinkled, flabby eggplants are old and the seeds will be dark and bitter-tasting.

When pressed with the thumb, the indentation in the flesh should not remain. The freshest eggplants will be those that are heaviest for their size, which indicates a juicy interior. Stems and caps should be bright green. Choose the smallest good quality eggplants available, as they will be the tenderest, with smaller seeds and thinner skins.

Unwashed, uncut eggplants stored in a loose plastic bag will stay fresh in the refrigerator for several days. Handle eggplants gently; they are delicate fruits that bruise easily, at which point decay accelerates.

Culinary Tips

- Eggplant acts like a sponge. It takes on flavor quite well, but will also soak up large quantities of oil or other fats. Try steam-sautéing, grilling, baking, or other lowfat cooking methods.

- Eggplant skin can be tough; you may want to peel large ones. White ones of any size have thicker skins and should always be peeled.

- Salting is sometimes called for to draw out the eggplant's natural juices before cooking. They absorb less fat if salted before cooking, and salting can eliminate the natural bitterness of a larger eggplant. Sprinkle sliced or diced pieces evenly with salt and set aside in a stainless steel colander for 30 minutes. Use about ½ teaspoon of salt for a pound of eggplant. Rinse off the salt, squeeze gently, and pat dry before proceeding with the recipe. Keep in mind, however, that salting is not always necessary or desirable. Don't cut eggplant until just before you cook it, as it will oxidize and begin to darken quite quickly.

- Stainless steel or enameled cast-iron cooking vessels, knives, and utensils are preferable for eggplants—carbon steel blades and iron pots will blacken the eggplant pulp.

- Unlike most vegetables, eggplant's flavor and texture are not harmed by longer cooking times, so be sure to cook thoroughly. Chewy, undercooked eggplant is not appetizing.
- As a rule of thumb, one small eggplant weighs ¾ pound; one medium eggplant weighs 1 pound; and one large eggplant weighs 1½ pounds.

Eggplant Spread with Gorgonzola, Capers, and Dill Seed

This is the perfect pungent appetizer to launch a Mediterranean menu. You may make it up to a day or two ahead of time. Store it tightly covered in the refrigerator; stir and bring to room temperature before serving. Decorative strips of lemon peel would make a nice garnish.

Yield: 6 appetizer servings

Eggplant	**1**	**pound (1 medium)**
Gorgonzola cheese, crumbled	**1½**	**ounces (⅓ cup)**
Capers, not drained	**2**	**teaspoons**
Garlic	**1**	**clove, minced**
Dill seed, crushed	**¼**	**teaspoon**
Cayenne		**A pinch**

Preheat the oven to 400 degrees F. Do not peel, but pierce the eggplant with a fork in several places and put it in the oven in a glass baking dish. Bake for 40 to 50 minutes, until the eggplant is quite soft. The skin will scorch slightly. Remove it from the oven and set aside to cool. When the eggplant is cool enough to handle, cut it in half lengthwise and scrape the pulp from the skin. If there are dense pockets of dark seeds, discard them. In a food processor, puree the eggplant with the Gorgonzola, capers, garlic, dill seed, and cayenne. Chill for at least a half hour before serving with crisp crackers or a sliced baguette.

Each serving provides:

42	Calories	4 g	Carbohydrate
2 g	Protein	126 mg	Sodium
2 g	Fat	5 mg	Cholesterol
1 g	Dietary Fiber		

Greek Eggplant Salad

VEGAN

This dish may be enjoyed in many ways. Here it is presented as a salad. However, it is also delicious as a spread on sweet French bread or as a dip for fresh vegetables. Any leftovers should be stored tightly covered in the refrigerator and enjoyed over the course of a few days.

Yield: 8 side-dish servings

Eggplant	2	**pounds (2 medium)**
White onion, diced	¼	**cup**
Garlic	2	**cloves, minced**
Fresh parsley, minced	¼	**cup**
Fresh oregano leaves, minced	1	**tablespoon**
Fresh-squeezed lemon juice	3	**tablespoons**
Olive oil	½	**cup**
Butter lettuce	8	**large leaves**

Preheat the oven to 400 degrees F. Do not peel the eggplants, but pierce them in several places with a fork and place in a glass dish. Bake for 40 to 50 minutes, until very soft. The skin will scorch slightly. Remove eggplants from the oven and set aside to cool. When they are cool enough to handle, cut in half lengthwise and scrape the pulp from the skin. If there are dense pockets of dark seeds, discard them.

Place the eggplant pulp in a food processor and pulse to coarsely chop, but do not puree. Drain off any liquid that may separate from the pulp. Add the onion, garlic, parsley, and oregano and pulse to combine. With the machine running, add the lemon juice and oil in a thin stream. Don't overprocess—the resulting mixture should be a thick, slightly chunky puree. Chill for several hours.

Line chilled salad bowls with the lettuce leaves and mound a scoop of eggplant on each. Garnish with olives or red pepper slices, if desired.

Each serving provides:

150	Calories	7 g	Carbohydrate
1 g	Protein	5 mg	Sodium
14 g	Fat	0 mg	Cholesterol
2 g	Dietary Fiber		

Grilled Eggplant and Bell Pepper Skewers with Peanut Dipping Sauce

VEGAN

The smoky and sweet flavors of the vegetables combine extremely well with the tangy peanut butter sauce in this showy side dish. You may make the dipping sauce as long as a day or two ahead of time; hold it in the refrigerator and bring to room temperature before serving.

Yield: 4 side-dish servings

The dipping sauce

Creamy peanut butter	1½	tablespoons
Rice wine vinegar	1	tablespoon
Mirin	2	teaspoons
White miso	2	teaspoons
Low-sodium soy sauce	½	teaspoon
Granulated garlic	½	teaspoon
Cayenne		A pinch

The skewers

Mirin	2	tablespoons
Dark sesame oil	1	teaspoon
Granulated garlic	¼	teaspoon
Eggplant	¾	pound (1 small)
Red bell pepper	1	medium

Combine the sauce ingredients in a small bowl with 1 tablespoon of water and whisk until smooth. Set aside at room temperature so the flavors can blend, or refrigerate for up to 2 days.

Soak 8 wooden skewers in cold water for 30 minutes. Preheat a coal or gas grill to medium-high. (To preheat a coal grill, start the charcoal at least 15 to 20 minutes before cooking begins, so the proper temperature can be achieved in time. Grill

The Best 125 Vegetable Dishes

is ready when the coals are glowing red and some gray ash is present on them. Preheat a gas grill at least 10 minutes, or according to the manufacturer's specific instructions.)

In a small bowl, stir together the mirin, sesame oil, and granulated garlic and set aside. Peel the eggplant and cut into 1-inch cubes. Cut the pepper in half lengthwise, discard the stem, seeds, and pithy membrane, and cut into ¾-inch pieces.

Thread alternating eggplant and pepper pieces onto the skewers. Brush the skewered vegetables on all sides with the mirin and sesame oil mixture and place directly on the grill. Cover the grill and cook for 12 minutes, turning and brushing the skewers every 4 minutes. Eggplant pieces should be nicely charred and soft inside. Transfer the skewers to a platter, leaving room at one end for the bowl of dipping sauce. Serve hot or at room temperature.

Each serving provides:

104	Calories	12 g	Carbohydrate
3 g	Protein	162 mg	Sodium
4 g	Fat	0 mg	Cholesterol
2 g	Dietary Fiber		

Roasted Eggplant and Red Bell Peppers with Creamy Pesto Sauce

This is a perfect choice for backyard grill parties, as summer is when eggplants and peppers are at their peak. As an alternative, you may cook the eggplant slices and peppers in a conventional broiler. Either way, when they are done, they may be held for several hours in the refrigerator, along with the sauce, but bring everything to room temperature before serving. Whatever the rest of the menu, be sure to serve a good crusty sourdough bread and a crisp red wine with this course.

Yield: 6 side-dish servings

Plain nonfat yogurt	⅓	cup
Basil Pesto (see page 14)	2	tablespoons
Balsamic vinegar	2	teaspoons
Garlic	1	clove, minced
Salt		A pinch
Pepper		A few grinds
Eggplant	1½	pounds (1 large)
Red bell peppers	2	large
Olive oil	1	tablespoon
Dried oregano	1	teaspoon
Granulated garlic	½	teaspoon
Cayenne	⅛	teaspoon

A few hours ahead of time, if possible, stir together the yogurt, pesto, vinegar, garlic, salt, and pepper. Cover and set aside in the refrigerator so the flavors can blend.

Rinse and dry the eggplant but do not peel it. Cut it crosswise into slices ½-inch thick. Rinse and dry the peppers and cut them in half lengthwise, discarding the stems, seeds, and white membrane. In a small bowl, beat the olive oil, oregano, granulated garlic, and cayenne until smooth and well combined. Rub the eggplant slices lightly on both sides with this mixture.

Preheat a gas or coal grill to medium-high. (To preheat a coal grill, start the charcoal at least 15 to 20 minutes before cooking begins, so the proper temperature can be achieved in time. The grill is ready when the coals are glowing red and some gray ash is present on them. Preheat a gas grill for at least 10 minutes, or according to the manufacturer's specific instructions.)

Place the eggplant slices and pepper halves on the grill and cook 6 minutes. Turn and cook for an additional 5 minutes. Remove the vegetables from the grill and allow to cool. Remove the blackened skin of the peppers. Cut the eggplant and peppers into strips and arrange on a serving platter. Top with the pesto sauce and serve.

Each serving provides:

99	Calories	11 g	Carbohydrate
3 g	Protein	57 mg	Sodium
5 g	Fat	1 mg	Cholesterol
2 g	Dietary Fiber		

Vermicelli with Curried Eggplant and Chard in Fresh Ginger Tomato Sauce

ALMOST INSTANT, VEGAN

Deliciously exotic-tasting, this pasta dish is a perfect balance of sweet and hot. Wait until you find really fresh eggplant and Swiss chard to try it—it makes a big difference in texture as well as taste.

Yield: 6 main-dish servings

Tomatoes	2	medium (1 pound)
Yellow onion, diced	1	cup
Garlic	2	cloves, chopped
Fresh ginger, grated	2	teaspoons
Salt	¼	teaspoon plus a pinch
Homemade Vegetable Stock*	1	cup
Swiss chard	½	pound
Eggplant	¾	pound (1 small)
Peanut oil	1	tablespoon
Cumin seed	½	teaspoon
Mustard seed	½	teaspoon
Ground cardamom	½	teaspoon
Ground turmeric	½	teaspoon
Currants	3	tablespoons
Dried vermicelli	8	ounces

*If you do not have Homemade Vegetable Stock on hand, make up a batch according to the directions on page 12, or simply substitute water.

Cut out and discard the stems of the tomatoes. Dice the tomatoes and combine them in a blender or food processor with the onion, garlic, ginger, ¼ teaspoon of the salt, and ⅓ cup of the stock. Puree to a smooth consistency and set aside.

Bring several quarts of water to a boil for the pasta. Meanwhile, carefully wash the chard; there is no need to dry it. Tear or cut the leaves into bite-size pieces and thinly slice the stems. Set aside separately. Trim off and discard the stem of the eggplant and cut it lengthwise into ¼-inch slices. Cut the slices lengthwise into ¼-inch strips, and cut the strips into 1-inch lengths.

Meanwhile, heat the oil over medium heat in a large saucepan that has a tight-fitting lid. Add the cumin and mustard seed, cardamom, and turmeric. Stir and cook the spices for about 2 minutes, then add the remaining ⅔ cup of stock and stir. Heat to the steaming stage, then stir in the eggplant, chard stems, and remaining pinch of salt. Immediately cover the pan tightly and cook for 5 minutes. Remove the lid and stir in the tomato sauce, chard leaves, and currants. Cover and cook 5 minutes, then remove the lid and cook, stirring frequently, 5 minutes longer.

Meanwhile, cook the pasta in the boiling water until al dente. Drain well and toss with the sauce. Serve very hot, offering cayenne for those who like very spicy food.

Each serving provides:

230	Calories	43 g	Carbohydrate
8 g	Protein	223 mg	Sodium
4 g	Fat	0 mg	Cholesterol
3 g	Dietary Fiber		

Eggplant Casserole Sicilian Style

Though we never ate this dish while traveling in Italy, it was described to us by a man from Taormina. Our Italian friend fried the eggplant in olive oil, but to lighten the dish a bit, we grill ours. Serve this with lightly dressed pasta for an authentic Italian meal.

Yield: 6 main-dish servings

Fresh pear tomatoes (or 2 28-ounce cans)	6	pounds
Olive oil	2	tablespoons
Garlic	4	cloves, minced
Dried oregano	1	teaspoon
Dried basil	1	teaspoon
Dried thyme	½	teaspoon
Salt	½	teaspoon
Pepper		Several grinds
Eggplant	1	pound (1 medium)
Eggs	4	medium, hard-boiled
Fresh basil leaves, chopped	½	cup
Part-skim mozzarella cheese	4	ounces, thinly sliced

Blanch and peel the tomatoes by immersing them in boiling water for 1 minute. Plunge them immediately into a bowl of cold water. When cool enough to handle, slip off and discard the skins and chop the tomatoes coarsely (if using canned tomatoes, drain off the juice, reserving for another use, and chop the tomatoes coarsely).

Heat 1 tablespoon of the oil over medium-high heat in a heavy-bottomed skillet and add the garlic. Sauté for about 1 minute, then add the tomatoes. Stir in the dried herbs and cook over medium-high heat about 5 minutes, stirring frequently. The tomatoes will release their juices and begin to break apart a bit. Add the salt and pepper, lower the heat to medium-low, and continue to cook about 10 minutes, stirring occasionally, until a thick, chunky sauce develops. Remove from the heat and set aside.

Meanwhile, preheat a coal or gas grill to medium. (To preheat a coal grill, start the charcoal at least 15 to 20 minutes before cooking begins, so the proper temperature can be achieved in time. The grill is ready when the coals are glowing red and are almost covered with gray ash. Preheat a gas grill for at least 10 minutes, or according to the manufacturer's specific instructions.)

Preheat the oven to 350 degrees F. Trim off and discard the stem of the eggplant and cut it into ¼-inch slices. Brush the grill with ½ tablespoon olive oil and place the eggplant on the oiled grill. Close the lid of the grill and cook 6 minutes. Turn, brushing the grill with the remaining ½ tablespoon oil, and cook an additional 5 minutes. Eggplant should be slightly charred on the outside but still somewhat firm. Remove from the grill and set aside.

Cut the eggs crosswise into ⅛-inch slices. Cover the bottom of a 9×13-inch baking dish with ⅓ of the tomato sauce and top with a single layer of eggplant. Arrange half the egg slices over the eggplant and sprinkle with half the chopped basil. Layer half the cheese on top, then repeat with the remaining ingredients, ending with tomato sauce. Cover and bake for 25 minutes. Serve immediately.

Each serving provides:

227	Calories	27 g	Carbohydrate
13 g	Protein	349 mg	Sodium
10 g	Fat	136 mg	Cholesterol
7 g	Dietary Fiber		

Pizza with Grilled Eggplant, Roasted Garlic, and Mozzarella

This pizza makes a great lunch or supper entrée in the summer, when our gardens yield fresh, sweet tomatoes and tender eggplant. There are several steps, but the process is not difficult. We like to bake the finished pizza on an outdoor gas grill to avoid heating up the kitchen, but a 425 degree F. oven will work just fine. You may also broil the eggplant instead of grilling it.

Yield: 6 main-dish servings

Pizza crust	1	12-inch crust
Garlic	1	bulb
Fresh pear tomatoes	3	large (about 6 ounces)
Dried oregano	¼	teaspoon
Salt		Scant ⅛ teaspoon
Pepper		Several grinds
Eggplant	1	pound (1 medium)
Olive oil	1	tablespoon plus 1 teaspoon
Part-skim mozzarella cheese grated	6	ounces (1½ cups)

Prepare Pizza Crust from the recipe on page 16 or use a commercial crust for an Almost Instant pizza. Preheat the oven or a toaster oven to 350 degrees F. and cut ¼ inch off the garlic bulb to barely expose the tops of the cloves. Do not peel. Use a clay garlic baker or wrap in foil and bake 30 to 45 minutes. When the garlic bulb is very soft, remove it from the oven and set aside to cool. When cool enough to handle, remove the garlic from the skins by squeezing the cloves from the bottom. The garlic will slide out the cut end as a soft paste. Spread this evenly over the bottom of the pizza crust and place the crust on a baking sheet or pizza pan.

Meanwhile, blanch and seed the tomatoes by immersing them in boiling water for 1 minute. Immediately plunge them into a bowl of cold water. When cool enough to handle, slip off the skins and chop the tomatoes. Place them in a small bowl and add the oregano, salt, and pepper, stirring to combine. Set aside.

Preheat a coal or gas grill to medium. (To preheat a coal grill, start the charcoal at least 15 to 20 minutes before cooking begins, so the proper temperature can be achieved in time. The grill is ready when the coals are glowing red and are almost covered with gray ash. Preheat a gas grill for at least 10 minutes, or according to the manufacturer's specific instructions.)

Remove the stem of the eggplant, but do not peel. Cut the eggplant lengthwise into ¼-inch slices. Brush one side of the eggplant slices with ½ tablespoon of the olive oil and place the eggplant on the grill, oil side down. Close the lid of the grill and cook 6 minutes. Turn, brushing the other side of the eggplant slices with the remaining ½ tablespoon of oil, and cook an additional 5 minutes. Remove from the grill and set aside. If you will be baking the pizza on the grill, increase the grill temperature to medium-high while you assemble the pizza. Otherwise, preheat the oven to 425 F.

Spoon the tomato sauce over the garlic on the pizza crust. Distribute half the mozzarella cheese evenly over the tomato sauce, then arrange the eggplant slices evenly in a fan pattern. Distribute the remaining cheese over the eggplant. Drizzle with the remaining teaspoon of olive oil and bake for 20 minutes, until the crust is golden. Serve immediately.

Each serving provides:

245	Calories	25 g	Carbohydrate
12 g	Protein	285 mg	Sodium
12 g	Fat	17 mg	Cholesterol
4 g	Dietary Fiber		

Green Beans

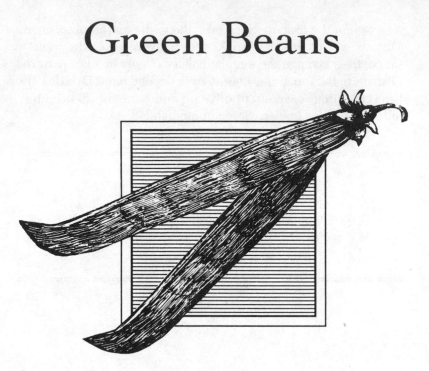

Beans are believed to have originated in what is today Indonesia. They found their way to Europe via the Spanish conquistadores and were originally prized in Spain as flowering ornamental plants. Beans were first raised commercially in the United States in 1836 near Utica, New York, though they had grown wild in the Americas for thousands of years. They have since become the fifth most popular vegetable in America.

Edible pod beans (usually referred to as green, string, or snap beans) are not a separate botanical group from dried shelling beans. The seed pods are simply harvested while immature, or green, and eaten whole. Left on the plant, seeds eventually grow to full size and dry in the pod. The basic botanical group is known as *Phaseolus vulgarus* (family: Legume), of which many different varieties have been developed over the centuries.

Bean plants have two basic growth habits—climbing vines (known as pole beans) and shrubs (known as bush beans). Pole beans mature sporadically for harvest over a longer period. Bush beans are preferred by commercial growers because all the pods are ready for harvest at the same time.

Not technically a green bean but often eaten fresh, fava beans (*Vicia faba*), also called broad beans, have a distinctive, succulent flavor. This drought-tolerant plant is an ancient crop of the Mediterranean region and is still widely grown there as a rotation crop and for fertilizer as well as for the table. Part of the culinary crop is eaten fresh and the remainder is dried. In most cases, unless the beans are harvested when quite small and tender, the pods are removed and the beans are blanched and peeled before using in recipes.

The Nutrition Picture

Green beans are a good source of beta carotene and vitamin C; dried ones are high in protein and carbohydrates in the form of starch. Beans also provide fair doses of potassium, calcium, and phosphorus. Green beans are low in calories, sodium, and fat and are a good vegetable source of iron. In addition, the edible pods provide good fiber. Fresh shelled fava beans also have ample fiber and are a good vegetable protein source.

Selection and Storage

Though green beans are available year-round, you will find the best quality and variety in summer and early fall. As a rule of thumb, a pound of green beans will yield six side-dish servings.

Select equal-size pods for uniform cooking. Avoid beans with rusty or mushy areas, or scars. Vivid color and plump, moist texture are signs of freshness, as is a barely detectable fuzz on the pods. Slender pods are preferable; fat, bulging pods usually mean the seeds are too mature to be tasty and the pods will be stringy. Fresh green beans should be crisp, not leathery or flaccid and should snap, not bend, when broken.

Rinse the beans, don't dry them, and wrap in plastic before refrigeration. Handled this way, they will retain their freshness for at least several days, and may keep for as long as two weeks.

Select fava bean pods that are bright green and glossy, with well-developed bulging seeds. Blackening at the ends of the pods is a sign that the beans will not be of good quality. Pods will feel spongy, but should appear juicy and fresh. Favas in their pods will stay fresh for a few days in a plastic bag in the refrigerator.

Culinary Tips

- Green beans may be enjoyed raw as well as cooked. Chop and toss with salads to add a satisfying crunch.
- Snap off both ends of green beans and pull away and discard any string that may be attached.
- Green beans may be cooked whole or cut at a slant crosswise to create bite-size pieces. French-cut beans are sliced vertically to mimic the shape of the extremely slender French cultivars known as haricots vert. Uncut beans are preferable, however, because they will retain more of their nutrients during cooking.
- Green beans are unappetizing when mushy, so cook until just fork tender. Properly cooked beans will still have a nice crunch.

- Unless you have just harvested small fresh fava bean pods from the garden, the beans should be shelled. Discard the pods and blanch the beans in boiling water for 2 minutes, rinse immediately in cold water, and peel off the tough skin before proceeding with the recipe.

Green Beans with Orange Allspice Glaze and Toasted Pecans

ALMOST INSTANT, VEGAN

This is a wonderful and unusual way to prepare green beans. Serve it with a curry-inspired meal, as a side dish at Thanksgiving dinner, or whenever you get a craving for it.

Yield: 6 side-dish servings

Green beans	1	pound
Salt	⅛	teaspoon plus a pinch
Unsalted raw pecans, chopped	3	tablespoons
Fresh-squeezed orange juice	½	cup
Dry sherry	2	tablespoons
Maple syrup	1	teaspoon
Ground allspice	⅛	teaspoon
Pepper		Several grinds
Arrowroot powder or cornstarch	1	teaspoon

Rinse off the green beans and remove the stems and any strings. Leave them whole. Bring ¼ cup water to a boil in a large skillet that has a tight-fitting lid. When it is simmering, add the beans and sprinkle on ⅛ teaspoon salt. Reduce the heat to medium, cover, and cook about 7 minutes, until beans are just fork tender.

Meanwhile, place the pecans in a dry, heavy-bottomed skillet over medium heat. Cook for several minutes, stirring or shaking the pan frequently, until the pecans are slightly browned and emit a roasted aroma. Remove from the pan and set aside.

When beans are done, transfer them to a serving dish and cover them to keep warm. Combine the orange juice, sherry, maple syrup, ground allspice, remaining pinch of salt, and pepper in a small saucepan over high heat. Dissolve the arrowroot powder in a tablespoon of water. When orange juice is simmering, whisk in the arrowroot mixture. Cook a moment longer, whisking constantly, until sauce is smooth and slightly thickened. Pour the sauce evenly over the beans and top with the toasted pecans.

Each serving provides:

65	Calories	9 g	Carbohydrate
2 g	Protein	93 mg	Sodium
2 g	Fat	0 mg	Cholesterol
1 g	Dietary Fiber		

Green Beans with Ginger Mushroom Sauté

ALMOST INSTANT

Any variety of fresh mushroom will work for this fantastic side dish; however, we especially like the intense flavor of shiitake or morel mushrooms. Serve it as an accompaniment to any grilled fish or Asian entrée.

Yield: 6 side-dish servings

Raw unsalted sunflower seeds	¼	cup
Green beans	1	pound
Mushrooms	¼	pound
Dark sesame oil	2	teaspoons
Mirin	1	tablespoon
Fresh ginger, grated	1	teaspoon
Light sour cream	¼	cup

Place the sunflower seeds in a single layer in a dry, heavy-bottomed skillet over medium-high heat. Shake the pan or stir frequently until the seeds begin to brown and emit a roasted aroma. Remove immediately from the pan and set aside.

Trim off the stem ends of the beans, string them if necessary, and cut them at a slant into 1-inch lengths. Place the beans on a steamer rack in a saucepan with a tight-fitting lid. Add about an inch of water, cover, and cook over medium-high heat 8 to 10 minutes, until just fork tender. Meanwhile, brush or wipe the mushrooms clean, trim off ¼ inch of their stems, and cut into ¼-inch slices.

Combine the oil, mirin, and ginger in a skillet over medium-high heat. Add the mushrooms and sauté for 5 minutes, stirring frequently. Lower the heat to medium-low and stir in the sour cream until just heated through, about 1 minute. Drain the beans and place them in a warm serving bowl. Add the mushroom mixture and toss to combine. Toss with the sunflower seeds and serve.

Each serving provides:

91	Calories	8 g	Carbohydrate
3 g	Protein	13 mg	Sodium
5 g	Fat	3 mg	Cholesterol
1 g	Dietary Fiber		

Green and Black Bean Salad with Oregano Cream Dressing and Avocado

ALMOST INSTANT

This is a refreshing twist on the more conventional bean salads. The flavors, textures, and colors are outstanding. This salad may be prepared up to a day ahead of time.

Yield: 6 side-dish servings

Green beans	1	pound
Black beans, cooked	2	cups (or 1 15-ounce can)
Red bell pepper, diced	1	cup
Red onion, minced	½	cup
Light sour cream	½	cup
Plain nonfat yogurt	½	cup
Apple cider vinegar	2	tablespoons
Fresh oregano leaves, minced	2	tablespoons
Cumin seed, crushed	½	teaspoon
Granulated garlic	¼	teaspoon
Mild chili powder	¼	teaspoon
Salt	¼	teaspoon
Pepper		Several grinds
Avocado	1	medium

Trim off the stem ends of the beans, string them if necessary, and cut them at a slant into 1-inch lengths. Place them on a steamer rack in a saucepan with a tight-fitting lid and cook over medium-high heat for 8 to 10 minutes, until just fork tender. Drain and plunge them into ice water to stop the cooking and set their bright green color.

If using canned black beans, rinse and drain them. In a serving bowl, combine the green and black beans with the bell pepper and onion. Whisk together the sour cream, yogurt, vinegar, oregano, cumin, garlic, chili powder, salt, and pepper. Pour this over the beans and toss to combine. Serve immediately, garnished with avocado slices, or refrigerate and garnish with the avocado just before serving.

Each serving provides:

207	Calories	27 g	Carbohydrate
10 g	Protein	115 mg	Sodium
8 g	Fat	7 mg	Cholesterol
4 g	Dietary Fiber		

Green Bean Salad with Asian Seasonings

ALMOST INSTANT, VEGAN

This simple dish turns green beans into something extraordinary. It is particularly good as a side dish with any Asian-inspired main course.

Yield: 4 side-dish servings

Raw sesame seeds	1	teaspoon
Green beans	1	pound
Rice wine vinegar	2	tablespoons
Olive oil	1	tablespoon
Mirin or dry sherry	1	tablespoon
Orange juice	1	tablespoon
Low-sodium soy sauce	2	teaspoons
Dark sesame oil	1	teaspoon
Garlic	1	clove, minced
Red onion, grated	3	tablespoons

Place the sesame seeds in a small, dry cast-iron skillet over medium-high heat. Shake the pan frequently and soon the seeds will begin to brown and emit a roasted aroma. Remove immediately from the pan and set aside until needed. Trim off the stem ends of the beans and string them, if necessary. Leave the beans whole. Bring 2 inches of water to a boil in a large saucepan or skillet with a tight-fitting lid. Add the beans, reduce heat to medium-low, cover, and cook until just fork tender, about 7 minutes. Rinse under cold water to stop the cooking and drain well.

The Best 125 Vegetable Dishes

Meanwhile, whisk together all remaining ingredients except the sesame seeds and onion until well combined. Toss the beans with the dressing and onion and serve immediately or allow to marinate in the refrigerator for up to a few hours (return to room temperature before serving). Transfer the beans to a pretty platter and sprinkle with the sesame seeds.

Each serving provides:

94	Calories	11 g	Carbohydrate
2 g	Protein	108 mg	Sodium
5 g	Fat	0 mg	Cholesterol
2 g	Dietary Fiber		

Stewed Green Beans
with Soft Cheese Polenta

Simple to prepare, yet utterly delicious, this hearty and wholesome casual dinner will make frequent appearances on your table. Leave out the polenta if you want to serve the beans as a side dish, perhaps with a creamy pasta.

Yield: 4 main-dish servings

Green beans	1	pound
Fresh pear tomatoes	1	pound, diced
Red onion	1	small, diced
Celery	1	rib, diced
Garlic	6	cloves, minced
Dried oregano	2	teaspoons
Salt	¼	teaspoon
Cayenne		A pinch
Fresh-squeezed lemon juice	1	tablespoon
Low-sodium vegetable broth cube	½	large
Granulated garlic	1	teaspoon
Coarse yellow cornmeal	1¼	cups
Part-skim mozzarella cheese, grated	3	ounces (¾ cup)

Trim off the stem ends of the beans and string them, if necessary. Cut them at a slant into 1-inch pieces. Set aside. Combine the tomatoes with the onion, celery, garlic, oregano, salt, and cayenne in a large saucepan, cover, and cook over medium-high heat 10 minutes. Remove the lid to stir the mixture midway through the cooking time. When 10 minutes is up, add the beans and ¼ cup water to the pot and stir. Reduce heat to medium, cover, and cook 10 to 15 minutes, until beans are fork tender. Stir in the lemon juice.

Meanwhile, bring 3 cups of water to a boil over high heat in a heavy-bottomed saucepan, along with the vegetable broth cube and granulated garlic. Reduce the heat to medium and pour the cornmeal into the water in a slow, steady stream, whisking constantly. Cook, whisking frequently, until the mixture is almost too thick to stir, then whisk in 1 cup cold water. Bring back to a bubble and cook, whisking frequently, until mixture is again almost too thick to stir. Add ½ cup cold water. When the mixture thickens up a third time, stir in the cheese until smoothly incorporated.

Divide the polenta equally among 4 shallow, warmed serving bowls. Spoon equal-size portions of the bean mixture over the polenta and serve very hot.

Each serving provides:

299	Calories	53 g	Carbohydrate
13 g	Protein	292 mg	Sodium
5 g	Fat	12 mg	Cholesterol
6 g	Dietary Fiber		

Green Bean, Fennel, and Tofu Stir-Fry with Fermented Black Bean Sauce

ALMOST INSTANT, VEGAN

All Asian markets and many well-stocked supermarkets carry the soba noodles and tofu, as well as the simple ingredients to prepare our homemade black bean sauce. Alternately, commercially prepared black bean sauce may be used. Stir-fries come together rapidly, and since these ingredients store well, this is a great standby dish.

Yield: 4 main-dish servings

Green beans	1	pound
White miso	3	tablespoons
Canola oil	1	tablespoon
Garlic	2	cloves, minced
Red onion, chopped	½	cup
Fresh fennel, chopped	1	cup
Dried red chili flakes	¼	teaspoon
Dried soba noodles (Japanese buckwheat)	8	ounces
Arrowroot powder or cornstarch	2	tablespoons
Firm-style tofu	10	ounces
Fermented Black Bean Sauce (see page 20)	¼	cup
Fresh-squeezed orange juice	½	cup

Trim off the stem ends of the beans, string them if necessary, and cut them into 1-inch lengths. Set aside. Bring several quarts of water to a boil in a stockpot for the noodles. Whisk the miso with ⅔ cup of water in a small bowl and set aside. Heat the oil in a wok or heavy skillet over medium-high heat. Stir in the garlic, onion, and fennel and cook 2 minutes, stirring frequently. Add the miso mixture along with the green beans and chili flakes. Stir to coat, then cover, and cook for 7 minutes, stirring occasionally.

Meanwhile, cook the noodles until tender but not mushy, about 15 minutes. Place 3 tablespoons of water in a small jar with a tight-fitting lid. Add the arrowroot or cornstarch and shake to dissolve. Set aside until needed. Drain and rinse the tofu and cut it into ½-inch cubes. Pat dry on a tea towel. Stir the tofu into the wok, along with the Fermented Black Bean sauce, orange juice, and arrowroot liquid. Continue to cook for 1 minute until a thick sauce develops. Place the drained noodles in warmed individual serving bowls and top with the bean mixture. Serve immediately.

Each serving provides:

481	Calories	70 g	Carbohydrate
24 g	Protein	911 mg	Sodium
13 g	Fat	0 mg	Cholesterol
5 g	Dietary Fiber		

Pasta with Fresh Fava Beans, Tomatoes, Rosemary, and Bleu Cheese

ALMOST INSTANT

Fava beans can become a nutritious, delicious, and unusual addition to your vegetable repertoire. In this recipe, the shelled beans are cooked with tomatoes, rosemary, and garlic and served with pasta, quite appropriate to their Sicilian heritage. The bleu cheese adds a rich, piquant note.

Yield: 4 main-dish servings

Fava beans, in their pods	1¼	pounds
Fresh pear tomatoes	1¼	pounds
Olive oil	2	tablespoons
Yellow onion	1	small, diced
Garlic	4	cloves, minced
Fresh rosemary leaves, minced	1	tablespoon
Dried red chili flakes	⅛	teaspoon
Dry white wine	⅓	cup
Salt	¼	teaspoon
Dried penne	12	ounces
Bleu cheese, crumbled	2	ounces (½ cup)

In a stockpot, bring several quarts of water to a boil. Shell the fava beans and plunge them into the boiling water for 2 minutes. Remove them with a slotted spoon and cool under cold running water. Peel the beans and set aside. (If the beans are small and just picked from the garden, there may be no need to blanch and peel them.)

Plunge the tomatoes into the boiling water for 2 minutes, then lift them out and transfer briefly to a bowl of cold water;

bring the water in the stockpot back to a boil for the pasta. When the tomatoes are cool enough to handle, remove their skins and stems and chop them coarsely into a bowl.

Heat 1 tablespoon of the olive oil in a heavy-bottomed skillet over medium-high heat and sauté the onion, garlic, rosemary, and chili flakes 5 minutes. Add the tomatoes, beans, white wine, and salt and bring to a simmer. Reduce the heat to medium-low, cover, and cook for about 10 minutes, until the beans are fork tender.

Meanwhile, cook the pasta in the boiling water until al dente and drain well. Toss the pasta with the remaining 1 tablespoon olive oil and the bleu cheese in a warmed serving bowl, then with the tomato sauce. Serve immediately.

Each serving provides:

517	Calories	79 g	Carbohydrate
18 g	Protein	377 mg	Sodium
13 g	Fat	11 mg	Cholesterol
4 g	Dietary Fiber		

Mushrooms

The edible fungi commonly called mushrooms are an ancient source of nourishment. Historians tell us they were considered royal food by Egyptian pharaohs. The French were the first to cultivate mushrooms as a crop, in caves and cellars during the seventeenth century. Most mushrooms for the commercial market today are grown indoors, where the environment can be carefully controlled. Shiitakes—the black mushrooms well-known in Asian cuisine—are cultivated primarily on artificial logs.

Mushrooms are prolific in the wild, springing up by the bushel wherever rich soil and damp weather combine to form the perfect fungus environment. Mushrooms have no roots or leaves. They don't bear flowers or seeds, but rather reproduce by scattering spores.

Of the approximately 38,000 varieties of mushrooms known to botanists, only a small percentage are edible. The common button mushroom, available in virtually every supermarket in the United States, is classified as *Agaricus bisporus*. Other popular varieties are occasionally available fresh and are often dried.

Plenty of species are capable of making us sick, and a few can kill us. It is advisable, therefore, to leave the gathering and eating of wild mushrooms to those who are expert at identifying them.

The Nutrition Picture

Mushrooms are low in calories and high in nutritive value, delivering considerable amounts of protein, B vitamins, copper, and other minerals. Since they contain no chlorophyl, they are devoid of beta carotene and vitamin C.

Recent studies have shown that mushrooms may have antibacterial and other medical uses, perhaps even tumor-inhibiting powers. Other studies, however, have linked very high consumption of *raw* mushrooms over an extended period of time with malignant tumor growth, so it may be prudent to usually cook mushrooms before eating them.

Mushrooms owe their rich taste in part to glutamic acid, a natural version of the flavor enhancer monosodium glutamate (MSG). However, whereas MSG contains sodium and other additives, fresh mushrooms are virtually sodium free.

Selection and Storage

Button mushrooms are available year-round and nationwide, with very little fluctuation in quality or price.

Select button mushrooms that are light and even in color, unbruised and unpitted, with caps tightly closed against the stems. Older mushrooms sometimes have a richer flavor and are suitable for stocks, but membranes under the caps should be light tan or pinkish, not dark brown or black. For garnish or for cooking whole, select small mushrooms. Medium-size ones are the best choice for slicing. For stuffing, choose the biggest you can find.

Some specialty varieties—notably shiitakes, oyster mushrooms, and crimini—are readily available in fresh form at gourmet shops or from time to time in supermarkets. When you see them in markets, seize the opportunity to enjoy their distinctive flavors. Fresh crimini and oyster mushrooms, shiitakes, chanterelles, porcinis, and morels should be dry to the touch, unwithered, firm and meaty, with a pleasant, earthy fragrance.

To keep moisture conditions just right, place fresh mushrooms in a loosely closed paper bag or shallow dish covered with a tea towel, not in a plastic bag. Don't wash or trim them before storing. Store on the shelf of the refrigerator, not in the crisper, to minimize humidity, and use as soon as possible. Don't discard mushrooms that have begun to dry out and shrivel in the refrigerator—they will add a wonderful richness to your next batch of Homemade Vegetable Stock (see page 12).

A few varieties of specialty mushrooms—particularly porcinis, shiitakes, and morels—are easy to obtain in dried form at gourmet markets. Dried mushrooms, stored in a tightly closed container in a cool, dark place, will keep almost indefinitely.

Canned mushrooms are much less nutritious than their fresh counterparts, and they often contain added sodium and fat. Since fresh are always available, there's no reason to resort to canned mushrooms.

Culinary Tips

- Wipe fresh mushrooms with a dry towel or sponge, or clean them with a soft brush, instead of washing. Never soak mushrooms, as they will absorb a lot of water, which may dilute the dish to which they are added.

- Peeling robs mushrooms of many of their nutrients and much of their flavor will be lost—there is no need to do so.

- If stems are particularly dirty, remove them in their entirety or simply trim off the tip. Stems, if removed, can be saved for soup stock.

- Overcooking turns mushrooms tough. Sauté them just until their juices are released for best results.

- To avoid discoloration, use stainless steel or enameled cast iron for cooking, wooden spoons for stirring, and nonmetallic bowls for marinating.

- Barely trim the root end of enoki mushrooms. We prefer them raw in salads or used as a garnish for soups, as they become tough when cooked.

- Reconstitute dried mushrooms by soaking them in warm water for about 30 minutes. Strain the soaking liquid and use as a stock, since it will have a wonderful intense mushroom flavor. Reconstituted mushrooms tend to have a chewier texture than their fresh counterparts.

Pickled Mushrooms

Small button mushrooms that are abundant in the markets around Eastertime are perfect for this recipe; however, larger ones may be halved or quartered with good results. Serve these morsels as an appetizer with cheese and crackers, as a salad atop butter lettuce leaves, or as part of a buffet spread.

Yield: 16 appetizer servings (about 1 quart)

Yellow onion	1	**small**
Mushrooms	1	**pound**
Red wine vinegar	⅓	**cup**
Olive oil	¼	**cup**
Honey	1	**tablespoon**
Dry mustard	1	**teaspoon**
Salt	½	**teaspoon**
Pepper		**Several grinds**
Green onions	2,	**minced**
Fresh parsley, minced	¼	**cup**

Peel the onion and cut in half lengthwise. Cut each half cross-wise into thin slices and set aside. Brush or wipe the mushrooms clean and trim off the stem end. Leave them whole if small, or cut them into quarters or halves. Place the vinegar, oil, honey, mustard, salt, and pepper in a small saucepan over medium heat. Bring just to the boiling point, then add the mushrooms, cover, and simmer 15 minutes, stirring occasionally. Remove from the heat and add the green onions and parsley, stirring gently to combine. Transfer to a bowl or jar and let cool at room temperature. Cover and refrigerate overnight, or for up to a few weeks. Bring to room temperature before serving.

Each serving provides:

46	Calories	3 g	Carbohydrate
1 g	Protein	70 mg	Sodium
4 g	Fat	0 mg	Cholesterol
1 g	Dietary Fiber		

Mushroom Tempeh Pâté
with Sage

Tempeh is available at all natural food stores and in some well-stocked supermarkets. It is produced from whole soybeans that have been fermented, creating a delicious nutty flavor. This pâté travels well, so we prepare it often as part of a picnic lunch. Enjoy it on a sunny spring day with fresh fruit, a good baguette, and Sonoma Chardonnay.

Yield: 10 appetizer servings

Mushrooms, chopped	¼	pound (1 cup)
Unsalted butter	2	tablespoons
Tempeh, cubed	4	ounces
Red onion, chopped	1	cup
Garlic	2	cloves, minced
Dry sherry	3	tablespoons
Low-sodium soy sauce	1	tablespoon
Rubbed sage	1	teaspoon
Ground allspice	⅛	teaspoon

Brush or wipe the mushrooms clean and chop them coarsely. Melt the butter in a medium skillet over medium-high heat and add the tempeh, mushrooms, onion, and garlic. Cook, stirring frequently, for 10 minutes. The mushroom liquid will evaporate and the mushrooms and onions will brown slightly. Stir in the sherry, soy sauce, sage, and allspice. Cook, stirring constantly, about 5 minutes, until the liquid is gone. Remove from the heat and allow to cool. Puree the mixture in a food processor to a thick, homogenous consistency. Spoon into a serving bowl, cover, and refrigerate for at least 1 hour, or up to 3 days. Serve at room temperature with crisp crackers or baguette slices.

Each serving provides:

61	Calories	5 g	Carbohydrate
3 g	Protein	64 mg	Sodium
3 g	Fat	6 mg	Cholesterol
0 g	Dietary Fiber		

Stuffed Mushrooms with Rosemary Pesto, Roasted Walnuts, and Couscous

Choose large mushrooms for this recipe—small ones will not do. We prepare batches of rosemary pesto and keep it in the freezer; its unique flavor is simply addictive! You may substitute commercially prepared basil pesto for good—but different—results. Serve these mushrooms as an appetizer, a first course, or a side dish. Any leftovers will be devoured the next day.

Yield: 10 appetizer servings

Raw, unsalted walnuts, chopped	½	cup
Couscous, uncooked	⅓	cup
Mushrooms	2	pounds
Olive oil	¼	teaspoon
Rosemary Pesto (page 15)	¼	cup
Plain nonfat yogurt	⅓	cup
Lowfat sour cream	2	tablespoons

Preheat the oven to 350 degrees F. Place the walnuts in a single layer in a dry, heavy-bottomed skillet over medium-high heat. Shake the pan or stir frequently until the nuts are golden brown and emit a wonderful roasted aroma. Immediately remove from the pan and set aside.

Place ⅔ cup of water in a small saucepan over high heat and bring it to a boil. Add the couscous, stir, cover, and remove from the heat. Set aside for 5 minutes. Meanwhile, brush or wipe the mushrooms clean and carefully remove the entire stem, leaving the cap intact. Finely dice the stems and set aside. Lightly oil a large baking sheet and place the mushrooms on it, cavity side up.

Stir the pesto, yogurt, and sour cream into the couscous along with ½ cup of the diced mushroom stems. Reserve the remaining stems for another use, such as soup stock. Fill each cavity and top with the toasted walnuts. Bake, uncovered, for 20 minutes. Serve immediately.

Each serving provides:

130	Calories	12 g	Carbohydrate
5 g	Protein	37 mg	Sodium
8 g	Fat	2 mg	Cholesterol
1 g	Dietary Fiber		

Mushrooms Cooked in Port with Garlic, Thyme, and Butter

ALMOST INSTANT

This is one the very best ways to eat button mushrooms. Quite simple to prepare, these succulent morsels will be quick to disappear at any meal for mushroom lovers.

Yield: 4 side-dish servings

Mushrooms	1	pound
Port wine	⅓	cup
Garlic	2	cloves, minced
Dried thyme	½	teaspoon
Unsalted butter	1	tablespoon
Salt	⅛	teaspoon
Pepper		A few grinds
Lemon wedges	1	per serving

Wipe or brush loose dirt particles from the mushrooms and slice them thinly. Place the mushroom slices in a stainless steel skillet that has a tight-fitting lid and pour the port over them. Add the garlic and thyme, cover, and cook over medium heat 5 minutes. Remove the lid, stir, cover, and cook an additional 5 minutes. Use a slotted spoon to transfer the mushrooms to a pretty serving dish and cover it to keep warm, or hold in a warm oven. Add the butter, salt, and pepper to the liquid in the pan and cook over medium-high heat for 3 to 4 minutes, until liquid is reduced by about half. Pour the reduced sauce over the mushrooms, garnish the bowl with lemon wedges, and serve very hot.

Each serving provides:

90	Calories	10 g	Carbohydrate
3 g	Protein	77 mg	Sodium
3 g	Fat	8 mg	Cholesterol
1 g	Dietary Fiber		

Mixed Mushroom Soup
with Nutmeg and Caraway

We like to use a variety of fresh mushrooms for this soup. Try fresh shiitake and morels or criminis if they are available, mixed with button mushrooms. Any ratio will work; however, more of the exotic mushrooms will intensify the flavor. Serve with a good rye bread, Gouda cheese, and a light zinfandel or Merlot.

Yield: 6 main-dish servings

Dried shiitake mushrooms	½	ounce
Caraway seed	1	teaspoon
Mushrooms	2	pounds
Unsalted butter	2	tablespoons
Dry sherry	2	tablespoons
Yellow onion	1	medium, diced
Unbleached flour	2	tablespoons
Lowfat milk	3	cups
Dried tarragon	1	tablespoon
Freshly grated nutmeg	¼	teaspoon
Salt	¼	teaspoon
Pepper		Several grinds

Soak the dried mushrooms in 2 cups of hot water for 30 minutes. Lift the mushrooms from the liquid and set aside. Strain the mushroom soaking liquid through a paper coffee filter and set aside. Rinse the mushrooms under a thin stream of cold running water to remove any grit lodged in the membranes under the caps. Squeeze the mushrooms gently to remove some of their liquid. Discard the mushroom stems and chop the caps.

Meanwhile, toast the caraway seed in a dry, heavy-bottomed skillet, stirring or shaking the pan frequently until the seeds begin to pop and emit a nutty aroma. Immediately remove from the pan and set aside.

Brush or wipe the fresh mushrooms clean and trim off the tips of the stems. Chop the mushrooms by hand or in a food processor. Heat 1 tablespoon of the butter along with the sherry in a large, heavy skillet over medium heat. When the butter has melted, add all of the mushrooms and the onion, and sauté for 15 minutes, until the liquid is released from the mushrooms. Stir frequently. Remove from the heat and spoon half the mushrooms into a food processor. Pulse until finely minced and paste-like, but not completely smooth. This may need to be done in several batches.

Place the reserved mushroom soaking liquid in a stockpot over medium-high heat. Add the pureed mushrooms and the remaining sautéed ones. Melt the remaining butter in a small saucepan over medium-low heat. Stir in the flour, cook for a moment, then gradually whisk in the milk. Cook for 15 minutes, stirring frequently—the sauce will be slightly thickened. Stir in the tarragon, nutmeg, salt, and pepper. Add this to the mushrooms in the stockpot. Add the caraway seeds, heat through but do not boil, and serve immediately.

Each serving provides:

172	Calories	20 g	Carbohydrate
8 g	Protein	160 mg	Sodium
7 g	Fat	20 mg	Cholesterol
2 g	Dietary Fiber		

Penne with Mushroom-Apple-Brandy Sauce and Gorgonzola

ALMOST INSTANT

Any variety of mushrooms may be used in this sauce. Try mixing cépes or shiitakes with button mushrooms, depending on availability. The sweet apple juice and pungent Gorgonzola cheese make a delicious marriage.

Yield: 4 main-dish servings

Mushrooms	1	pound
Unsalted butter	2	tablespoons
Garlic	2	cloves, minced
Dried penne	12	ounces
Unsweetened apple juice	⅔	cup
Arrowroot powder or cornstarch	1	tablespoon
Brandy	3	tablespoons
Gorgonzola cheese, crumbled	2	ounces (½ cup)

Bring several quarts of water to a boil in a large stockpot. Brush or wipe the mushrooms to remove any dirt particles. Trim off the tips of the stems, then thinly slice the mushrooms. Melt the butter in a large skillet over medium heat and add the garlic and mushrooms. Sauté for about 15 minutes, stirring frequently, until they release their liquid and become limp. The cooking time may vary a few minutes depending on the type of mushrooms used.

Meanwhile, cook the pasta until al dente. Place 3 tablespoons of the apple juice in a jar that has a tight-fitting lid. Add the arrowroot and shake to dissolve. Set aside. Stir the remaining apple juice and brandy into the skillet with the mushrooms and increase the heat to medium-high. Pour in the arrowroot mixture and stir constantly for a moment or two, until the sauce thickens. Place the cooked pasta in a warmed serving bowl and toss with the mushroom sauce. Top with the crumbled cheese, toss again, and serve immediately.

Each serving provides:

499	Calories	76 g	Carbohydrate
16 g	Protein	210 mg	Sodium
12 g	Fat	26 mg	Cholesterol
4 g	Dietary Fiber		

Risotto with Mushrooms, Leeks, Madeira, and Pine Nuts

VEGAN

This dish is a winning combination of flavors and textures, and a very special treat for friends and family. Each bite begins with a rosemary rush, then the other flavors kick in for a perfectly balanced finish.

Yield: 4 main-dish servings

Pine nuts	2	**tablespoons**
Mushrooms	1	**pound**
Leeks	½	**pound (2 small)**
Madeira	⅓	**cup**
Dried rosemary	2	**teaspoons, crushed**
Salt	⅛	**teaspoon**
Pepper		**A few grinds**
Olive oil	1	**tablespoon**
Garlic	2	**cloves, minced**
Arborio rice, uncooked	1	**cup**
Homemade Vegetable Stock*	3½	**cups**

Place the pine nuts in a single layer in a dry, heavy-bottomed skillet and toast over medium-high heat for several minutes. Stir or shake the pan frequently, until the nuts are lightly browned and emit a wonderful roasted aroma. Set aside.

Brush or wipe the mushrooms clean and cut them into thick slices. Set aside. Trim off the root end and the green portions of the leeks. Cut them in half lengthwise and rinse well

---

*If you do not have Homemade Vegetable Stock on hand, make up a batch according to the directions on page 12, or dissolve 1 large, low-sodium vegetable broth cube in 3½ cups of hot water.

The Best 125 Vegetable Dishes

under running water to remove any grit between the layers. Slice crosswise into thin half-rounds. Set aside. Bring the stock to a simmer, turn off the heat, and keep it handy in a warm spot on the stove.

In a stainless steel or enameled cast-iron skillet, combine the mushrooms, leeks, Madeira, rosemary, salt, and pepper. Bring to a simmer over medium-high heat, reduce heat to low, and sauté, stirring frequently, about 10 minutes, until mushrooms have released their liquid and most of it has evaporated. Do not overcook or the mushrooms will turn rubbery.

In a large, heavy-bottomed saucepan, heat the olive oil over medium heat. Stir in the garlic, then add the rice and stir and sauté for about a minute. Add the stock ½ cup at a time, stirring almost constantly and waiting until the liquid is absorbed before each addition. When the last addition of stock has been absorbed and the rice is tender, transfer it to a warmed serving bowl or tureen, stir in the mushroom mixture and the pine nuts, and serve hot.

Each serving provides:

335	Calories	53 g	Carbohydrate
8 g	Protein	175 mg	Sodium
8 g	Fat	0 mg	Cholesterol
2 g	Dietary Fiber		

Onions

Onions are believed to have originated in central or western Asia. They were widely consumed there, and by the Babylonians, ancient Egyptians, Romans, and Greeks. Civilized Europeans didn't discover the wonders of the onion in the cooking pot until the seventeenth century. The first onion seeds arrived in America with the Pilgrims.

Revered as a sacred symbol of the universe (the word onion stems from the Latin *unus*, meaning *the one*), onions have long been used for purposes other than culinary. Ancient man rubbed onion juice on his body to repel predators. In Caesar's time, athletes ate nothing but onions for breakfast before great games as it was believed this would fortify their blood. Greeks also used onions for tonic purposes. In the Middle Ages, onions were used to counteract the effects of certain poisonous animal and insect bites.

A member of the lily family, common red, white, and yellow onions are classified as *Allium cepa*. They are slow to mature in the garden, requiring two years' growth before harvest. Young onion plants thinned from the beds are bundled for market and sold as green onions or scallions. Other small onions include pearl onions, less than 1 inch in diameter, and boiling onions, 1 to 1½ inches in diameter. These succulent miniatures are not immature, but are separate varieties bred for their small size.

Leeks, chives, and shallots are also members of the vast *Allium* genus. The leek (*Allium ampeloprasum porrum*) has no bulb and only the slender white part is eaten. The best quality leeks are 1½ inches or less in diameter. The shallot (*Allium ascalonicum*) is mild and aromatic, with a more delicate flavor than an onion. Chives (*Allium schoenoprasum*) are an onion-flavored herb used primarily as a piquant, raw addition to salads and other dishes. Garlic (*Allium sativum*), the ubiquitous pungent seasoning, is considered by many to be the star of the *Allium* clan.

The Nutrition Picture

Onions are low in calories as well as most nutrients. A number of recent studies, however, have associated onion consumption with improvement of blood pressure and cholesterol levels, and a decrease in the formation of blood clots. There is some evidence to suggest onions may also be useful cancer fighters and may help in the treatment of asthma and allergies. Research is ongoing, but the evidence is mounting that the onion is a health promoter as well as a flavor enhancer.

Bulb onions provide good amounts of potassium and phosphorus. Green onions contain some vitamin A. Leeks shine as the nutritional star in this group, providing respectable amounts of potassium, calcium, phosphorus, and vitamin A.

Selection and Storage

Spring and early summer onions are shipped to market immediately after harvest and are available March through September. They have soft flesh and a mild, sweet taste suitable for raw, as well as cooked, uses. Storage onions are harvested in late summer and early fall, stored for several months, and shipped to markets from late fall to early spring. They are firmer, with dry, crackly outer skins, and more pungent flavors, suitable for long cooking. White onions tend to be more pungent than yellow and red ones, though color is not necessarily a reliable guide.

Leeks are available year-round in some areas, though they may disappear from the markets in the summer. Pearl and boiling onions do not have a peak season and are generally in good supply. Green onions and shallots are likewise available year-round. Chives are a wonderful home garden crop, but are not always available in markets, since their delicacy gives them a short shelf life. They die back in the winter, but regenerate in early spring.

Bulb onions should feel dry and solid, with no mushy spots or sprouts. The onion's neck should be tightly closed. The skins of storage onions should be crackly and shiny, with no dark blotches underneath. Good quality onions will have no smell at all or a very mild aroma; a strong onion odor usually indicates bruising under the skin.

Store bulb onions out of direct sunlight in a cool, dry place with good air circulation. A loosely woven basket is ideal. Buy bulb onions in small quantities you will use quickly. They ferment naturally—don't store them in a damp or humid environment, which will accelerate their demise. Likewise, avoid storing onions near potatoes, which give off a gas that hastens their spoilage. Tightly wrap cut onions and store in the refrigerator.

Green onions, chives, and leeks should be wrapped in plastic and refrigerated. Store shallots as you would bulb onions, and buy only what you intend to use within a few days—they tend to spoil quickly.

Culinary Tips

- Onions contain volatile compounds that irritate the eyes, but cooking renders them much milder. Peeling an onion under cold water will reduce eye irritation; refrigerating first also helps.

- If onions begin to sprout, use them immediately. You may use the sprout itself as a scallion substitute.

- The onion's flavor mellows with long cooking; some varieties become quite sweet.

- Use no more than 2 inches of the green portion of leeks, since the upper part is quite tough. Slice them in half lengthwise and carefully rinse out the layers to remove any grit.

- Blanch pearl onions for easy peeling by immersing them in a pot of boiling water for about 1 minute, then plunging them into cold water. When they are cool enough to handle, slip off their skins.

- As a rule of thumb, one small onion weighs ¼ pound; one medium onion weighs ½ pound.

Grilled Onions with Red Wine Vinaigrette

VEGAN

Yield: 4 side-dish servings

Yellow onions	1	pound (4 small)
Olive oil	2	tablespoons
Red wine vinegar	1	tablespoon
Fresh-squeezed lemon juice	1	tablespoon
Garlic	1	clove, minced
Cayenne		A pinch

Preheat a coal or gas grill to medium-high. (To preheat a coal grill, prepare the charcoal at least 15 to 20 minutes before cooking begins, so the proper temperature can be achieved in time. The grill is ready when the coals are glowing bright red and a small amount of gray ash is present on them. Preheat a gas grill for at least 10 minutes, or according to the manufacturer's specific instructions.)

Trim off the ends of the onions and peel them. Place them on the grill with one cut end down. Cover and cook for 45 minutes, turning every 10 to 12 minutes to brown evenly. The onions are done when they are soft and slightly charred.

Meanwhile, whisk together the olive oil, vinegar, lemon juice, garlic, and cayenne. Place the cooked onions on a serving platter and drizzle with the dressing. Serve immediately.

Each serving provides:

101	Calories	10 g	Carbohydrate
1 g	Protein	3 mg	Sodium
7 g	Fat	0 mg	Cholesterol
2 g	Dietary Fiber		

Onions in Sherry with Baby Potatoes and Dill

VEGAN

This earthy concoction fits the bill in chilly weather served piping hot, but it can also be served at room temperature in warm weather as a kind of salad, with lemon wedges and dill sprigs for garnish. Either way, it is delicious and filling.

Yield: 6 side-dish servings

Yellow onions	1½	**pounds (3 medium)**
Baby red potatoes	½	**pound**
Olive oil	2	**tablespoons**
Garlic	3	**cloves, minced**
Salt	¼	**teaspoon**
Dried rosemary	1	**teaspoon**
Dill seed	½	**teaspoon**
Dry sherry	½	**cup**
Fresh parsley, minced	¼	**cup**
Pepper		**Several grinds**
Lemon wedges	1	**per person**

Trim off the ends of the onions and peel them. Cut each one into 8 lengthwise wedges. Set aside. Scrub the potatoes but do not peel them; cut each one into quarters. Set aside.

Heat the olive oil in a large, heavy-bottomed skillet over medium-high heat. Sauté the garlic for 2 minutes, stirring constantly, then add the onions and salt. Cook, stirring frequently, 2 to 3 minutes, until onions begin to brown. Turn the heat down to medium, add the potatoes, rosemary, and dill seed and sauté 10 minutes, stirring frequently.

In a small bowl, combine the sherry with ¼ cup water. Holding the lid to the pan in one hand, pour in the sherry mixture and immediately cover the pan tightly. Reduce heat to low and cook for 10 minutes. Remove the lid and cook a little longer, if necessary, until the liquid is almost gone—no more than 5 minutes will be needed. Transfer to a serving bowl, sprinkle with the parsley and pepper, and garnish with lemon wedges. Serve hot, or allow to come to room temperature before serving.

Each serving provides:

147	Calories	20 g	Carbohydrate
2 g	Protein	100 mg	Sodium
5 g	Fat	0 mg	Cholesterol
2 g	Dietary Fiber		

Leeks Braised in Sherry with Juniper Berries and Rosemary

ALMOST INSTANT

Leeks are often overlooked as a main ingredient or a stand-alone side dish, but this recipe will show you just how wonderful they are. The juniper berries have a delicate pine-pepper flavor that works perfectly with the rosemary. They are available in the spice section of any well-stocked market.

Yield: 4 side-dish servings

Leeks	**1¼**	**pounds (5 medium)**
Unsalted butter	**1**	**tablespoon**
Dry sherry	**2**	**tablespoons**
Fresh rosemary leaves	**1**	**teaspoon**
Dried juniper berries	**1**	**teaspoon**

Trim off the root ends and all but about 2 inches of the green portion of the leeks. Slice them in half lengthwise and rinse under cold water to remove any dirt that may be lodged between the layers. Melt the butter in a skillet that has a tight-fitting lid over medium-low heat. Add the sherry, 2 tablespoons water, and the whole rosemary leaves. Crush the juniper berries in a mortar and pestle and add them along with the leeks. Cover and cook for 12 to 15 minutes. Remove the lid after 12 minutes to make sure there is still a little liquid in the pan; you want the leeks to brown slightly, but not to scorch. If the liquid is gone but the leeks are not yet tender, add a tablespoon or two of water and replace the lid. If the leeks are tender and there is still liquid in the pan, stir and cook, uncovered, for a minute or two longer, until it has evaporated. Serve immediately.

Each serving provides:

75	Calories	10 g	Carbohydrate
1 g	Protein	14 mg	Sodium
3 g	Fat	8 mg	Cholesterol
1 g	Dietary Fiber		

Pearl Onions Pickled
in Balsamic Vinegar

VEGAN

This recipe makes at least 12 servings; however, not all of the onions need to be eaten immediately. They store very well in the refrigerator for several weeks and improve with age. If you preserve foods, this is an excellent recipe to double or triple and seal in canning jars, processing 15 minutes in a boiling water bath.

Yield: 12 appetizer servings

Pearl or boiling onions	1½ pounds
Salt	¼ cup
White wine vinegar	2 cups
Balsamic vinegar	½ cup
Honey	1 tablespoon
Olive oil	2 tablespoons
Bay leaves	2 to 4
Dried oregano	1 teaspoon
Whole cloves	½ teaspoon
Dried red chili flakes	Scant ⅛ teaspoon
Whole peppercorns	½ teaspoon

Blanch the onions by immersing them in boiling water for about a minute, then plunge them into ice water and drain in a colander. Trim a very small amount off the tip end and peel. Place the onions in a deep glass bowl or a small crock. Bring 4 cups of water to a boil and add the salt; stir until dissolved. Remove from the heat, allow to cool slightly, then pour over the onions. Place a plate over the onions and weight it down to keep the onions completely submerged in the brine. Allow to cure in the brine at room temperature for 48 hours.

Drain the onions in a colander and rinse with cold water to remove the salt. Place them in a bowl or pack into quart jars. Pour the vinegars into a nonaluminum saucepan and add the honey, olive oil, bay leaves, oregano, whole cloves, chili flakes, and peppercorns. Bring to a boil over high heat, then reduce heat and simmer for 5 minutes. Pour the vinegar mixture over the onions, cover, and cool to room temperature before storing in the refrigerator. Allow to marinate for at least a day before serving. They will keep for at least 2 months in tightly closed containers in the refrigerator.

Each serving provides:

54	Calories	8 g	Carbohydrate
1 g	Protein	189 mg	Sodium
2 g	Fat	0 mg	Cholesterol
0 g	Dietary Fiber		

Onion Sorrel Soup

Most onion soup recipes call for beef stock; however, we prefer the vegetarian approach. In this version, sorrel provides the unique flavor note. The sorrel plant is easy to grow and has attractive green foliage. If you don't have a home garden, look for it in the fresh herb section of specialty markets. Serve this wonderful soup with garlic bread and Caesar salad for a perfect cool evening meal.

Yield: 6 main-dish servings

Yellow onions	**2½**	**pounds (5 medium)**
Unsalted butter	**3**	**tablespoons**
Brandy	**½**	**cup**
Homemade Vegetable Stock*	**6**	**cups**
Worcestershire sauce	**2**	**tablespoons**
Maggi Seasoning	**½**	**teaspoon**
Liquid Smoke	**5**	**drops**
Fresh sorrel leaves	**8**	**large**
Salt	**¼**	**teaspoon**

Trim off the ends of the onions and peel them. Cut them in half lengthwise, then cut each half into thin slices. Melt the butter in a very large skillet over medium-high heat. (If you do not have a skillet large enough, use two smaller ones.) Cook uncovered for 10 minutes, reduce the heat to medium, and continue to cook for 10 minutes, until onions are very limp and transparent. Stir frequently. Pour in the brandy, increase the heat to medium-high, and cook 5 minutes, or until the brandy evaporates.

*If you do not have Homemade Vegetable Stock on hand, make up a batch according to the directions on page 12, or dissolve 3 large, low-sodium vegetable broth cubes in 6 cups of hot water.

Meanwhile, put the stock in a stockpot and bring to a boil over high heat. Add the Worcestershire sauce, Maggi Seasoning, Liquid Smoke, and the cooked onions. Return to a boil, reduce the heat to medium, and simmer 20 minutes. Finely chop the sorrel and add with the salt during the last 2 minutes of cooking. Serve immediately, garnished with chopped sorrel leaves, if desired.

Each serving provides:

200	Calories	17 g	Carbohydrate
4 g	Protein	290 mg	Sodium
8 g	Fat	16 mg	Cholesterol
3 g	Dietary Fiber		

Polenta and Onion Casserole with Fennel Seed and Mozzarella

The preparation of this dish requires two burners and the oven, but it is not difficult. The resulting casserole is warming, rich, and delicious—a great meal to share with friends in front of a roaring fire.

Yield: 8 main-dish servings

Fennel seed	2	teaspoons
Dried red chili flakes	¼	teaspoon
Olive oil	1	tablespoon plus ¼ teaspoon
Garlic	4	cloves, minced
Red onions	1½	pounds (3 medium)
Salt	⅛	teaspoon
Low-sodium whole tomatoes	1	28-ounce can
Capers, drained and minced	2	tablespoons
Granulated garlic	¼	teaspoon
Pepper		A few grinds
Coarse yellow cornmeal	1½	cups
Part-skim mozzarella cheese, grated	4	ounces (1 cup)

Use a mortar and pestle or small food processor to coarsely grind the fennel seed with the dried red chili flakes. In a large, heavy-bottomed skillet, heat the olive oil over medium heat. Add the ground spices and the garlic and stir for a minute before adding the onions and salt. Sauté, stirring frequently, about 8 minutes, until the onions become rather soft. Add the tomatoes along with their juice and the capers. Bring to a simmer, reduce heat to medium-low, and cook 15 minutes, stirring occasionally. Break up the large pieces of tomato with a wooden spoon as the mixture cooks down.

Meanwhile, preheat the oven to 375 degrees F. Rub a 2-quart casserole dish with the remaining ¼ teaspoon olive oil. Bring 3½ cups of water to a boil in a heavy saucepan over high heat, along with the granulated garlic and pepper. Reduce heat to medium and pour the cornmeal into the water in a slow, steady stream, whisking constantly. Cook, whisking almost constantly to prevent sticking, until the mixture is very thick, then whisk in ½ cup cold water and bring back to a bubble. Stir in half the cheese and pour into the oiled dish. Top with the onion mixture and the remaining mozzarella. Bake for 25 minutes, then allow to sit for 5 minutes before serving.

Each serving provides:

206	Calories	33 g	Carbohydrate
8 g	Protein	328 mg	Sodium
5 g	Fat	8 mg	Cholesterol
3 g	Dietary Fiber		

Peas

The edible pea is one of the world's most ancient vegetables. Some form of the plant is known to have existed during the Bronze Age in what is now northeastern Europe. Dried peas have been found in Egyptian tombs and were known in ancient Rome and Greece. In the sixteenth century, varieties for fresh eating were developed in France and spread from there to the rest of Europe, and eventually to the Americas.

A prolific annual, *Pisum sativum* is technically a legume, but it is packaged and prepared like other fresh vegetables. Varieties for fresh eating include shelling peas (also called English peas) as well as edible-pod types like snow peas. The sugar snap pea, a cross between snow peas and English peas, is a wonderfully sweet edible-pod variety created in the 1970s.

The Nutrition Picture

The pea itself is a seed that will produce new generations if it is planted after being allowed to mature and dry on the vine. As such, it contains all the nutrients necessary for the growth of new plants—and is also very nourishing to people. The pea is a terrific source of lowfat, low-calorie, low-sodium protein. It also provides good doses of potassium, vitamins C and A, and dietary fiber.

Snow peas are eaten when the seeds are still quite immature, so their protein content is reduced, but they are higher in calcium and vitamin C than shelled peas.

Selection and Storage

For fresh green shelling peas the season is short, from April through July. Most of the domestic crop of shelling peas is frozen or canned—only 5 percent of the crop is sold fresh. Pea varieties with edible pods are more readily available most of the year than shelling peas. A pound of peas in pods will yield one cup of shelled peas—enough for two generous servings. With sugar snap or snow peas, plan on ¼ pound per serving.

Select pods for shelling that are quite plump, with fat, visible bulges indicating well-developed and sweet peas. Pods should not rattle, and should be velvety and bright green. Pass over any puffy, yellowish pods. Snow peas, on the other hand, should be quite flat, with shiny skin and crisp texture. The smaller ones will be sweeter. Sugar snaps should have crisp, plump, juicy pods. In all varieties, avoid mushy, rubbery, or limp pods.

At room temperature, half the sugar in green peas will turn to starch within 6 hours of picking, so use them the day you buy them, if possible. Otherwise, you may store peas in a loosely closed plastic bag in the refrigerator for a day or two. Don't wash or shell peas before storing.

Frozen peas retain their flavor and nutrients well and are quite useful when shelling peas are out of season. Avoid canned peas, however, which are usually mushy or grainy in texture. Their color is also unappealing, and undesired salt and sugar are often added. Please don't judge the virtue of peas by the canned variety you may have experienced as a child—the crisp sweetness of fresh peas will win you over.

Culinary Tips

- Rinse pods before shelling if they are dirty. To shell peas, snap off the stem and pull away the string—the pod will pop open. Dislodge the peas with your thumb and collect them in a bowl. If you wish, you may use the pea pods in your next batch of Homemade Vegetable Stock (see page 12).
- Remove the stem and string of sugar snap peas, but eat the entire pod.
- Barely trim off the stem of snow peas. Before using them in salads or as a garnish, you may enliven their color and tenderize them slightly by immersing them in boiling water for about 1 minute, then immediately plunging them into cold water to set their bright color.
- All varieties of peas can be eaten raw and are good additions to salads.
- Thawed but not cooked, frozen peas can be used in salads or for other uses that call for fresh peas. To thaw frozen peas, separate clumps with your fingers, rinse with warm water, and allow to drain in a colander.
- Don't overcook peas—they have a delicate texture and their nutrients are quickly lost.

Peggy's Pea Salad with Cashews

ALMOST INSTANT

The British love their fresh peas, and Peggy Hadler has been making this wonderful dish as long as we can remember. It is a delicious way to use the first fresh spring peas that show up in the market or the garden. However, we often make it using frozen peas with excellent results.

Yield: 6 side-dish servings

Peas, with pods	2	**pounds (2 cups shelled)**
Celery	2	**ribs, diced**
Red onion, minced	⅓	**cup**
Lowfat sour cream	½	**cup**
Garlic	1	**clove, minced**
White wine vinegar	2	**teaspoons**
Cashews, salted and roasted	½	**cup, minced**

Shell the peas; discard the pods or save them for your next batch of soup stock. Place the peas, celery, and onion in a bowl and toss to combine. Whisk together the sour cream, garlic, and vinegar. Pour this over the peas and celery and toss well to combine. Serve immediately or cover and store in the refrigerator for up to a day. Just before serving, add the nuts and toss again.

Each serving provides:

138	Calories	14 g	Carbohydrate
5 g	Protein	105 mg	Sodium
7 g	Fat	5 mg	Cholesterol
0 g	Dietary Fiber		

Pea Pods with Bleu Cheese and Pimiento Filling

Inspired by our favorite bleu cheese dressing, this appetizer is somewhat labor-intensive because of the stuffing procedure, but the effect is showy enough to make it worthwhile. It will go more quickly and appear prettier if you use a pastry bag to extrude the filling precisely and quickly. If you don't have time for this, you can thin the filling out with more yogurt or nonfat milk and use it as a dip for raw vegetables. It can also become a wonderful reduced-fat bleu cheese salad dressing when thinned with additional lemon juice.

Yield: 10 appetizer servings

Firm-style tofu	5	ounces
Snow peas	½	pound
Bleu cheese, crumbled	2	ounces (½ cup)
Plain nonfat yogurt	2	tablespoons
Fresh-squeezed lemon juice	2	teaspoons
Garlic	1	clove, minced
Dried dill weed	½	teaspoon
Lemon zest, minced	½	teaspoon
Minced pimiento peppers	1	2-ounce jar

Cut the tofu into ¼-inch slices and set them aside for about 30 minutes between two tea towels so they will release some of their moisture. Meanwhile, soak the peas in ice water for 15 to 20 minutes to crisp and chill them.

Puree the tofu, cheese, yogurt, lemon juice, garlic, dill, and lemon zest in a food processor or blender until smooth. The mixture will be thick. Stir in the minced pimientos and set aside in the refrigerator.

Pull the strings from the pea pods and use a sharp knife to slit them open on the curved side. Leave about ¼ of one end unslit to serve as a kind of handle for picking the peas up from the platter. Fill a pastry bag with the bleu cheese mixture and use it to lightly fill each pea pod. Arrange the pods on a pretty serving platter and chill if they are not to be served immediately.

Each serving provides:

53	Calories	3 g	Carbohydrate
4 g	Protein	85 mg	Sodium
3 g	Fat	4 mg	Cholesterol
1 g	Dietary Fiber		

Peas and Orzo with Olives, Garlic, Tarragon, and Pecans

ALMOST INSTANT, VEGAN

Here is another comfort food creation. It comes together very quickly and you'll find yourself making it frequently from ingredients you will want to keep on hand. Orzo, the rice-shaped pasta of Greek cuisine, is available at any market with a good pasta selection. Oil-cured olives are actually packaged dry, not in a brine. A well-stocked deli counter or gourmet food store will have them.

Yield: 4 side-dish servings

Salt		A pinch
Fresh-squeezed lemon juice	2	tablespoons
Oil-cured olives, minced	2	tablespoons
Fresh tarragon leaves, minced	1	tablespoon
Garlic	1	clove, minced
Pepper		Several grinds
Raw unsalted pecans, chopped	3	tablespoons
Dried orzo	1	cup
Petite peas, frozen	1	pound
Olive oil	2	teaspoons
Lemon wedges	1	per serving

Bring 6 cups of water to a boil in a large saucepan with the salt. Meanwhile, in a small bowl, combine the lemon juice, olives, tarragon, garlic, and pepper and set aside at room temperature. Place the pecans in a single layer in a dry, heavy-bottomed skillet over medium-high heat and cook, stirring frequently, for several minutes, until nuts are browning and emit a wonderful roasted aroma. Remove them from the pan and set aside.

Cook the orzo in salted boiling water for about 10 minutes, until it is al dente, then add the frozen peas. As soon as the water comes back to a boil, transfer the orzo and peas to a colander and drain very well. In a warmed serving bowl, toss the orzo and peas with the olive oil until well combined, then with the olive mixture and the pecans. Garnish with lemon wedges and serve hot or at room temperature.

Each serving provides:

333	Calories	53 g	Carbohydrate
12 g	Protein	338 mg	Sodium
9 g	Fat	0 mg	Cholesterol
6 g	Dietary Fiber		

Spicy Snow Pea Sauté with Fermented Black Bean Sauce

ALMOST INSTANT, VEGAN

The delectable edible pods called snow peas can age quickly in the supermarket bin. If the ones you purchase are a little limp, you can refresh them by soaking them in ice water for at least 15 minutes before proceeding with the recipe. This is a classic Asian-inspired side dish, best served with rice.

Yield: 4 side-dish servings

Snow peas	½	pound
Mushrooms	¼	pound
Fresh mung bean sprouts	1	cup
Dry sherry	2	tablespoons
Mirin	2	teaspoons
Low-sodium soy sauce	1	teaspoon
Chili oil	¼	teaspoon
Dark sesame oil	1	teaspoon
Garlic	1	clove, minced
Salt		A pinch
Fermented black beans	2	teaspoons, minced
Arrowroot powder or cornstarch	1½	teaspoons
Homemade Vegetable Stock*	¼	cup

*If you do not have Homemade Vegetable Stock on hand, make some according to the directions on page 12, or simply use ¼ cup water.

Pull the stem ends and strings from the snow peas and slice each one in two at a slant crosswise. Brush or wipe loose dirt particles from the mushrooms and thickly slice them. Rinse the bean sprouts and set aside in a colander to drain.

Stir together the sherry, mirin, soy sauce, chili oil, sesame oil, and garlic and place this mixture in a wok or skillet. Bring to a simmer over medium heat, add the mushrooms and salt, cover, and cook 3 minutes. Add the snow peas, cover, and cook 3 minutes longer. Add the bean sprouts and black beans and stir and cook about 1 minute to barely heat up the bean sprouts. Most of the liquid should have evaporated.

Meanwhile, dissolve the arrowroot powder in the stock. Pour this mixture into the skillet and toss until the vegetables are evenly coated with the thin, translucent sauce. This will take only a moment; do not overcook the arrowroot or it will turn gummy. Serve very hot, with rice or Asian noodles.

Each serving provides:

79	Calories	10 g	Carbohydrate
3 g	Protein	168 mg	Sodium
2 g	Fat	0 mg	Cholesterol
2 g	Dietary Fiber		

Fresh Pea and Potato Soup
with Ginger and Mint

ALMOST INSTANT

This simple yet rich soup is addicting. The sweet heat of ginger enlivens the delicate flavor of spring peas, and fresh mint sprinkled on top ties it all together. We haven't tried it with frozen peas, but they would probably work in a pinch.

Yield: 4 first-course servings

Raw sesame seeds	½	teaspoon
English peas, in their pods	2	pounds
Red potatoes	¾	pound, peeled and diced
Half-and-half	½	cup
Fresh ginger, grated	2	teaspoons
Garlic	2	cloves, minced
Salt	¼	teaspoon
Fresh mint leaves, minced	2	tablespoons

Place the sesame seeds in a small, dry cast-iron skillet over medium-high heat. Shake the pan frequently and soon they will begin to brown and emit a roasted aroma. Remove immediately from the pan and set aside until needed. Shell the peas; discard the pods or save them for your next batch of soup stock. In a stockpot, combine the peas, potatoes, half-and-half, ginger, garlic, and salt with 1½ cups water. Bring to a simmer over medium heat, cover, and cook about 10 minutes, until very tender. The cream may curdle, but this is all right. Transfer in small batches to a blender or food processor and puree to a thick, smooth consistency. Add another tablespoon or two of water if the soup seems too thick. Return to the pot and cook over low heat for 2 minutes, to just heat through. Ladle portions into individual warmed bowls and sprinkle evenly with minced mint and sesame seeds. Serve immediately.

Each serving provides:

174	Calories	24 g	Carbohydrate
6 g	Protein	156 mg	Sodium
6 g	Fat	20 mg	Cholesterol
1 g	Dietary Fiber		

Pea Pods and Penne with Mushrooms, Paprika, Dill, and Feta

ALMOST INSTANT

Italy meets Hungary in this colorful and delicious main dish. It's a fine choice when you want to serve a hearty meal in a hurry.

Yield: 4 main-dish servings

Sugar snap peas	3/4	pound
Red cabbage, finely shredded	2	cups
Dried penne	8	ounces
Unsalted butter	1	tablespoon
Garlic	2	cloves, minced
Paprika	2	teaspoons
Dried dill	1	teaspoon
Mushrooms	1/2	pound, sliced
Salt	1/8	teaspoon
Dry sherry	1/4	cup
Fresh-squeezed lemon juice	1/3	cup
Feta cheese, crumbled	2	ounces (1/2 cup)
Pepper		Several grinds

In a large stockpot, bring several quarts of water to a boil for the pasta. Pull the strings from the pea pods; leave them whole. Place the pea pods and the cabbage shreds on a steamer rack in a saucepan that has a tight-fitting lid. Add about 1 inch of water and cook over medium-high heat for 4 minutes. Remove the lid from the steaming pot and set aside.

Cook the penne in the boiling water until al dente. Meanwhile, in a skillet over medium heat, combine the butter, garlic, paprika, and dill. Heat until the butter melts and sizzles, then add the mushrooms and stir to coat with butter and seasonings. Add salt and stir. Sauté 2 minutes, stirring once or twice during this time. Add the sherry and stir and sauté 2 minutes longer. Turn off the heat and stir in the lemon juice.

When the pasta is done, drain briefly, allowing some water to cling to the tubes. Toss with the mushroom mixture until well combined, then toss with the vegetables and feta. Transfer to a warmed serving bowl, grind on some pepper, and serve very hot.

Each serving provides:

383	Calories	63 g	Carbohydrate
14 g	Protein	246 mg	Sodium
7 g	Fat	20 mg	Cholesterol
7 g	Dietary Fiber		

Peppers

Peppers are native to the western hemisphere and have been cultivated for thousands of years in tropical regions. It is believed they were introduced to Europe about 500 years ago by Columbus.

They got their name from Spanish explorers, who were actually in search of peppercorns. Peppers, however, belong to the nightshade family, along with tomatoes, potatoes, and eggplants, and are unrelated to the peppercorns used as a seasoning.

Peppers—generally divided into the hot and sweet categories—are grouped under the botanical name *Capsicum annuum*. The hot varieties are usually called chili peppers, or just chilies, and are used to lend a spicy flavor to other foods. The heat comes from substances called capsaicinoids, contained mostly in the white interior membranes of the pepper. As chili peppers mature on the plant, thcy turn from green to red—the redder the pepper, the hotter its bite. Soil and climate conditions affect hotness, so even within the same variety, intensity can vary.

Sixty percent of the domestic pepper crop are of the sweet type known as bell peppers. The different bell pepper colors—ranging from yellow to purple to bright red—depend on variety and stage of ripeness. Green bell peppers are fully developed, but not technically ripe. Most will continue to ripen and will eventually turn red if left on the vine. Red bell peppers are more expensive due to the longer growing time, and because they are more delicate than the less ripe green ones and therefore require more careful handling. Bell peppers don't contain capsaicinoids, so the more mature red peppers of this variety are actually sweeter.

The Nutritional Picture

By weight, green peppers contain twice as much vitamin C as oranges. Red peppers contain 3 times as much, while chili peppers contain even more. Red peppers are also an excellent source of beta carotene, providing nearly 11 times as much as green peppers. All pepper varieties are low in calories, sodium, and fat.

Selection and Storage

Fresh peppers, particularly green bells, are generally available year-round, though their season peaks in the summer. Serving size varies for peppers, depending on their preparation. If serving a stuffed pepper, plan on one per person.

Regardless of variety, peppers should be firm, glossy, smooth, and symmetrical, with unwithered stems. Bell peppers should feel heavy for their size. Beware of soft or bruised areas. Green bells may show some red coloration—these will be slightly sweeter than all-green ones, but will not continue to ripen after harvest.

Store sweet peppers unwashed in a loosely closed plastic bag in the refrigerator for up to a week. Green ones will keep slightly longer, and hot ones longer still.

Dried hot chilies should not be crumbly and broken (unless, of course, you are looking for a crushed variety). Their appearance will be wrinkled and glossy. They may be stored at room temperature for several months in a tightly closed container.

Culinary Tips

- Wash uncut sweet or hot peppers just before using. The seeds may be bitter and should be discarded. Cut peppers in half lengthwise for easy removal of the pithy membranes, stems, and seeds.

- Roasting peppers develops a wonderful smoky flavor. Wash and dry the peppers and cook directly on the grill, over an open burner, or under the broiler, turning frequently, until the peppers are charred black all over and are beginning to collapse. Transfer to a paper bag, fold the bag closed, and set aside until cool enough to handle. When cooled, remove the skin, stems, and seeds. Cut the pepper pulp as directed in the specific recipe.

- The color of purple peppers changes to an unappetizing gray when cooked, so select them only for raw uses.

- Since the heat of chilies can vary even within a single variety, use sparingly at first and add more if you wish. Chili peppers can be soaked in cold, salted water to reduce their fire.

- Don't allow the membranes, seeds, or juices of hot chilies to come in contact with your skin because they cause a painful burning sensation. Wearing rubber gloves is a reasonable precaution. If your skin does come in contact, wash the area carefully with a diluted bleach solution or mild soap and water to minimize discomfort. Be especially careful to avoid touching your eyes.

- When grinding or crushing dry hot peppers, be careful not to inhale the dust or get it into your eyes.
- To subdue fire in the mouth after consuming a particularly hot pepper, eat bread or rice rather than drinking water. Better yet, drink milk, which contains a substance that will neutralize capsaicinoids.
- As a rule of thumb, one large bell pepper weighs ½ pound.

Grilled Peppers with Balsamic Vinaigrette

ALMOST INSTANT, VEGAN

We prefer to use a variety of different colors of sweet peppers for this salad. The subtle difference in flavors is pleasing and the colors create a pretty dish. Serve fresh French bread to sop up the extra dressing.

Yield: 6 side-dish servings

Olive oil	3	tablespoons
Balsamic vinegar	1	tablespoon
Fresh-squeezed lemon juice	1	tablespoon
Garlic	1	clove, minced
Fresh basil leaves, minced	1	tablespoon
Fresh mint leaves, minced	1	tablespoon
Salt		Scant ⅛ teaspoon
Pepper		Several grinds
Sweet peppers	2	pounds (4 large)

Preheat a coal or gas grill to medium. (To preheat a coal grill, start the charcoal at least 15 to 20 minutes before cooking begins so the proper temperature can be achieved in time. The grill is ready when the coals are glowing bright red and there is a fairly thick coating of gray ash on them. Preheat a gas grill at least 10 minutes or according to the manufacturer's specific instructions.)

Whisk together the olive oil, vinegar, and lemon juice. Add the garlic, basil, mint, salt, and pepper. Whisk again and set aside.

Cut the peppers in half, discard the stems, seeds, and pithy membranes, then slice each half in thirds lengthwise. Place on a rack on the grill, cover the grill, and cook 12 to 15 minutes, turning several times during the cooking time. They will char slightly and become limp. Arrange on a serving platter and pour the dressing over them. Serve immediately, or allow to marinate at room temperature for up to several hours. They may also be covered and refrigerated for up to 2 days.

Each serving provides:

96	Calories	9 g	Carbohydrate
1 g	Protein	49 mg	Sodium
7 g	Fat	0 mg	Cholesterol
2 g	Dietary Fiber		

Sautéed Pepper Medley with Sherry, Oregano, and Almonds

ALMOST INSTANT, VEGAN

Simple, pretty, and delicious—what else could we desire? Any combination of peppers will work for this dish, but try to include different colors for the visual effect. You can even include a seeded jalapeño if you enjoy hot and spicy food.

Yield: 4 side-dish servings

Raw unsalted almond slivers	2	tablespoons
Sweet peppers	1½	pounds (3 large)
Olive oil	1	tablespoon
Garlic	2	cloves, minced
Dried oregano	1	teaspoon
Salt	⅛	teaspoon
Pepper		A few grinds
Dry sherry	¼	cup
Lemon wedges	1	per serving

Toast the almonds in a dry, heavy skillet over medium-high heat. Shake the pan or stir frequently until the nuts are lightly browned and emit a roasted aroma. Remove from the pan and set aside.

Cut the peppers in half lengthwise, discard their stems, seeds, and pithy membranes, and cut the halves crosswise into ¼-inch strips. Heat the olive oil over medium heat in a large, heavy-bottomed skillet that has a tight-fitting lid. Sauté the garlic for a minute, then add the peppers and stir. Add the oregano, salt, and pepper and sauté, stirring frequently, for 6 to 7 minutes, until peppers are beginning to brown. Add the sherry, stir, and immediately cover the pan. Reduce heat to medium-low and cook for 3 to 5 minutes. Transfer the peppers to a serving bowl or platter and top with the almonds. Serve hot or at room temperature, with lemon wedges alongside.

Each serving provides:

121	Calories	14 g	Carbohydrate
2 g	Protein	74 mg	Sodium
6 g	Fat	0 mg	Cholesterol
2 g	Dietary Fiber		

Curry Sautéed Peppers
with Chutney Cream

ALMOST INSTANT

Any combination of sweet peppers will work for this simple, strongly seasoned side dish. We like to use at least two colors for a prettier effect. Add the cayenne to the cream mixture only if you enjoy hot and spicy food.

Yield: 4 side-dish servings

Raw sesame seeds	2	teaspoons
Sweet peppers	1½	pounds (3 large)
Garlic	2	cloves, minced
Curry powder	1½	teaspoons
Red onion	1	medium, diced
Salt	⅛	teaspoon plus a pinch
Light sour cream	⅓	cup
Plain nonfat yogurt	⅓	cup
Mango Chutney (page 18)	2	tablespoons
Fresh cilantro, minced	¼	cup
Cayenne		A pinch
Dry sherry	3	tablespoons

Toast the sesame seeds in a dry, heavy-bottomed skillet over medium heat, stirring or shaking the pan frequently, until the seeds are lightly browned and emit a nutty aroma. Remove from the pan and set aside.

Wash and dry the peppers. Discard the stem ends, white membranes, and seeds and chop the peppers into roughly uniform chunks. In a heavy-bottomed skillet with a tight-fitting lid, combine the garlic and curry powder with ¼ cup water and bring to a simmer over medium heat. Add the peppers, onion,

The Best 125 Vegetable Dishes

and ⅛ teaspoon salt and stir to combine well. Cover the pan and cook 5 minutes, then remove the lid and stir. Put the lid back on and cook for about 4 minutes longer, until peppers have begun to brown and all the liquid is gone.

Meanwhile, stir the sour cream, yogurt, chutney, cilantro, cayenne, and remaining pinch of salt together in a small bowl and set aside. Place the dry sherry in a small bowl. When pepper cooking time is up, turn off the heat and deglaze the pan by pouring the sherry into the pan all at once, stirring rapidly so the liquid covers the bottom of the pan. It will sizzle and steam, loosening any browned bits that may be stuck to the pan. This takes only a moment. Transfer the contents of the pan to a pretty serving bowl and toss with the cream mixture until well combined. Sprinkle with the sesame seeds and serve.

Each serving provides:

146	Calories	23 g	Carbohydrate
5 g	Protein	126 mg	Sodium
4 g	Fat	7 mg	Cholesterol
3 g	Dietary Fiber		

Roasted Peppers and Couscous Salad with Capers, Lime, and Thyme

VEGAN

This stunning dish deserves a place of honor at a summer buffet dinner. Any color bell pepper can be used for this dish, though we especially enjoy the sweetness of the red and yellow varieties.

Yield: 8 side-dish servings

Olive oil	3	tablespoons plus 2 teaspoons
Granulated garlic	½	teaspoon
Dried thyme	¾	teaspoon
Salt	⅛	teaspoon plus ¼ teaspoon
Cayenne		A pinch
Dried couscous	1½	cups
Fresh-squeezed lime juice	2	tablespoons plus 1 teaspoon
Balsamic vinegar	1	tablespoon
Capers, not drained	2	tablespoons
Honey	2	teaspoons
Garlic	3	cloves, minced
Pepper		Several grinds
Bell peppers	1	pound (2 large)
Fresh parsley, minced	½	cup
Green onions, minced	⅓	cup
Tomato	1	large, diced

Bring 2¼ cups water to a boil in a medium saucepan, along with 2 teaspoons of the olive oil, granulated garlic, ¼ teaspoon of the thyme, ⅛ teaspoon of the salt, and the cayenne. When it is boiling rapidly, pour in the couscous and stir. Immediately turn off the heat, cover the pan, and allow to stand 10 minutes. Remove to a large bowl and use a fork to gently break up most of the clumps. Allow to cool to room temperature.

Meanwhile, make the dressing by combining the remaining 3 tablespoons olive oil, lime juice, balsamic vinegar, capers, honey, garlic, remaining ½ teaspoon thyme, remaining ¼ teaspoon salt, and pepper in a small food processor. Puree to a smooth sauce consistency. Preheat the oven to 400 degrees F. Rinse and dry the peppers. If they are large ones, cut in half from stem end to tip, then cut each piece in half crosswise. If the peppers are small, cut in half from stem end to tip. Discard the stems, seeds, and pithy membrane. Use your fingers or a brush to lightly coat the inside of the pepper pieces with a small amount of the dressing. Place cut side up in a single layer in a glass baking dish and bake for about 30 minutes—you want the peppers to be somewhat limp and tender. Remove from the oven and allow to cool a bit.

When couscous has cooled to room temperature, toss with the parsley, onions, and tomato, reserving a tablespoon or so of the parsley for garnish. Toss with the remaining dressing until well combined. Arrange the peppers on a large platter and mound the couscous mixture over them. Garnish with the reserved parsley and the lemon wedges. Serve immediately, or hold in the refrigerator for up to a few hours. Return to room temperature before serving.

Each serving provides:

207	Calories	32 g	Carbohydrate
5 g	Protein	167 mg	Sodium
7 g	Fat	0 mg	Cholesterol
1 g	Dietary Fiber		

Roasted Pepper and Chard Pizza with Cumin, Jalapeños, and Cilantro

A spicy delight, this dish combines some classic south-of-the-border flavors on a crust. For a wonderful summer meal, serve it with a lime-infused black bean and jicama salad. This pizza may also be cooked on a hot outdoor grill to avoid heating up the kitchen.

Yield: 6 main-course servings

Pizza crust	1	12-inch crust
Red bell pepper	½	pound (1 large)
Fresh Swiss chard	1	pound
Olive oil	1	tablespoon
Yellow onion	1	small
Garlic	6	cloves, minced
Cumin seed	1½	teaspoons
Salt		A pinch
Monterey Jack cheese, grated	2	ounces (about ⅔ cup)
Parmesan cheese, finely grated	¼	cup
Pickled jalapeños, seeded and minced	1	tablespoon
Fresh cilantro, minced	2	tablespoons

Prepare a pizza crust from the recipe on page 16, or use a commercial crust for an Almost Instant pizza.

Roast the pepper over a gas burner, under a broiler, or on a hot grill, turning frequently until the skin is charred black all over and the pepper has begun to collapse. Place immediately in a paper bag and fold the bag closed; set aside. The steam in the bag will finish cooking the pepper.

258

Wash the chard leaves well, but do not dry them. Thinly slice the stems and coarsely chop the leaves; set the stems and leaves aside separately. Heat the olive oil in a heavy-bottomed skillet over medium heat. Add the onion, garlic, and cumin seed and sauté for a moment, then stir in the chard stems and salt. Sauté for 5 minutes, then mound the greens on top, cover tightly, and cook an additional 5 minutes. Remove the lid. Greens should be wilted; stir to combine them with the other ingredients in the pan. Continue to cook for a minute or two, stirring constantly, until all the liquid has evaporated. Remove from the heat.

Preheat the oven to 450 degrees F. When the pepper is cool enough to handle, remove the skin, discard the stem and seeds, and thinly slice the pulp. Distribute the cooked greens evenly over the pizza crust, and arrange the pepper slices on top in a pretty pattern. In a small bowl, toss the cheese with the jalapeños and the cilantro. Distribute this mixture evenly over the pizza. Place on a baking sheet and bake for 12 minutes, until the cheese is melted and the crust is lightly browned. Serve very hot.

Each serving provides:

206	Calories	21 g	Carbohydrate
9 g	Protein	405 mg	Sodium
11 g	Fat	13 mg	Cholesterol
3 g	Dietary Fiber		

Stuffed Chilies with Savory Chocolate Tomato Sauce

An exotic masterpiece, the sauce combines chocolate, cinnamon, and nutmeg with tomatoes for a dense, rich, mysterious flavor. Serve this wonderful version of chili rellenos with Spanish rice, seasoned black beans, and flour tortillas for a delicious meal. We use the traditional ranchero cheese available in Mexican markets; if you are unable to locate it, substitute farmers cheese. Poblano chilies are the perfect choice for stuffing, though any long, mild green pepper—like Anaheim—could be substituted.

Yield: 8 main-dish servings

Poblano chilies	1½	pounds (about 8 large)
Peeled and crushed pear tomatoes	1	28-ounce can
Yellow onion	½	medium, chopped
Garlic	3	cloves, minced
Unsweetened powdered cocoa	2	teaspoons
Ground cinnamon	½	teaspoon
Chili powder	½	teaspoon
Ground cumin	½	teaspoon
Dry mustard		Scant ⅛ teaspoon
Ground cloves		Scant ⅛ teaspoon
Part-skim ranchero cheese, crumbled	10	ounces (2½ cups)

Egg whites	3	large
Whole egg	1	large
Unbleached flour	1	tablespoon
Bread crumbs	1	tablespoon
Canola oil	2	tablespoons

Roast the peppers on a hot grill or under a broiler for about 5 minutes, or until the skin is uniformly charred. Turn and blacken the other side, being careful not to tear the peppers. Carefully lay them on a glass platter and cover with a paper bag or plastic wrap. Set aside at room temperature; the steam inside the wrapping will finish cooking the peppers.

Meanwhile, place the tomatoes, onion, and garlic in a blender or food processor and puree until smooth. Pour into a large skillet and add the cocoa, cinnamon, chili powder, cumin, mustard, and cloves. Cook over medium heat, stirring frequently, 8 to 10 minutes, until thickened. Set aside.

When the peppers are cool enough to handle, gently remove the skin. Carefully make a slit lengthwise through only one side of each chili, starting ½ inch from the stem end. Use a spoon to carefully scrape out and discard the seeds and membranes, but be careful to not detach the stems from the peppers. Stuff the chilies with equal portions of cheese, compacting the cheese in your hands to conform to the shape of the chilies as you do so. Overlap the slit edges of each chili slightly as you fill it and set aside.

Beat all of the egg whites until they are stiff but not dry. Add the egg yolk and beat to incorporate. Add the flour and bread crumbs, then beat again to incorporate. Pour the batter onto a large platter or a pie pan. Heat 1 tablespoon of the oil in a large cast-iron skillet over medium-high heat. Carefully dip four of the chilies in the batter, one at a time, to generously coat them, and gently place them in the hot pan. (Use a pan large enough to cook all 4 at a time.) Fry the stuffed peppers 4 to 5 minutes, until golden brown, then turn and cook 4 to 5 minutes on the other side.

Meanwhile, reheat the tomato sauce and pour it into a large, shallow dish. Slide the cooked chilies into the tomato sauce and hold in a warm oven. Repeat the process with the remaining four chilies. Immerse them in the sauce and serve immediately, or keep them warm in the oven while you complete the rest of the meal.

Each serving provides:

165	Calories	17 g	Carbohydrate
10 g	Protein	317 mg	Sodium
8 g	Fat	39 mg	Cholesterol
2 g	Dietary Fiber		

Potatoes

Potatoes were cultivated and eaten, mostly raw, as far back as 3000 B.C. in the Aztec and Incan civilizations. They arrived in Europe from South America in the sixteenth century, where they became an important source of inexpensive nutrition to peasant populations, especially in Ireland. Irish peasants came to depend on this crop exclusively, and the blight in 1846 caused 600,000 deaths and a mass exodus of Irish people to America. Today the potato is the world's most commonly consumed vegetable and continues to be an economical source of good nutrition.

The fruit and foliage of the potato vine—*Solanum tuberosum,* a member of the nightshade family—are not edible; the plant is grown exclusively for its edible tubers. More than 400 varieties are currently known, and you can occasionally find unusual potatoes like Finnish Yellow or Blue Carib in the market, in addition to the more common russet, red, and white types.

The Nutrition Picture

Potatoes are a good source of cholesterol-lowering dietary fiber and are quite high in potassium, which is associated with lowering blood pressure and reducing the risk of strokes. (However, half the potato's potassium is lost if boiled; it leaches into the cooking water.) Potatoes are also high in complex carbohydrates and provide considerable amounts of phosphorus, copper, iron, and B vitamins, as well as protein. The skin of potatoes is particularly nourishing, so learn to enjoy them without peeling.

When prepared properly, potatoes are low in fat and sodium. Their reputation as fattening is unfair; the fat comes from what they are commonly topped with or fried in.

Selection and Storage

Potatoes are grown commercially in forty-eight states, and there is a year-round harvest for American markets. Potatoes keep well and may be stored for up to a year by growers before being shipped to market, so there is no period of inadequate supply for the most popular types. Not as widely available are *new potatoes,* those that are freshly harvested and brought immediately to market. New potatoes are not necessarily tiny ones—they may be as large as a standard russet. They are characterized by very thin, tender skins. Potatoes that have been in cold storage, conversely, have thicker, though still edible, skins. New potatoes are lower in starch so they cook more quickly, are more tender, and have a sweeter flavor than their long-stored counterparts.

Select individual potatoes, if possible, rather than those packaged in plastic bags, so you can inspect them well. Potatoes should be smooth, heavy, firm, and well-shaped, with no discoloration or wounds. Avoid green-hued potatoes—they contain a substance called solanine, which causes gastrointestinal distress in some people and contributes a bitter flavor. Pass over sprouting potatoes; the sprouts are indicative of age and often increased solanine levels.

Store potatoes in a basket or brown paper bag in a cool, dark place, but not in the refrigerator. Avoid storing potatoes in plastic bags, where moisture can collect and accelerate spoilage. Discard any potatoes that are softened or sprouting, since they will contaminate the good ones. Don't store near apples or onions, which emit a gas that will affect the freshness and taste of potatoes. Storage potatoes will stay fresh for up to two months under optimum conditions at home. Use new potatoes within a few days.

Unfortunately, the majority of the potato crop in America is sold in processed form, not fresh. Most forms of frozen or dehydrated potatoes, or potato chips, are high in fat and sodium, and may contain other undesirable additives. So eat potatoes in abundance, if you like them, but always eat them fresh and avoid high-fat and high-sodium cooking methods and condiments. Whatever the preparation, plan on about ½ pound per serving.

Culinary Tips

- Scrub potatoes well, but don't peel them, or important nutrients will be lost.
- Cut potatoes oxidize and darken quickly, so cook them as soon as possible after chopping. If necessary, hold them in a bowl of ice water to which a few drops of lemon juice or vinegar have been added to prevent darkening

until you are ready to begin cooking them. For the same reason, it is best to use noncarbon knives and stainless steel or enameled cast-iron pots.

- The more delicate flavor and texture of new potatoes make them especially suitable for roasting and for potato salad. The starchier storage potatoes have thicker skins and a mealier texture, and are particularly good for baking.

- When baking whole potatoes, pierce the surface in several places with a fork. You may lightly oil the skin of the potatoes before baking for a crisper effect, but there is no reason to wrap them in foil. Excellent healthy condiments for baked potatoes include nonfat yogurt, lowfat cottage cheese, fresh chives or tarragon, and black pepper. It's fine to add salt, but keep the amount to a minimum. Quite tasty, and lower in fat than the traditional butter and sour cream, are a drizzle of olive oil and a sprinkle of freshly grated Parmesan or cheddar cheese.

- As a rule of thumb, one medium potato weighs ¼ pound and one large potato weighs ½ pound.

Parsley Potatoes

ALMOST INSTANT, VEGAN

We have been eating a version of this quickie side dish for years. The parsley adds a bright color note and a fresh flavor.

Yield: 4 side-dish servings

New potatoes	1 **pound (4 medium)**
Olive oil	1 **tablespoon**
Fresh parsley, minced	¼ **cup**
Granulated garlic	⅛ **teaspoon**
Pepper	**A few grinds**
Salt	**A pinch**

Wash the potatoes and cut into 1-inch cubes. Drop into boiling water and cook about 10 minutes, until tender but not mushy. Drain well and toss in a bowl with the olive oil, then with the parsley, garlic, pepper, and salt. Serve hot.

Each serving provides:

123	Calories	21 g	Carbohydrate
2 g	Protein	43 mg	Sodium
4 g	Fat	0 mg	Cholesterol
2 g	Dietary Fiber		

Grilled Red Potatoes

ALMOST INSTANT, VEGAN

Here is a wonderful side dish to accompany a grilled entrée. It is easy and versatile. Though we usually use red potatoes, you may substitute white ones or russets.

Yield: 6 side-dish servings

Red potatoes	2	**pounds (8 medium)**
Olive oil	1	**tablespoon**
Granulated garlic	¼	**teaspoon**

Preheat a coal or gas grill to medium-high. (To preheat a coal grill, start the charcoal at least 15 to 20 minutes before cooking begins, so the proper temperature can be achieved in time. The grill is ready when the coals are glowing red and some gray ash is present on them. Preheat a gas grill for at least 10 minutes, or according to the manufacturer's specific instructions.)

Scrub the potatoes, but do not peel them. Cut into ½-inch slices. Use your hands to rub the oil on the potato slices. Sprinkle with half of the granulated garlic. Place garlic side down on the grill. Cover the grill and cook for 5 minutes, then sprinkle with the remaining garlic, turn, and continue to cook for 5 minutes. Turn and cook about 5 additional minutes on each side, until potatoes are fork tender and golden brown. Serve immediately.

Each serving provides:

143	Calories	27 g	Carbohydrate
3 g	Protein	12 mg	Sodium
3 g	Fat	0 mg	Cholesterol
3 g	Dietary Fiber		

Chive Potato Salad with Cucumbers

Cucumbers and chives are used generously to make this a fresh, crunchy potato salad. The flavors of celery seed and red wine vinegar are carried by the olive oil and potatoes, pleasantly surprising the palate.

Yield: 8 side-dish servings

Red potatoes	2	pounds (8 medium)
Olive oil	2	tablespoons
Red wine vinegar	¼	cup
Celery seed	1	teaspoon
Salt	¾	teaspoon
Pepper		Several grinds
Cucumbers	2	medium
Reduced-calorie mayonnaise	½	cup
Plain nonfat yogurt	½	cup
Fresh chives, minced	¼	cup
Celery	2	ribs, diced

Scrub the potatoes and cut into large bite-size pieces. Place them in a pan, cover with water, and bring to a boil over high heat. Cook until just fork tender, about 12 minutes. Do not overcook, or they will fall apart when tossed. Drain well and transfer to a large bowl.

Meanwhile, whisk together the olive oil and 2 tablespoons of the vinegar. Crush the celery seed with a mortar and pestle and add to the oil and vinegar, along with ¼ teaspoon of the salt and the pepper. Pour this over the hot, drained potatoes and toss well. Set aside at room temperature to cool.

Peel the cucumbers and quarter them lengthwise. Scrape out the seeds and cut the cucumbers crosswise into thick slices. Place in a colander and sprinkle with the remaining ½ teaspoon of salt. Allow to sit for 30 minutes, then rinse well and pat dry.

Meanwhile, mix together the mayonnaise, yogurt, remaining 2 tablespoons of vinegar, and the chives. Toss the celery, cucumber, and green onions with the cooled potatoes, then evenly pour on the mayonnaise dressing and toss again. Serve immediately, or cover and refrigerate until needed.

Each serving provides:

182	Calories	25 g	Carbohydrate
4 g	Protein	317 mg	Sodium
8 g	Fat	5 mg	Cholesterol
3 g	Dietary Fiber		

Cream of Potato Soup with Leeks, Tarragon, and Edam

Serve this rich soup with hot French bread and a mixed green salad for a perfect early spring meal. It is also delightful served cold as a summer luncheon entrée or starter course for 8 people.

Yield: 6 main-dish servings

Leeks	1½	pounds (4 medium)
Olive oil	1	tablespoon
Dry sherry	3	tablespoons
Garlic	2	cloves, minced
Salt	½	teaspoon
Pepper		Several grinds
Ground mace	½	teaspoon
Russet potatoes	2	pounds (4 large)
Unsalted butter	2	tablespoons
Unbleached white flour	2	tablespoons
Lowfat milk	2	cups
Edam cheese, grated	3	ounces (1½ cups)
Fresh tarragon leaves, minced	1	tablespoon

Trim off the root ends of the leeks and all but about 2 inches of the green portion. Slice them in half lengthwise and rinse under cold water to remove any dirt that may be lodged between the layers. Cut crosswise into thin slices.

Heat the oil and sherry in a large skillet over medium heat. Stir in the garlic, salt, pepper, and mace. Sauté for about a minute, then add the leeks. Cover and cook for 10 minutes, stirring occasionally, until they are very limp. If the moisture evaporates completely before they are limp, add 1 tablespoon of water. Remove from the heat and set aside.

Meanwhile, scrub the potatoes and dice them. Place in a stockpot with 4 cups of water and bring to a boil over high heat. Reduce heat to medium and cook, uncovered, for 20 minutes until they are very tender and beginning to fall apart. The liquid will be quite starchy and thick. Stir occasionally during the cooking time.

Place the butter in a small saucepan and melt over low heat. Stir in the flour, cook for a moment, then gradually whisk in the milk. Cook, stirring frequently, for 5 minutes, until sauce begins to thicken. Add the cheese, a handful at a time, stirring to incorporate it. Stir in the tarragon, then pour the sauce into the stockpot with the potatoes. Add the sautéed leeks, heat through for a minute, and serve immediately.

Each serving provides:

315	Calories	42 g	Carbohydrate
10 g	Protein	383 mg	Sodium
11 g	Fat	26 mg	Cholesterol
3 g	Dietary Fiber		

South-of-the-Border Potato Pancakes

VEGAN

Once you discover potato pancakes, you will begin to invent versions to accommodate whatever ingredients you have on hand. Guy Hadler is credited with this combination, and it is one of our favorites. These are wonderful with poached eggs for a delicious brunch, or as a side dish with broiled or grilled fish. Salsa fresca is a nice accompaniment. Any leftovers, tightly wrapped, will keep for a day or two in the refrigerator. Be sure to use a well-seasoned cast-iron pan so you will need minimal oil for frying.

Yield: 8 side-dish servings

Russet potatoes	2	pounds (4 large)
Lowfat milk	¼	cup
Corn kernels, fresh or frozen	1	cup
Red bell pepper, diced	½	cup
Fresh cilantro leaves, minced	¼	cup
Granulated garlic	¼	teaspoon
Ground cumin	¼	teaspoon
Chili powder	¼	teaspoon
Salt	⅛	teaspoon
Pepper		Several grinds
Canola oil	2	teaspoons

Peel and dice the potatoes. Place them in a medium saucepan, cover with water, and bring to a boil. Once boiling, cook for 8 to 10 minutes, until fork tender. Drain the potatoes well, place in a bowl, add the milk, and mash them. Stir in the corn and red bell pepper, along with the seasonings. Form into 2- to 3-inch patties. Place a heavy bottomed skillet over medium-high heat and lightly coat with some of the oil. Fill the pan with patties, cook until golden, then turn and brown the other side. Place on a platter in a warm oven and continue to cook the remaining patties, adding additional oil as necessary. You should use no more than 2 teaspoons total oil. Serve hot.

Each serving provides:

116	Calories	23 g	Carbohydrate
3 g	Protein	50 mg	Sodium
2 g	Fat	1 mg	Cholesterol
2 g	Dietary Fiber		

Garlic Mashed Potatoes

ALMOST INSTANT, VEGAN

This spiked version of basic mashed potatoes is addicting, but so nutritious that you can eat as much as you like.

Yield: 6 side-dish servings

Russet potatoes	2	**pounds (4 large)**
Garlic	6	**cloves, peeled**
Olive oil	1	**tablespoon**
Salt	¼	**teaspoon**
Cayenne	⅛	**teaspoon**

Scrub and dice the potatoes, and put them in a large pot with the peeled whole garlic cloves and enough water to cover them. Bring to a boil over high heat, reduce to medium-high, and cook until very tender, about 15 minutes. Drain, but reserve ¼ cup of the cooking water.

Whip the potatoes with a whisk or whir in a food processor with a tablespoon of the reserved potato water, oil, salt, and cayenne. Continue adding potato water a little at a time until you've achieved your desired consistency. Serve very hot.

Each serving provides:

147	Calories	28 g	Carbohydrate
3 g	Protein	102 mg	Sodium
3 g	Fat	0 mg	Cholesterol
3 g	Dietary Fiber		

The Best 125 Vegetable Dishes

Spinach

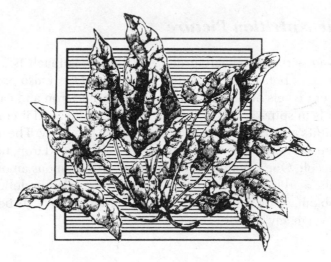

It is believed that spinach was originally cultivated in Persia, some time after the birth of Christ. From there it made its way to China and India. Spinach was introduced into Spain in the twelfth century, and probably came to the Americas with Columbus or with the Pilgrims on the *Mayflower*. However, it was not widely cultivated and enjoyed on the table in America until the nineteenth century.

Botanically, spinach is known as *Spinacia oleracea*. There are three distinct types: Savoy has crinkly leaves; flat-leafed or smooth-leafed varieties are unwrinkled and spade-shaped; semi-savoy types have slightly crinkled leaves. The major suppliers of spinach for domestic markets are California and

Texas, where it is grown as a cool-season crop in regions where winters are mild.

The Nutrition Picture

Along with other leafy green vegetables, spinach is a good source of beta carotene and vitamins A and C. It also provides decent levels of protein and potassium. The iron and calcium levels in spinach are also good, but the oxalic acid it contains inhibits absorption of these minerals by the body. Therefore, there are better vegetable sources for calcium and iron, notably broccoli. One would have to consume an enormous amount of oxalic acid to experience an overall iron or calcium deficiency problem, so there's no need to avoid eating spinach. Its benefits outweigh any concern about oxalic acid.

Selection and Storage

Fresh spinach is readily available year-round. Greens cook down a great deal, so it will take 2 to 3 pounds of fresh spinach to yield 2 cups of cooked. Plan on ½ cup cooked spinach as an average serving size.

Fresh spinach should look moist and succulent and should smell fresh, not sour. Don't buy wilted, yellowed, or dehydrated spinach. Select spinach with thin stems and small leaves for the best flavor.

Spinach should not be washed before storing. Simply remove any bruised or mushy leaves from the bunch, wrap loosely in a plastic bag, and store in the refrigerator crisper for up to 3 or 4 days.

Though its flavor and texture are not optimum, frozen spinach has its uses. However, all of our recipes have been tested using fresh spinach. Avoid using the canned variety—its taste and texture bear little resemblance to those of fresh-cooked spinach, and undesirable additives may be present.

Culinary Tips

- Spinach's gritty reputation suggests the importance of careful cleaning. Discard the stems and immerse the leaves in a large basin of cold water. Gently but thoroughly agitate the leaves, then allow to sit in the basin for several minutes while the dirt sinks to the bottom. Carefully lift out the spinach and place it in a colander. Rinse well. Repeat the process if you are washing a large quantity of spinach or if the spinach seems particularly dirty.
- Spinach is delicious raw. We frequently add it to salads and sandwiches. For raw uses, carefully wash the leaves and dry them in a spinner or with a tea towel. Tear larger leaves into bite-size pieces for salads. Leaves can be left whole for sandwiches.
- If steaming spinach, don't dry the leaves after washing. Place the wet leaves in a nonaluminum pot and cover. Cook over medium heat until the spinach has wilted, usually no longer than 5 minutes.
- Spinach becomes an unappetizing mush when overcooked, so add it to soups, stews, and other hot dishes toward the end of the cooking time.
- Generally speaking, other leafy greens such as Swiss chard and mustard are suitable for the same types of preparation as spinach and can be substituted with good results in our recipes. Keep in mind, however, that Swiss chard is slightly bitter and mustard greens have a spicy bite, so the flavor of the finished dish will be quite different from that achieved with spinach.

Grilled Spinach Rolls Stuffed with Tofu, Feta, and Fresh Nutmeg

Shop for large leaves of spinach for this recipe, or use early spring Swiss chard. Prepare the rolls as an appetizer for a grill party, or serve them as a side dish. The preparation is simple and may be done in advance and the presentation is delightful.

Yield: 6 side-dish servings

Spinach or chard	12	**large leaves (about ¼ pound)**
Firm-style silken tofu	5	**ounces**
Feta cheese, crumbled	3	**ounces (¾ cup)**
Granulated garlic	¼	**teaspoon**
Pepper		**Several grinds**
Freshly grated nutmeg	⅛	**teaspoon**
Fresh chives	12	**long ones**
Olive oil	¼	**teaspoon**
Lemon wedges	1	**per serving**

Preheat a coal or gas grill to medium-high. (To preheat a coal grill, start the charcoal at least 15 to 20 minutes before cooking begins, so the proper temperature can be achieved in time. The grill is ready when the coals are glowing red and some gray ash is present on them. Preheat a gas grill for at least 10 minutes, or according to the manufacturer's specific instructions.) If you will not be cooking the rolls on a grill, preheat the oven to 375 degrees F.

Wash the spinach leaves and remove the thick stems. Pat dry. If using chard, wash the leaves and cut away the stems. In either case, take care not to tear the leaves. Pat them dry with a tea towel.

Rinse the tofu and pat dry. Cut into cubes and place in a food processor with the feta, garlic, pepper, and nutmeg. Puree until well combined but still lumpy. Spoon $\frac{1}{12}$ of the filling in the center of a spinach or chard leaf, tuck in the sides, and roll up. Tie one of the chives around the bundle to secure it. Repeat this process to make the rest of the rolls.

Coat your hands with the olive oil and gently rub each roll. Wrap the rolls in foil in a single layer. Place the foil packet on the grill or in the oven and cook for 10 minutes. Remove from the foil and serve immediately with the lemon wedges.

Each serving provides:

82	Calories	4 g	Carbohydrate
7 g	Protein	177 mg	Sodium
5 g	Fat	13 mg	Cholesterol
1 g	Dietary Fiber		

Spinach with Ginger
and Shiitake Mushrooms

VEGAN

This classic Chinese spinach preparation is simple and quick to prepare. It would be the perfect accompaniment to any Asian entrée, with rice on the side.

Yield: 4 side-dish servings

Dried shiitake mushrooms	1	ounce
Spinach	1½	pounds (about 2 bunches)
Peanut oil	2	teaspoons
Yellow onion	½	medium, chopped
Fresh ginger, grated	1	tablespoon
Low-sodium soy sauce	2	teaspoons
Arrowroot powder or cornstarch	2	teaspoons

Soak the mushrooms in 2 cups of hot water for 30 minutes. Rinse the mushrooms under a thin stream of cold, running water, rubbing to remove any grit lodged in the membranes under the caps. Squeeze the mushrooms gently to remove some of their liquid. Discard the mushroom stems and sliver the caps. Set aside. Strain the soaking liquid through a paper coffee filter. You will need ⅓ cup for this recipe. Save the rest in the refrigerator for soup stock or another use.

Carefully wash the spinach (see page 279), discarding the stems. Set the wet leaves aside.

In a heavy-bottomed skillet or wok that has a tight-fitting lid, heat the oil for a minute or so over medium-high heat, then add the onion and ginger and stir to combine. Sauté for about 3 minutes, stirring almost constantly, until the onion begins to wilt. Pile in the spinach leaves and immediately cover the pan. Reduce heat to medium and cook 4 minutes. Meanwhile, combine the soy sauce and arrowroot with ⅓ cup of the mushroom soaking liquid until the arrowroot has dissolved. When spinach cooking time is up, turn off the heat, remove the lid, and immediately stir the arrowroot mixture into the hot pan, stirring around to combine with the spinach; a thick sauce will develop. Transfer the spinach to a warmed bowl and serve very hot.

Each serving provides:

83	Calories	13 g	Carbohydrate
5 g	Protein	199 mg	Sodium
3 g	Fat	0 mg	Cholesterol
4 g	Dietary Fiber		

Spinach with Radicchio and Warm Dried-Tomato Vinaigrette

VEGAN

The radicchio makes a beautiful pink bed for the spinach in this unusual Mediterranean-inspired side dish. Once you have washed the spinach, it comes together in just a few moments.

Yield: 4 side-dish servings

Dried tomato, minced	¼	cup
Spinach	2	pounds (about 2½ bunches)
White wine	3	tablespoons
Balsamic vinegar	2	tablespoons
Olive oil	1	tablespoon
Garlic	1	clove, minced
Salt		A pinch
Pepper		A few grinds
Arrowroot powder or cornstarch	1	teaspoon
Radicchio, finely shredded	1	cup

Reconstitute the dried tomatoes if they are too dry to mince by soaking them in hot water for 15 to 30 minutes. Drain them well and mince them. Carefully wash the spinach (see page 279), discarding the stems. Place the wet leaves in a large pot and cover tightly. Turn the heat on to medium-high and cook the spinach until it has wilted, about 5 minutes. Transfer to a colander to drain.

Meanwhile, in a very small saucepan, combine the wine, vinegar, olive oil, garlic, salt, and pepper. Bring to a simmer and remove from the heat. Immediately whisk in the arrowroot powder until thickened, then stir in the dried tomato and set aside in a warm spot on the stove.

Make a ring of the radicchio on a serving plate. Mound the spinach in the center and drizzle everything with the warm vinaigrette. Serve hot or at room temperature.

Each serving provides:

96	Calories	11 g	Carbohydrate
6 g	Protein	171 mg	Sodium
4 g	Fat	0 mg	Cholesterol
5 g	Dietary Fiber		

Spinach Soup with Oregano and Calamata Olives

VEGAN

The influences for this soup are decidedly Greek, yet the flavor and lightness are spa cuisine. The preparation is simple; washing the spinach is the most time-consuming part. Serve this soup as a delightful, early spring starter course, or as a light summer meal along with good bread and a salad.

Yield: 4 first-course servings

Spinach	1½ pounds (about 2 bunches)
Olive oil	2 tablespoons
Yellow onion, diced	½ cup
Garlic	3 cloves, minced
Dried oregano	1 teaspoon
Salt	¼ teaspoon
Pepper	Several grinds
Fresh-squeezed lemon juice	¼ cup
Calamata olives, pitted and diced	¼ cup
Fresh oregano leaves	1 tablespoon

Carefully wash the spinach (see page 279) and discard the stems. Stack several leaves on top of each other and cut them into ½-inch strips. Repeat until all the spinach is sliced. Set aside.

Place the olive oil in a stockpot over medium heat. Add the onion, garlic, and dried oregano. Sauté for about 2 minutes, then add 4 cups of hot water. Bring to a boil over high heat and add the spinach. Return to a boil, reduce the heat to medium, cover, and cook about 5 minutes, until the spinach wilts. Stir in the salt, pepper, lemon juice, olives, and fresh oregano and simmer about 3 minutes longer. Serve immediately.

Each serving provides:

113	Calories	9 g	Carbohydrate
4 g	Protein	307 mg	Sodium
8 g	Fat	0 mg	Cholesterol
4 g	Dietary Fiber		

Spinach, Kiwi, and Grapefruit Salad with Cilantro Sherry Vinaigrette

VEGAN

This composed salad is light, refreshing, and stunning on the plate. If you have calendulas in your garden, pick one and scatter the edible petals over each salad. Kiwis are often hard when purchased, and are not ripe and ready to eat until they soften up enough to yield to light pressure. Purchase them a few days ahead of time, if necessary, and allow them to ripen in a basket in your kitchen.

Yield: 4 side-dish servings

Pink grapefruit	1	**medium**
Kiwis	2	**medium**
Fresh-squeezed orange juice	2	**tablespoons**
Olive oil	1	**tablespoon**
Sherry vinegar	2	**teaspoons**
Dijon mustard	¼	**teaspoon**
Salt		**A pinch**
Red onion, grated	2	**teaspoons**
Fresh cilantro leaves, minced	1	**heaping teaspoon**
Spinach	6	**ounces (about ½ bunch)**

Chill the grapefruit and kiwi for several hours before preparing the salad. In a small bowl, whisk together the orange juice, olive oil, vinegar, mustard, and salt until well combined and creamy. Stir in the red onion and cilantro and set aside at room temperature.

Carefully wash the spinach (see page 279), discarding the stems. Dry thoroughly and set aside in the refrigerator. Peel the grapefruit and divide it into individual sections. Remove and discard the membrane from each section, discard any seeds, and break the fruit into bite-size pieces. Set aside in the refrigerator. Peel the kiwis and cut crosswise into thin slices.

Arrange a bed of spinach on each of 4 chilled salad plates. Artfully arrange portions of grapefruit and kiwi on top of the spinach. Drizzle each salad with dressing and garnish with calendula petals, if available.

Each serving provides:

83	Calories	12 g	Carbohydrate
2 g	Protein	69 mg	Sodium
4 g	Fat	0 mg	Cholesterol
2 g	Dietary Fiber		

Curried Spinach with Tomatoes and Pureed Chickpeas

VEGAN

In this colorful dish, the spinach is very briefly cooked and retains its fresh, bright flavor. Serve it with steamed rice and a tart, leafy salad for a very hearty and satisfying meal.

Yield: 6 main-dish servings

Salt	½	teaspoon
Green onions	4,	minced
Pepper		Several grinds
Brown basmati rice, uncooked	1½	cups
Low-sodium whole tomatoes	1	28-ounce can
Cooked garbanzo beans (chickpeas)	2	cups
Garlic	6	cloves, minced
Cumin seed	1	teaspoon, crushed
Ground turmeric	1	teaspoon
Ground ginger	½	teaspoon
Fennel seed	¼	teaspoon, crushed
Cayenne	¼	teaspoon
Spinach	2	pounds (about 2½ bunches)
Fresh-squeezed lemon juice	1	tablespoon
Fresh cilantro, minced	¼	cup

Combine 3 cups of water with ¼ teaspoon salt, 2 of the green onions, and the pepper in a medium saucepan over high heat and bring to a boil. Add the rice, bring back to a boil, reduce heat to low, cover, and cook 25 minutes.

Meanwhile, combine the tomatoes with the garbanzo beans, garlic, cumin, turmeric, ginger, fennel, cayenne, and remaining ¼ teaspoon salt in a large skillet or saucepan over medium-high heat. When it comes to a simmer, reduce heat to medium-low and cook, stirring frequently, 10 minutes. Transfer half the mixture in small batches to a food processor or blender and puree briefly to a chunky sauce consistency. Return the puree to the pan.

Meanwhile, carefully wash the spinach (see page 279), discarding the stems. Place the wet spinach in a large stockpot over medium-high heat, cover, and steam 5 minutes. Transfer it to a colander and rinse with cold water. When the spinach is cool enough to handle, squeeze it gently to remove most of the juice (this can be saved for another use, if you wish, such as soup stock). Chop the spinach coarsely. Stir the spinach, lemon juice, and cilantro into the bean mixture and cook over low heat for 2 minutes, to just heat through. Place portions of rice on warmed serving plates, top with the spinach mixture, and top evenly with the remaining green onions.

Each serving provides:

323	Calories	63 g	Carbohydrate
13 g	Protein	296 mg	Sodium
4 g	Fat	0 mg	Cholesterol
8 g	Dietary Fiber		

Risotto of Spinach, Strawberries, Ricotta, and Poppy Seeds

An unusual combination of flavors, this risotto is well-balanced, not overly sweet. It is quite beautiful and delicious, and makes the most of spring's abundance of spinach and strawberries. This is a fine way to use berries that are slightly overripe.

Yield: 6 main-dish servings

Spinach	1½	pounds (about 2 bunches)
Fresh strawberries, very ripe	½	pound
Fresh-squeezed orange juice	3	tablespoons plus ⅓ cup
Poppy seeds	2	teaspoons
Homemade Vegetable Stock*	5	cups
Olive oil	1	tablespoon
Arborio rice, uncooked	1½	cups
Freshly grated nutmeg	1½	teaspoons
Dry white wine	½	cup
Salt	⅛	teaspoon
Part-skim ricotta cheese	½	cup
Fresh tarragon leaves, minced	2	teaspoons

Carefully wash the spinach (see page 279) and discard the stems. Place the wet leaves in a large pot and cover tightly. Turn the heat on to medium-high and cook the spinach until it has wilted, about 5 minutes. Transfer to a colander to cool. When cool enough to handle, squeeze gently to remove as much

*If you do not have Homemade Vegetable Stock on hand, make up a batch according to the directions on page 12, or dissolve ½ of a large, low-sodium vegetable broth cube in 5 cups of hot water.

water as possible and chop coarsely. Set aside. Remove the stems from the strawberries and dice them. Toss the berries with 3 tablespoons of the orange juice and the poppy seeds and set aside at room temperature.

Combine the stock with the remaining ⅓ cup orange juice, heat the mixture in a small saucepan for a few minutes, and keep this broth handy near the stove. In a large, heavy-bottomed saucepan, heat the olive oil over medium heat. Add the rice and nutmeg and stir for a moment or two. Add the wine and stir gently until it is absorbed. Add the broth ½ cup at a time, stirring almost constantly and waiting until the liquid is absorbed before each addition. When the last addition of broth has been absorbed and the rice is tender, stir in the salt, spinach, strawberry mixture, ricotta, and tarragon until well combined. Heat through for 1 minute. Serve immediately in warmed, shallow bowls.

Each serving provides:

292	Calories	49 g	Carbohydrate
9 g	Protein	156 mg	Sodium
5 g	Fat	6 mg	Cholesterol
3 g	Dietary Fiber		

Summer Squash

All squashes, winter and summer varieties alike, are Native American foods. The North American Indians introduced squash to the Pilgrims, who considered it uncivilized due to the unwieldy size of the plant, but still depended on it because of its prolific production. Botanical remnants excavated in Mexico date the squash to about 3000 B.C.

The botanical species called *Cucurbita pepo* includes all of what we think of as summer squash, in addition to the pumpkin. However, we have discussed the pumpkin in the winter squash chapter of this book because it more closely resembles the acorn, butternut, or hubbard squash than the zucchini or crookneck. Summer squashes are related to melons and cucumbers.

Summer squash is harvested at a tender age, when skin and seeds are less developed and are still edible. When left on the plant too long, they become overly large, stringy, and unappetizing.

Experienced home gardeners know better than to sow many summer squash plants, as they are abundant producers and take up a great deal of space. It is a good idea to check the plants daily, since squashes grow quickly. Pick elongated varieties like zucchini or crookneck when they are no more than seven or eight inches long. Patty pans, with their graceful scalloped edges, should be no more than about four inches across. Blossoms at the end of the squashes are delicious and nutritious when fresh; try eating them raw in salads or adding them to sautés or stews at the end of the cooking time.

The Nutrition Picture

Summer squashes are high-water-content foods, low in calories, fat, and sodium. They provide moderate amounts of vitamin C, potassium, and beta carotene.

Selection and Storage

Summer squash got its name because it flourishes in hot, dry weather. Today, however, it is available in most markets year-round, with a peak season of May through August. A pound will serve about four people as a side dish. If you are stuffing and baking squash, select ones of uniform size and plan on one per person.

Summer squashes should be glossy, plump, crisp, and firm, not bruised or rubbery. For the best flavor and most satisfying texture, select small squashes. They should, however, be heavy for their size, which indicates a juicy interior.

Stored unwashed in a loosely closed plastic bag in the refrigerator crisper, summer squashes will keep for up to a week. Since the fresh ones are available nearly year-round and nationwide, there is no need to resort to frozen or canned varieties.

Culinary Tips

- Since they are are so similar in flavor and texture, summer squashes can be used interchangeably in most recipes.
- Don't overcook summer squashes, especially tiny ones.
- Rinse and dry squashes before using, but don't peel them—much of their nutrition is in the skin.
- Because of their high water content, summer squashes give off a lot of liquid when cooked. If you're using them in a casserole, you may want to salt them to leach out some of their juice before proceeding. Simply sprinkle grated, sliced, or diced squash evenly with salt and set aside in a stainless steel colander for 30 minutes. Use about ½ teaspoon of salt per pound of squash. Rinse off the salt, squeeze gently, and pat dry before proceeding with the recipe. Salting, however, is not necessary for most summer squash recipes.

Zucchini with Garlic and Chili Flakes

ALMOST INSTANT, VEGAN

This versatile vegetable lends itself to many different preparations. This one is a wonderfully crisp side dish for any Italian entrée. The recipe may easily be cut in half, if you wish; however, leftovers are good cold the next day.

Yield: 8 side-dish servings

Zucchini	3	**pounds (9 medium)**
Olive oil	2	**tablespoons**
Garlic	4	**cloves, minced**
Dried red chili flakes		**Scant ⅛ teaspoon**
Salt	⅛	**teaspoon**
Pepper		**Several grinds**

Wash the zucchini, trim off the stem ends, and cut into ½-inch slices. Place on a steamer rack in a large saucepan that has a tight-fitting lid. Add about an inch of water, cover, and cook over high heat for 8 minutes, until almost fork tender.

Heat the olive oil in a skillet over medium heat and sauté the garlic, chili flakes, salt, and pepper for about 1 minute. Drain the zucchini and add to the skillet. Cover, reduce heat to low and cook about 5 to 6 minutes, tossing frequently to coat all sides with the oil and seasonings. Serve immediately.

Each serving provides:

55	Calories	5 g	Carbohydrate
2 g	Protein	40 mg	Sodium
4 g	Fat	0 mg	Cholesterol
1 g	Dietary Fiber		

Skewers of Summer Squash in Pineapple Ginger Marinade

VEGAN

This is a simple yet fanciful presentation of zucchini. Serve it along-side any grilled entrée. Select squashes that are no larger than about 7 inches in length and 1½ inches in diameter.

Yield: 6 side-dish servings

The marinade

Unsweetened pineapple juice	½	cup
Low-sodium soy sauce	2	tablespoons
Fresh-squeezed lemon juice	2	tablespoons
White wine vinegar	1	tablespoon
Honey	1	tablespoon
Canola oil	1	tablespoon
Fresh ginger, grated	1	tablespoon
Garlic	2	cloves, minced

The skewers

Zucchini	¾	pound (3 small)
Yellow crookneck squash	1	pound (3 medium)
Mushrooms	½	pound
Olive oil	1	teaspoon

Combine the marinade ingredients in a glass bowl and whisk together. Trim the ends off the zucchini and cut crosswise into about ½-inch slices. Trim the ends and the narrow necks from the crookneck squash, saving them for soup stock. Cut the squash crosswise into ½-inch slices. Place the squashes in the marinade, toss to coat, and set aside at room temperature for 1 hour.

If the mushrooms are small, remove the stems and leave the caps whole. If using larger ones, remove the stems and cut the caps in half. Add the mushrooms to the marinade, toss gently to coat, and allow to sit 30 more minutes.

Meanwhile, soak 6 wooden skewers in water for about 30 minutes. Preheat a coal or gas grill to medium-high. (To preheat a coal grill, start the charcoal at least 15 to 20 minutes before cooking begins, so the proper temperature can be achieved in time. The grill is ready when the coals are glowing red and some gray ash is present on them. Preheat a gas grill for at least 10 minutes, or according to the manufacturer's specific instructions.)

Distribute the vegetables equally among the skewers and lightly brush with the olive oil. Reserve the marinade for a dipping sauce. Place the skewers on the grill, cover the grill, and cook for 20 minutes, turning every 5 minutes, until they are fork tender. Place the reserved marinade in small bowls. Remove the skewers from the grill and serve immediately along with the dipping sauce.

Each serving provides:

87	Calories	14 g	Carbohydrate
3 g	Protein	205 mg	Sodium
4 g	Fat	0 mg	Cholesterol
2 g	Dietary Fiber		

Summer Squashes en Papillote with Tex-Mex Seasonings

ALMOST INSTANT, VEGAN

You may use any type of summer squash for this dish, but it's an especially nice way to prepare patty pans. If you can locate squashes no bigger than a bite or two in size, cook them whole for a stunning feast of sweetness.

Yield: 4 side-dish servings

Cumin seed	1	**teaspoon**
Chili powder	1	**teaspoon**
Granulated garlic	½	**teaspoon**
Salt	⅛	**teaspoon**
Pepper		**Several grinds**
Summer squashes	1	**pound (3 medium)**
Red bell pepper	½	**medium, slivered**
Red onion	1	**small, diced**
Fresh cilantro, minced	2	**tablespoons**
Husked raw pumpkin seeds	2	**tablespoons**
Parchment paper	4	**12 × 18-inch pieces**

Preheat the oven to 400 degrees F. Use a mortar and pestle or spice grinder to crush the cumin seed. In a small bowl, stir together the chili powder, cumin seed, garlic, salt, and pepper. Set aside. Trim the stems off the squashes and cut into bite-size pieces (if using baby squashes, leave them whole).

Fold each piece of parchment in half and crease to create 9 × 12-inch rectangles. Use scissors to cut each rectangle into a half-heart shape. Open out the hearts and distribute the squash pieces evenly among the 4 papers, positioning them near the center of each crease. Sprinkle equal portions of the spice mixture evenly over the squash. Lay a quarter of the red bell pepper strips and onion pieces over each portion and sprinkle equal portions of cilantro over each. Close the heart so that the edges of the paper meet. Beginning at the round end, fold over about ½ inch of the paper and crease sharply. Work your way around the shape of the heart, folding in the edges and creasing sharply in overlapping pleats. Twist the pointy end to seal everything tightly in the paper packet. Repeat this process with the remaining packets. Place the packets in a single layer on a baking sheet and bake for 12 minutes.

Meanwhile, place the pumpkin seeds in a single layer in a heavy, dry skillet over medium heat. Shake or stir the seeds frequently. When seeds begin to pop, stay close to the pan and keep the seeds moving almost constantly. You want them all to pop, if possible, but do not let them get too brown. Remove from the pan, cool a bit, mince, and set aside.

Transfer the packets to warmed serving plates and instruct your guests to pinch and tear the paper to release the aromatic steam. The contents may then be lifted out onto the plate and the paper removed from the table and discarded. Serve very hot, passing the pumpkin seeds to sprinkle on top.

Each serving provides:

51	Calories	10 g	Carbohydrate
2 g	Protein	82 mg	Sodium
1 g	Fat	0 mg	Cholesterol
2 g	Dietary Fiber		

Zucchini Apple Slaw

VEGAN

This unlikely combination yields a fresh and clean flavor. The apples lend nice tartness and the celery a delightful crunch. The lemon juice prevents the apples from oxidizing and turning brown. We use Granny Smith apples; if these are not available, seek out another crisp variety.

Yield: 8 side-dish servings

Zucchini	1	**pound (3 medium)**
Salt	1	**tablespoon**
Celery seed	¼	**teaspoon**
Apple cider vinegar	2	**tablespoons**
Light sesame oil	3	**tablespoons**
Pepper		**Several grinds**
Green apples	1	**pound (2 medium)**
Fresh-squeezed lemon juice	2	**tablespoons**
Celery	2	**ribs, thinly sliced**

Wash the zucchini and remove the stem ends. Coarsely grate them and place in a colander. Sprinkle with the salt and allow to sit for 30 minutes. Rinse well, then squeeze gently in a tea towel to remove as much liquid as possible. Place in a medium bowl.

Meanwhile, crush the celery seed with a mortar and pestle. Whisk together the vinegar, oil, pepper, and celery seed.

Peel the apples and coarsely grate them, discarding the cores. Place in a separate small bowl and sprinkle with the lemon juice, then add to the zucchini, along with the celery. Pour the dressing over the salad, cover, and chill for 30 minutes or longer before serving.

Each serving provides:

83	Calories	10 g	Carbohydrate
1 g	Protein	148 mg	Sodium
5 g	Fat	0 mg	Cholesterol
1 g	Dietary Fiber		

Summer Squash and Apricot Soup with Fresh Basil and Pine Nuts

VEGAN

This dish is the perfect combination of flavors that sing of summer. If you are using squash picked from your garden, all the better. This soup is good hot or chilled. You may make it using only zucchini if you wish, but we prefer the golden yellow of crookneck with the basil, so use a combination, if possible.

Yield: 4 first-course servings

Pine nuts	2	tablespoons
Dried apricots, chopped	½	cup
Yellow onion	1	medium, diced
Bell pepper (any color)	½	medium, diced
Salt	¼	teaspoon
Summer squash	1½	pounds (3 large)
Paprika	½	teaspoon
Fresh basil leaves, whole	1	cup
Pepper		A few grinds

Place the pine nuts in a single layer in a dry, heavy-bottomed skillet and heat over medium-high heat. Shake the pan or stir frequently until they are slightly browned and emit a roasted aroma. Remove pine nuts from the pan, cool a bit, mince, and set aside. Trim off the ends of the squashes, dice them, and set aside.

Combine the apricots, onion, bell pepper, and ⅛ teaspoon of the salt with 5 cups of water in a stockpot over high heat and bring to a boil. Reduce heat to medium and simmer 10 minutes. Add the squash, paprika, and the remaining ⅛ teaspoon salt. Bring to a simmer over medium-high heat, reduce heat to medium, and simmer 20 minutes. Transfer the soup in small batches to a blender or food processor and puree.

Return the soup to the stockpot over medium heat and stir in the basil, reserving 4 nice leaves for garnish. When the basil has wilted, stir in the pepper. Serve immediately in warmed bowls, or chill for an hour or so before serving in chilled bowls. In either case, divide the pine nuts evenly among the bowls, sprinkling on top of the soup. Garnish each bowl with a reserved basil leaf before serving.

Each serving provides:

127	Calories	25 g	Carbohydrate
5 g	Protein	143 mg	Sodium
3 g	Fat	0 mg	Cholesterol
4 g	Dietary Fiber		

Zucchini, Tofu, and Butter Lettuce Stir-Fry with Fermented Black Beans

ALMOST INSTANT, VEGAN

Seasoned with the rice wine vinegar, mirin, and smoky sesame oil, delicate zucchini matchsticks are delicious. The secondary flavor of the fermented black beans and the crunch of the butter lettuce are nice surprises, so be careful not to overcook the lettuce. Look for dried Asian noodles that do not contain eggs, to avoid the added fat and cholesterol.

Yield: 6 main-dish servings

Zucchini	2	pounds (6 medium)
Firm-style tofu	1	pound
Dark sesame oil	2	tablespoons
Mirin	3	tablespoons
Rice wine vinegar	2	tablespoons
Reduced-sodium soy sauce	1	tablespoon
Garlic	3	cloves, minced
Fresh ginger, grated	2	tablespoons
Fermented black beans, chopped	½	cup
Dried asian-style noodles	16	ounces
Butter lettuce	1	head
Arrowroot powder or cornstarch	2	tablespoons
Fresh cilantro, minced	½	cup

In a stockpot, bring several quarts of water to a boil for the noodles. Trim the ends from the zucchini and cut into 3-inch matchsticks. Set aside. Pat the tofu dry and cut into cubes. Heat the oil, mirin, vinegar, and soy sauce in a wok or large skillet over medium-high heat and add the garlic and ginger. Cook for a minute or two, then add the zucchini, tofu, and black beans, along with ½ cup water. Cover and cook over medium heat for about 10 to 12 minutes, tossing frequently, until zucchini is fork tender.

Meanwhile, cook the noodles in the boiling water until tender and drain well. Roll up the lettuce leaves, beginning with the stem end and cut into ¼-inch strips. Set aside until needed. Place 3 tablespoons of water in a jar with a tight-fitting lid. Add the arrowroot powder and shake to dissolve.

When zucchini is tender, pour the arrowroot mixture into the wok, increase the heat to high, and cook about a half minute, stirring constantly, until thickened. Turn off the heat, add the lettuce and cilantro, and toss in the hot wok until just combined. Serve immediately over the hot noodles.

Each serving provides:

483	Calories	72 g	Carbohydrate
27 g	Protein	1,298 mg	Sodium
13 g	Fat	0 mg	Cholesterol
1 g	Dietary Fiber		

Zucchini Stuffed with Greek Olives, Feta, and Tomatoes

Choose zucchini that weigh about ½ pound each for this Mediterranean feast. The colors are lovely and the flavors combine to create a truly delicious dish. It makes four ample main-dish servings with the addition of salad and bread; alternately, you may serve it as a side dish for eight.

Yield: 4 main-dish servings

Dried tomatoes, minced	2	tablespoons
Olive oil	1	tablespoon
Yellow onion, minced	2	tablespoons
Garlic	2	cloves, minced
Long-grain brown rice, uncooked	½	cup
Dried oregano	1	teaspoon
Salt	⅛	teaspoon
Pepper		Several grinds
Zucchini	2	pounds (4 large)
Plain nonfat yogurt	2	tablespoons
Lowfat sour cream	2	tablespoons
Feta cheese, crumbled	2	ounces (½ cup)
Calamata olives, pitted and minced	¼	cup

If the dried tomatoes are too dry to mince, reconstitute them by soaking for 15 to 30 minutes in hot water. Drain them well and mince them. Set aside.

Heat the olive oil in a saucepan over medium heat and add the onion and garlic. Sauté about a minute, then stir in the rice, tomatoes, and oregano. Add 1⅛ cups water, increase the heat to high, and bring to a boil. Season with the salt and pepper. Cover, reduce heat to low, and cook for 35 minutes.

Meanwhile, preheat the oven to 350 degrees F. Cut the zucchinis in half lengthwise. Using a melon baller or spoon, scrape out the zucchini flesh, leaving a ¼-inch shell. Discard the zucchini flesh or save for another use, such as soup stock. Arrange the zucchini halves, cut side up, in a single layer in a glass baking dish, and add hot water to measure ½ inch up the side of the dish.

Stir the yogurt and sour cream into the rice. Combine the cheese and olives in a small bowl. Fill each zucchini half with the rice mixture, then top with equal portions of the cheese-olive mixture. Cover and bake for 30 minutes. Serve immediately.

Each serving provides:

197	Calories	25 g	Carbohydrate
6 g	Protein	320 mg	Sodium
9 g	Fat	15 mg	Cholesterol
2 g	Dietary Fiber		

Sweet Potatoes

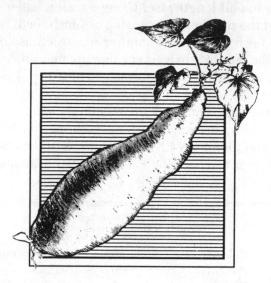

It is generally agreed that the sweet potato is a tropical American plant that was eventually carried to Europe by Columbus. Sweet potatoes were widely cultivated in colonial America, and were a chief source of nutrition to homesteaders and soldiers in the Revolutionary War.

Sweet potatoes contain an enzyme that converts their starch to sugar, hence the name. Red-skinned sweet potatoes are commonly referred to as yams in America, so named by African slaves for their resemblance to the immense tubers they had loved in their homeland. These were called by the African word "to eat"—*nyami* in certain dialects. True yams don't grow in the continental United States. They require an exceptionally long growing period and thrive in the extreme heat found in central Africa. Common usage, however, has made the terms *sweet potato* and *yam* interchangeable to Americans.

The sweet potato—*Ipomoea batatas*—is not related to regular potatoes, but is rather a member of the morning glory family. It is grown not from seeds, but from sprouts saved from the prior year's crops. Sweet potatoes grow best in warm, dry climates. The primary producers in the United States are California, Louisiana, and New Jersey.

The Nutrition Picture

The sweet potato is generally agreed to be among the most nutritious of vegetables. Its cancer-fighting potential, associated with extraordinarily high vitamin A content, is becoming well-accepted. It is also a good source of potassium, calcium, and vitamin C.

As vegetables go, sweet potatoes are not particularly low in calories, but they contain no more than a common russet potato of comparable size. They are low in fat when not smothered in butter or candied.

Storage and Selection

There are two varieties of sweet potato: the dry, tan-skinned, yellow-fleshed variety; and the more moist, red-skinned, orange-fleshed one, typically called a yam. The orange-fleshed kind tends to be sweeter, so a yam is a sweeter sweet potato. Both varieties are common in markets year-round, though they peak in the fall. Purchase one small sweet potato per person for use as a side dish.

Look for sweet potatoes that are heavy for their size, hard, and smooth-skinned. Those with bruised, mushy, or dark spots and ones that are sprouting should be avoided. Medium-size specimens that taper at the ends are usually superior in flavor and texture. Buy similar-size potatoes if you plan to cook them whole.

Store sweet potatoes in a cool, dry place, but never in the refrigerator, where they may develop a hard core and an unpleasant taste. Brush off excess dirt before storing, but don't wash them until just before cooking. Sweet potatoes will stay fresh for months if stored at around 55 degrees, but use them within a week if stored at room temperature. Handle sweet potatoes gently, since their skin is delicate and thin, and is easily damaged.

If you discover that sweet potatoes stored at home have sprouted or developed rotten spots, discard the whole thing; don't just trim off the bad parts. The entire potato may have developed a bitter taste.

Since fresh sweet potatoes are available year-round, there is no need to use the less-nutritious canned or frozen ones.

Culinary Tips

- Red-skinned and tan-skinned sweet potatoes are interchangeable in recipes, but don't combine them in a single recipe because the red ones take a bit longer to cook. Adjust cooking time accordingly, if necessary. We generally prefer the sweeter taste, deeper color, and moister flesh of the red-skinned variety.
- Scrub sweet potatoes before cooking, but do not peel. It is best to cook them in their skins so nutrients are retained, then eat the skins for greatest benefit, or peel after cooking.
- Pierce whole sweet potatoes with a fork and place them on a pan before baking to catch the juices.
- One medium sweet potato weighs ½ pound.

Fettuccine with Sweet Potatoes, Roasted Red Peppers, and Vermouth

When cooked on a grill, the sweet potatoes take on a pleasing smoky flavor. They puree smoothly into the sauce, which is topped with the bright red sweet peppers. This dish is a delicious way to increase the beta carotene in our diets.

Yield: 6 main-dish servings

Red-skinned sweet potatoes	1½	pounds (3 medium)
Red bell pepper	2	medium
Lowfat milk	2	cups
Unsalted butter	2	tablespoons
Unbleached flour	1½	tablespoons
Salt	¼	teaspoon
Pepper		Several grinds
Freshly grated nutmeg	⅛	teaspoon
Ground mace	⅛	teaspoon
Dried fettuccine	1	pound
Dry vermouth	¼	cup

Preheat a coal or gas grill to medium-high. (To preheat a coal grill, start the charcoal at least 15 to 20 minutes before cooking begins, so the proper temperature can be achieved in time. The grill is ready when the coals are glowing red and a small amount of gray ash is present on them. Preheat a gas grill for at least 10 minutes, or according to the manufacturer's specific instructions.)

Wash the sweet potatoes and pierce them in several places with a fork. Place the whole sweet potatoes on the grill, cover the grill, and cook about 45 minutes, until they are soft, turning occasionally. Remove from the grill, allow to cool slightly, then peel off the skin and chop the pulp. Simultaneously place the peppers on the grill. Turn them every 10 minutes to blacken and blister the skin, cooking for about 30 minutes total. Place the peppers in a paper bag, fold the bag closed, and allow them to cool. Peel off the blackened skin and remove the seeds. Slice into ½ inch strips and set aside. Place the sweet potato in a food processor with ½ cup of the milk and ¼ cup water. Puree until smooth and set aside. Meanwhile, put several quarts of water on to boil for the pasta in a stockpot over high heat.

Melt the butter in a large skillet over medium-high heat and stir in the flour. Allow it to cook a moment, then gradually whisk in the remaining 1½ cups of milk. Add the salt, pepper, nutmeg, and mace. Cook the sauce for about 10 minutes, stirring often, until it begins to thicken. Meanwhile, cook the pasta in the boiling water until al dente.

Add the sweet potato puree and the vermouth to the white sauce and heat through. Drain the fettuccine well and place in a large, warmed serving bowl. Toss with the sweet potato sauce and arrange the grilled red pepper strips over the top. Serve immediately, passing Parmesan cheese, if desired.

Each serving provides:

473	Calories	81 g	Carbohydrate
15 g	Protein	159 mg	Sodium
9 g	Fat	89 mg	Cholesterol
5 g	Dietary Fiber		

Grilled Sweet Potatoes

ALMOST INSTANT

Have you ever wondered what to do with sweet potatoes in the summertime? The grill is the answer. This preparation is very easy and most delicious. Serve them hot with any grilled entrée, or at room temperature as a finger-food appetizer.

Yield: 6 side-dish servings

Red-skinned sweet potatoes	2	**pounds (4 medium)**
Olive oil	1	**tablespoon**
Granulated garlic	¼	**teaspoon**
Lowfat sour cream	¼	**cup**
Paprika	¼	**teaspoon**

Preheat a coal or gas grill to medium-high. (To preheat a coal grill, start the charcoal at least 15 to 20 minutes before cooking begins, so the proper temperature can be achieved in time. The grill is ready when the coals are glowing red and a small amount of gray ash is present on them. Preheat a gas grill for at least 10 minutes, or according to the manufacturer's specific instructions.)

Scrub the potatoes, but do not peel them. Slice crosswise into ½-inch disks. Use your hands to rub the oil on the potato slices. Sprinkle one side of the slices with half of the granulated garlic and place garlic side down on the grill. Cover the grill and cook for 3 minutes, then sprinkle with the remaining garlic, turn, and continue to cook for 3 minutes. Turn and cook an additional 3 minutes on each side. Arrange the potato slices on a warm platter and dollop a small amount of sour cream on top of each. Sprinkle with the paprika and serve immediately.

Each serving provides:

191	Calories	38 g	Carbohydrate
3 g	Protein	28 mg	Sodium
3 g	Fat	3 mg	Cholesterol
5 g	Dietary Fiber		

Sesame Sweet Potato Sauté with Hijiki

VEGAN

What a marvelous way to enjoy sweet potatoes! Don't let the exotic combination deter you—it is rich and absolutely delicious, particularly with a teriyaki dish or another Japanese entrée. Hijiki is a dried seaweed available at Asian markets and some natural food stores.

Yield: 6 side-dish servings

Dried hijiki seaweed	⅓	cup (about ⅓ ounce)
Raw sesame seeds	1	teaspoon
Red-skinned sweet potatoes	1¼	pounds (2 large)
Canola oil	1	tablespoon
Dark sesame oil	1	tablespoon
Salt		A pinch
Cayenne		A pinch
Low-sodium soy sauce	2	tablespoons
Mirin	2	tablespoons
Green onions	2,	minced

Rinse the hijiki briefly under cold running water, then place it in 2 cups of warm water and soak for 30 minutes. Rinse again and drain well.

Meanwhile, toast the sesame seeds in a dry, heavy-bottomed skillet over medium heat, stirring or shaking the pan frequently, until they are lightly browned and emit a wonderful roasted aroma. Immediately remove from the pan and set aside.

Peel the sweet potatoes, cut crosswise into ¼-inch slices, then cut the slices into ¼ inch strips. Heat the oils together in a heavy-bottomed skillet or wok with a tight-fitting lid over medium heat. When the oil is hot enough to sizzle a piece of sweet potato, add the sweet potato strips to the pan, along with the salt and cayenne, and stir. Sauté, stirring frequently, for 5 minutes. Add the hijiki and continue to sauté, stirring frequently, 3 minutes.

Meanwhile, combine the soy sauce and mirin with ¼ cup water in a small bowl. Holding the lid of the skillet in one hand, add the soy sauce mixture to the sweet potatoes and immediately cover the pan. Reduce heat to low and cook for 4 minutes. Remove the lid, increase the heat to medium-high, and cook, stirring constantly, until almost all the liquid is gone—about 2 to 3 minutes. Transfer to a warmed bowl and serve hot, sprinkled evenly with the green onions and toasted sesame seeds.

Each serving provides:

136	Calories	20 g	Carbohydrate
2 g	Protein	252 mg	Sodium
5 g	Fat	0 mg	Cholesterol
2 g	Dietary Fiber		

Sweet Potato and Pear Puree
with Butter, Rum, and Nutmeg

*The sautéed pears, honey, and nutmeg bring out the sweetness of the
potatoes, with the rum providing the counterpoint. We think you'll
agree that this is a great variation on the sweet potato theme.*

Yield: 4 servings

Red-skinned sweet potatoes	¾	**pound (1 large)**
Pears	¾	**pound (2 small)**
Unsalted butter	1	**tablespoon**
Dark rum	2	**tablespoons**
Honey	½	**teaspoon**
Freshly grated nutmeg	1	**teaspoon**
Salt	⅛	**teaspoon**

Wash the sweet potatoes and cut them in half crosswise. Place
them in a saucepan with enough water to cover them completely
and bring to a boil. Cook for about 25 minutes, until they are
very soft all the way through. Remove from the water and set
aside to cool.

Meanwhile, peel the pears, cut them in half lengthwise,
and remove the cores. Dice the pears. Melt the butter in a
heavy-bottomed skillet over medium heat. Add the pears and
stir and sauté for 3 minutes, then add the rum and sauté
1 minute longer.

When sweet potatoes are cool enough to handle, peel them and place them in a food processor or blender. Add the sautéed pears, using a rubber spatula to scrape out all the pan juices. Add the nutmeg, honey, and salt and puree to a smooth consistency. Serve hot.

Each serving provides:

158	Calories	28 g	Carbohydrate
1 g	Protein	78 mg	Sodium
4 g	Fat	8 mg	Cholesterol
4 g	Dietary Fiber		

Sweet Potatoes Baked in Orange Sauce

This has become a traditional Thanksgiving recipe in our homes over the years. It is a wonderful alternative to the sticky-sweet brown sugar and marshmallow version.

Yield: 8 side-dish servings

Red-skinned sweet potatoes	3	**pounds (6 medium)**
Unsalted butter	2¼	**tablespoons**
Fresh-squeezed orange juice	½	**cup**
Orange peel, grated	½	**medium orange**
Cornstarch	1	**teaspoon**
Honey	½	**cup**
Freshly grated nutmeg	¼	**teaspoon**

Rinse the sweet potatoes and cut into large cubes. Place on a steamer rack in a large saucepan that has a tight-fitting lid. Add enough water to cover the bottom of the rack and bring to a boil over high heat. When the water boils, reduce heat to medium-high, cover, and cook for 25 to 30 minutes, until barely fork tender (they will finish cooking in the oven). Remove from the pan and allow to cool. Peel the sweet potatoes and cut them into ¼-inch slices. Using ¼ teaspoon of the butter, lightly rub a 9 × 13-inch (3-quart) glass baking dish. Arrange the slices in layers.

Preheat the oven to 350 degrees F. Melt the remaining 2 tablespoons of butter in a small saucepan and stir in the orange juice and peel. Whisk in the cornstarch, honey, and nutmeg. Bring to a boil over medium-high heat and cook several minutes, until thickened. Pour the sauce over the yams, cover, and bake 45 minutes. Serve steaming hot.

Each serving provides:

231	Calories	49 g	Carbohydrate
2 g	Protein	17 mg	Sodium
4 g	Fat	9 mg	Cholesterol
4 g	Dietary Fiber		

Tomatoes

The tomato is a native South American plant, discovered growing among the maize by the Incas. Initially, they considered it a weed, though eventually they discovered its usefulness. The Incas, as well as the Mayans and Aztecs, cultivated seeds, which were carried to Europe by explorers in the fifteenth or early sixteenth century.

The tomato received the nickname "love apple" because it was originally mistaken by the Spanish for an apple, and because of its aphrodisiac reputation. A resourceful Italian chef brought it from Spain to Florence, Italy, in the middle sixteenth century, where he called it *pomo d'oro* (apple of gold). This makes sense, considering the fact that early varieties were yellow.

Tomatoes were long believed by many Europeans and by American settlers to be poisonous, and they were not eaten extensively until the nineteenth century. Thomas Jefferson is thought to have been the first American to plant tomatoes; nevertheless, they remained uncommon until the late 1800s.

Though botanically a berry, the tomato—*Lycopersicum esculentum*—is used as a vegetable. Indeed, the Supreme Court officially proclaimed it a vegetable in 1893 as the result of a tariff dispute. This member of the nightshade family includes thousands of varieties, ranging from marble-size cherry tomatoes to hefty beefsteaks, and from red to yellow and even white.

The tomato is the third most popular supermarket vegetable, and the single most popular vegetable for home gardens. If you have never tasted one from a farm stand or backyard vine, you are in for a special treat. A bonus for home tomato growers is the crop of tart green tomatoes at the end of the season that are delicous stuffed or sautéed.

By the way, tomatillos (little tomatoes), the lemony-flavored husk tomatoes common to Mexican cuisine, are also nightshades, but are quite distinct from the common garden tomato.

The Nutrition Picture

Tomatoes provide considerable quantities of potassium, as well as beta carotene and vitamins A and C. Though they contain only half as much vitamin C, by weight, as oranges, tomatoes are the leading plant source of vitamin C in the American diet, by virtue of the quantities we consume. They are low in fat and sodium.

Selection and Storage

Tomatoes are at their best in the summer and early fall. Winter producers, like Florida and Latin America, have developed thick-skinned varieties that ship well, but lack flavor, so we enjoy as many fresh tomatoes in season as possible. The tomato is grown commercially in almost every state and is the most common greenhouse vegetable in the United States. Thousands of varieties are known, but typically you will find only cherry, pear (or plum), and round slicing tomatoes in the markets.

Select tomatoes that are plump, heavy, smooth-skinned, and unbruised. A sweet tomato fragrance should be noticeable.

Pinkish tomatoes may be acceptable if not mushy, but they will need a few days of ripening at home before using. Hold unripe tomatoes at room temperature, but out of the sun, or they may scorch in spots. If you place them in a paper bag with a banana or apple, the gas emitted by the other fruit will hasten the tomato's ripening.

Once tomatoes have turned a uniform bright red color, use them immediately or refrigerate for several days, but for the best flavor return them to room temperature before serving.

A wide variety of tomato products is available canned and they are good items to keep on hand in the pantry. We prefer low-sodium brands. Canned tomatoes can be successfully substituted for fresh in many cooked dishes during the winter months or when time is extremely short.

Culinary Tips

- Wash tomatoes gently in cold water and dry before serving.
- Add raw tomatoes to salad at the last moment; exposure to salt will draw out their moisture and will water down your dressing.
- When possible, cook tomatoes in a cast-iron pan. Tomato acids will react with the minerals in the pan, increasing the iron content of the dish.

- To remove the seeds from a raw tomato, cut in half cross-wise and squeeze gently over the compost pail or garbage can to dislodge the seed pockets.
- Ripe tomatoes can be chopped and frozen for use over the winter or made into a sauce for canning or freezing.
- Plum or pear tomatoes are less juicy, have fewer seeds, and are meatier than round slicing varieties, making them ideal for use in sauces.
- If peeling is called for, first blanch the tomato in boiling water for about 1 minute, then immerse it in cold water. When cool enough to handle, peel off the skin.
- Dried tomatoes have an intensified flavor and a chewy texture. Different varieties are available—the driest ones may be extremely tough and should be reconstituted before using. Place them in a small bowl and cover with hot water for 15 to 30 minutes. Drain, reserving the liquid for soup stock, if desired.
- As a rule of thumb, one medium tomato weighs ½ pound.

Crostini with Topping of Tomatoes, Fresh Basil, Garlic, and Capers

ALMOST INSTANT, VEGAN

Crostini is nothing more than toast, but it must be made with an excellent fresh bread. We have classified this as a side-dish because it works well as the salad course of any Mediterranean-inspired summer feast. However, we often make a light meal of it, with the addition of fresh mozzarella cheese and a fruity Italian red wine. There is one cardinal rule here—you must use vine-ripened, round salad tomatoes and basil leaves that are fresh from the plant. You may adjust the amount of garlic to your liking—several large cloves would not be too much for a garlic lover.

Yield: 6 side-dish servings

Tomatoes	1½	pounds (3 medium)
Fresh basil leaves	1	cup, firmly packed
Garlic	3	cloves, minced
Capers, drained	2	tablespoons
Olive oil	2	tablespoons
Fresh-squeezed lemon juice	2	teaspoons
Salt	¼	teaspoon
Pepper		Several grinds
Fresh sourdough baguette	1	1-pound loaf

Cut the tomatoes in half crosswise and squeeze out the seed pockets. Cut out the stems and discard them. Dice the tomatoes uniformly. Wash and dry the basil leaves and mince them with a sharp knife. Toss with the tomatoes in a bowl. Add the garlic, capers, olive oil, lemon juice, salt, and pepper and stir to combine well. Set aside in the refrigerator to chill.

Preheat the broiler. Cut the baguette crosswise into ½-inch slices and arrange the slices in a single layer on the broiler pan. Broil about 2 minutes per side, until the bread is lightly browned and crisp on the outside. Alternately, you may toast the bread slices on a hot grill. (Crostini may be made several hours or a day ahead of time, and held at room temperature in a loosely closed paper bag.)

Set out the tomato mixture in a shallow serving dish and serve the crostini alongside in a basket. Diners serve themselves, mounding the topping onto the bread and devouring one slice at a time.

Each serving provides:

281	Calories	47 g	Carbohydrate
8 g	Protein	635 mg	Sodium
7 g	Fat	0 mg	Cholesterol
3 g	Dietary Fiber		

Tomatoes with Fresh Dill

ALMOST INSTANT, VEGAN

Garden-fresh tomatoes, with their vine-ripened sweetness, are the preferred choice for this salad. If you do not have a garden, buy tomatoes from a farm stand or allow purchased tomatoes to sit at room temperature for several days to fully ripen (see page 326). You may use either globe or pear tomatoes.

Yield: 8 side-dish servings

Tomatoes	2	pounds (4 medium)
Red onion, minced	¼	cup
Fresh basil leaves, minced	2	tablespoons
Fresh dill weed, minced	2	tablespoons
Fresh parsley, minced	2	tablespoons
Olive oil	3	tablespoons
White wine vinegar	2	tablespoons
Granulated garlic	½	teaspoon
Salt	½	teaspoon
Pepper		Several grinds

Remove the stem ends and slice or quarter the tomatoes. Put them in a bowl with the onion, basil, dill, and parsley. Toss gently to coat the tomatoes with the herbs. Whisk together the oil, vinegar, garlic, salt, and pepper. Pour the dressing over the tomatoes and toss again. Serve immediately, or cover and chill for up to several hours, but return to room temperature before serving.

Each serving provides:

71	Calories	6 g	Carbohydrate
1 g	Protein	147 mg	Sodium
5 g	Fat	0 mg	Cholesterol
1 g	Dietary Fiber		

Cherry Tomato Sauté with Golden Raisins, Shallots, and Blackberries

ALMOST INSTANT, VEGAN

This simple and succulent sauté is like a hot chutney and makes a quintessential summer side dish or topping for grilled fish. The berries must be at their peak of sugar for best results, so watch the market offerings and buy only the best (better yet, pick them yourself). The dish will be most beautiful if you combine red and yellow cherry tomatoes, but red only will work fine.

Yield: 4 side-dish serving

Cherry tomatoes	¾	pound
Olive oil	2	teaspoons
Shallots	2	medium, slivered
Golden raisins	3	tablespoons
Dry white wine	2	tablespoons
Salt		A pinch
Ripe blackberries	1	cup
Ground allspice	½	teaspoon
Pepper		Several grinds

Rinse and dry the cherry tomatoes. Remove their stems, but leave the tomatoes whole. Heat the olive oil in a heavy-bottomed skillet over medium heat. Add the shallots and sauté for a minute, then add the tomatoes, raisins, wine, and salt. Stir and sauté for about 6 minutes, until the tomatoes are beginning to soften. Add the blackberries, allspice, and pepper and cook, stirring gently, for no longer than 2 minutes. You want the berries to barely begin cooking so they will not release all their liquid. Transfer to a warmed serving bowl and serve hot or at room temperature.

Each serving provides:

86	Calories		15 g	Carbohydrate
1 g	Protein		43 mg	Sodium
3 g	Fat		0 mg	Cholesterol
3 g	Dietary Fiber			

Tomatoes and Couscous en Papillote with Sherry and Cilantro

VEGAN

The vibrant red, green, and white of this meal in a packet make a beautiful presentation. And that is just the beginning—the aromas and flavors are also sure to satisfy. Serve this as a main dish along with bread and cheese, or as a side dish with your favorite grilled entrée.

Yield: 4 main-dish servings

Pear tomatoes	2	pounds
Dry sherry	¼	cup
Granulated garlic	½	teaspoon
Ground cumin	¼	teaspoon
Mild chili powder	¼	teaspoon
Dried couscous	¾	cup
Shelled peas, fresh or frozen	1	cup
Green onions	4	
Fresh cilantro, minced	¼	cup
Parchment paper for baking	4	12 × 16-inch pieces

Blanch the tomatoes by immersing them in boiling water for 1 minute. Immediately plunge them into cold water. Peel the tomatoes when they are cool enough to handle and chop them coarsely, retaining their juices. Set them aside in a bowl.

Preheat the oven to 425 degrees F. Combine the sherry, ¼ cup water, granulated garlic, cumin, and chili powder in a small bowl and set aside. Fold each piece of parchment in half and crease to create 8 × 12-inch rectangles. Use scissors to cut each rectangle into a half-heart shape. Open out the hearts and place equal portions of couscous near the center of each crease. Top with equal portions of tomatoes along with their liquid, then with the peas. Cut the green onions into 1-inch lengths and distribute among the packets, along with the cilantro. Pour the sherry sauce equally over the vegetables and couscous. Close the heart so the edges of the paper meet. Beginning at the round end, fold over ½-inch of paper and crease sharply. Work your way around the shape of the heart, folding in the edges and creasing sharply in overlapping pleats. Twist the pointy end and seal everything tightly in the paper packet. Repeat this process for the remaining packets.

Place the packets in a single layer on a baking sheet and bake for 15 minutes. Place each packet on a warmed serving plate and instruct your guests to pinch and tear the paper to release the aromatic steam. The contents may then be lifted out onto the plate and the paper removed from the table and discarded.

Each serving provides:

235	Calories	45 g	Carbohydrate
9 g	Protein	30 mg	Sodium
1 g	Fat	0 mg	Cholesterol
3 g	Dietary Fiber		

Tomatoes Stuffed with Orzo, Fresh Fennel, and Gorgonzola

This is a lovely, refreshing, summer main course. We have enjoyed it as a special lunch break during hectic book production seasons. If you are making a dinner entrée of it, you may want to include grilled vegetables and a good bread and wine on the menu.

Yield: 4 main-dish servings

Dried orzo	½	cup
Tomatoes	2	pounds (4 medium)
Fresh fennel bulb, thinly sliced	1	cup
Gorgonzola cheese, crumbled	2	ounces (½ cup)
Fresh parsley, minced	¼	cup
Olive oil	1	tablespoon
Sherry vinegar	1	tablespoon
Garlic	1	clove, minced
Salt	⅛	teaspoon
Pepper		Several grinds

Bring 4 cups of water to a boil in a large saucepan. Add the orzo and cook for 10 minutes after the water returns to the boil. Meanwhile, use a small, sharp knife to slice off the stem end of the tomato, creating a large opening on top. Carve out the inside of each tomato with a sharp knife leaving a ¼-inch shell. Discard the seed pockets and mince the tomato flesh. Combine the minced tomato with the fennel, Gorgonzola, and parsley. Toss this mixture with the olive oil, then with the vinegar, garlic, salt, and pepper and set aside. When the orzo is cooked, rinse under cold water and drain very well. Add to the tomato mixture and toss until well distributed. Stuff the tomato shells with this mixture, and garnish each with a parsley or fennel sprig, if desired. Serve immediately or chill for a few hours, but return to room temperature before serving.

Each serving provides:

223	Calories	30 g	Carbohydrate
8 g	Protein	316 mg	Sodium
9 g	Fat	11 mg	Cholesterol
4 g	Dietary Fiber		

Broiled Tomato and Leek Soup with Peppercorns, Madeira, and Tarragon

This pretty soup would be a perfect starter course for a Southwestern-inspired feast, or serve it as a lunch entrée, enhanced by good bread and cheese, and perhaps a salad. Of course, you must use excellent, vine-ripened slicing tomatoes for best results. The sour cream is a marvelous addition, but is not essential. The broiler does a fine job of charring the vegetables, but you may use a hot grill, if you prefer.

Yield: 4 first-course servings

Tomatoes	3	pounds (6 medium)
Leeks	¾	pound (3 medium)
Madeira	¼	cup
Fresh tarragon leaves, minced	1	tablespoon
Pickled peppercorns, drained	2	teaspoons
Salt	¼	teaspoon
Sour cream	¼	cup
Nutmeg, freshly grated		Several grinds

Preheat the broiler. Cut the tomatoes in half crosswise and squeeze gently to remove the seed pockets. Arrange the tomato halves cut side up on a broiler pan. Remove the root end and most of the green portion of the leeks, then cut them in half lengthwise. Clean carefully under a stream of cold running water to remove any dirt that is lodged between the layers. Arrange the leek halves cut side up alongside the tomatoes. Broil for 15 to 20 minutes, until well charred and softened. Check every 5 minutes, removing leek strips as they char and rearranging the vegetables so they will char evenly. When the cut surfaces are well charred, use tongs to carefully remove the tomatoes to a plate—you want to retain their juice, so try to spill as little as possible. Set the tomatoes and leeks aside separately to cool.

When cool enough to handle, pull the skins off the tomatoes as you scrape the pulp into a bowl. Cut out and discard the stems. Mash the pulp well to break up any large chunks and transfer half the tomato pulp to a blender jar, along with any juices that have collected on the plate. Add the Madeira, tarragon, peppercorns, and salt and puree to a smooth consistency. Place the tomato puree and remaining tomato pulp in a large saucepan. Mince the broiled leeks, including the blackened parts, and stir into the tomatoes. Heat through over medium heat and serve in warmed bowls, topped with a dollop of sour cream and a good grind of nutmeg.

Each serving provides:

143	Calories	22 g	Carbohydrate
4 g	Protein	216 mg	Sodium
4 g	Fat	6 mg	Cholesterol
4 g	Dietary Fiber		

Fresh Tomato Oregano Sauce
with Fusilli and Zucchini

VEGAN

This quick and light sauce takes advantage of the summer garden's bounty of pear tomatoes and fresh herbs. It is delicious served with pasta, as in this recipe, but can also be used as an ingredient in other recipes where tomato sauce is called for. To enjoy this year-round, you may substitute one fifteen-ounce can of pear tomatoes and one and one-half teaspoons dried oregano for the fresh. In the wintertime, the chives are optional.

Yield: 4 main-dish servings

Fresh pear tomatoes	1½	pounds
Olive oil	1	tablespoon
Yellow onion	1	small, minced
Garlic	2	cloves, minced
Fresh lemon	1	slice
Fresh oregano leaves	1	tablespoon
Fresh chives, minced	1	tablespoon
Dry white wine	½	cup
Salt	⅛	teaspoon
Pepper		A few grinds
Dried pasta spirals	8	ounces
Zucchini	1	cup, diced

Blanch the tomatoes by immersing them in boiling water for 1 minute. Immediately plunge them into cold water. Retain the blanching water. Peel the tomatoes when they are cool enough to handle, and cut each one in half crosswise. Gently squeeze to remove the seed pockets. Coarsely chop the tomatoes.

Heat the olive oil in a large skillet and sauté the onion and garlic for a minute or two. Add the tomatoes and lemon. Simmer over low heat 15 minutes, then crush the tomatoes with a wooden spoon and stir in the herbs, wine, salt, and pepper. Continue to cook until reduced to a chunky sauce consistency. This should take no more than 10 minutes.

Meanwhile, bring the tomato blanching water back to a boil and cook the pasta until al dente, adding the zucchini for the last 3 minutes of cooking time. Drain well and toss with the hot tomato sauce. Serve immediately, passing Parmesan cheese, if desired.

Each serving provides:

312	Calories	54 g	Carbohydrate
9 g	Protein	91 mg	Sodium
5 g	Fat	0 mg	Cholesterol
4 g	Dietary Fiber		

Cinnamon Tomato Lasagnette

Lasagnette noodles, or mafalda, are narrow, long ribbons resembling skinny lasagna noodles. Look for them in well-stocked supermarkets or Italian specialty stores. Bake this casserole in a glass dish or, for a particularly pretty presentation, in individual oval baking dishes, decreasing the cooking time by five minutes. The ranchero cheese is a dry, crumbly variety; if you cannot locate it, substitute ricotta.

Yield: 6 main-dish servings

Peeled and crushed pear tomatoes	1	28-ounce can
Yellow onion	½	medium, chopped
Garlic	3	cloves, minced
Ground cinnamon	½	teaspoon
Mild chili powder	½	teaspoon
Ground cumin	½	teaspoon
Dry mustard		Scant ⅛ teaspoon
Ground cloves		Scant ⅛ teaspoon
Dried lasagnette noodles	8	ounces
Firm-style tofu	8	ounces
Part-skim ranchero cheese crumbled	8	ounces (2 cups)
Plain nonfat yogurt	½	cup
Fresh basil leaves, minced	3	tablespoons
Olive oil	¼	teaspoon
Parmesan cheese, finely grated	¼	cup

Bring several quarts of water to a boil for the pasta. Use a large pan as these noodles require lots of movement for even cooking and to prevent sticking. Place the tomatoes, onion, and garlic in a blender or food processor and puree until smooth. Pour the mixture into a medium saucepan and add the cinnamon, chili powder, cumin, mustard, and cloves. Cook over medium-low heat for about 10 minutes, stirring frequently.

Preheat the oven to 350 degrees F. Cook the pasta until almost al dente. It will finish cooking in the oven. Rinse the tofu, cut it into ½-inch slices, and pat dry. Crumble the tofu into a bowl and combine with the ranchero cheese, yogurt, and basil. Drain the noodles and lay out to dry on a tea towel. Rub a 9 × 9 × 2-inch pan with the olive oil and spread half the sauce evenly over the bottom. Layer with half the noodles, and spread evenly with the tofu-cheese mixture. Top with the remaining noodles and sauce. Sprinkle with the Parmesan cheese, cover, and bake 20 minutes. Uncover and bake 5 minutes longer. Serve hot.

Each serving provides:

312	Calories	41 g	Carbohydrate
19 g	Protein	351 mg	Sodium
8 g	Fat	15 mg	Cholesterol
2 g	Dietary Fiber		

Winter Squash

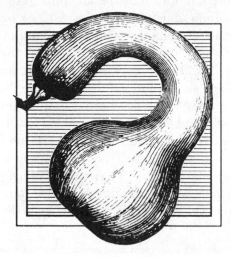

Like their summer counterparts, most winter squashes are ancient Native American foods. Cave relics in Mexico date them as far back as 3000 B.C. Winter squashes became a staple of colonial Americans because of their abundance and long storage time. Spaghetti squash is a more recent variety, however. It was originally developed in Italy, and traveled from there to Japan and eventually to America.

Winter squashes belong to the botanical species *Cucurbita maxima,* part of the gourd family. The pumpkin has the same botanical name as summer squash—*Cucurbita pepo*—but is discussed in this chapter because its consistency and cooking methods more closely resemble those of winter squash varieties.

Winter squashes stay on the plant for a long time, developing a hard, inedible skin, large, mature seeds, and a pronounced sweetness in the pulp. They become sweeter the longer they stay on the vine.

The Nutrition Picture

Winter squashes deliver more nutrients than summer varieties. Though the nutrition picture varies among the different types, most are excellent sources of complex carbohydrates, vitamin C, and fiber. In addition, they contain considerable beta carotene, which continues to develop after harvest.

Selection and Storage

As the name implies, the peak season for winter squashes is fall and winter. They can be stored for months, however, so are generally in good supply year-round.

Winter squash comes in many shapes, colors, and sizes. The acorn squash is vertically ridged, pointy-ended, and uniformly orange in color, or deep green with orange patches. The butternut is an elongated pear shape and is smooth-skinned and tan; some varieties have stripes. The spaghetti squash is smooth-skinned, pale yellow, and oblong. The hubbard has bumpy skin, is usually orange or dark green, and the average size range is about 5 to 15 pounds. Hubbards are frequently offered in the market already cut into more manageable weights. Turban, kabocha, and delicata are some other interesting varieties, though they are usually found only in specialty markets.

The familiar, much-loved pumpkin, though botanically a summer squash, is available only in the autumn. Almost all domestic pumpkins are a variety bred for size and are purchased for use as Halloween jack-o'-lanterns. Small pumpkins are superior for cooking as they are less stringy. Stored in a cool place, pumpkins will last for at least a month if their skin is intact. Once cut, they tend to develop mold rapidly, so use up as soon as possible.

Select winter squashes that are not bruised or blemished, and check carefully for mold and mushy spots. All winter squashes should be heavy for their size—lightness probably indicates a dry, stringy interior. Except in the case of spaghetti squash, which is a uniform pale yellow, good quality winter squashes have a rich, deep color. All should have dull, not shiny, surfaces. Select winter squashes with their stems intact, if possible. The stems should be firmly attached and dry, not black or damp.

Winter squash will keep for up to three months in a cool, dark place. When buying cut squash, look for deep color and dense flesh. Tightly wrapped in plastic and stored in the refrigerator, cut squash will stay fresh for up to a week.

Culinary Tips

- Rinse and dry squashes, and use a heavy knife or cleaver to cut them. Remove the seeds and pithy membranes before cooking.

- Large squashes with particularly thick rinds are easier to cut if you first make a shallow slit to guide the knife and keep it from slipping. Then place the blade in the slit and use whatever force is necessary to push the blade through the squash—a mallet or hammer could be called into service, if necessary. Hard-shell squashes are sometimes easier to peel after cooking, or you can cut the rind off before chopping the flesh.

- Spaghetti squash has a mild taste and crisp texture, and separates into individual, pastalike strands when cooked. Its flavor is delicate, so combine it with mild sauces and seasonings.

- Though winter squashes can generally be substituted one for the other in recipes, their flavors and textures are quite distinct from each other. The texture of a butternut squash, for instance, might be similar enough to pumpkin to substitute in a pie, but the flavor will be quite different. Spaghetti squash is in a class by itself, and substituting another variety for it in recipes would be disastrous.
- Raw pumpkin seeds are high in protein and can be oven roasted and hulled for snacks. Toasted hulled pumpkin seeds make a nice crunchy addition to sweet or savory dishes.

Grilled Butternut Squash Soup with Fresh Shiitake Mushrooms

This exotic-tasting soup combines the sweetness of winter squash with the woody richness of shiitake mushrooms. Wood chips added to the grill accentuate the earthy flavor. Delicious!

Yield: 4 main-course servings

Hickory or apple wood chips	1	**cup**
Butternut squash	1	**pound**
Canola oil	1	**teaspoon**
Fresh shiitake mushrooms	¼	**pound**
Dark sesame oil	1	**teaspoon**
Mirin	1	**tablespoon**
Garlic	2	**cloves, minced**
Homemade Vegetable Stock*	2½	**cups**
Salt	⅛	**teaspoon**
Pepper		**Several grinds**
Lowfat milk	2½	**cups**
Dried pastina	⅓	**cup**
Fresh cilantro, minced	¼	**cup**

Place the wood chips in a bowl and cover them with water. Set aside to soak for at least 15 minutes. Preheat the grill to medium. (To preheat a coal grill, start the charcoal at least 15 to 20 minutes before cooking begins, so the proper temperature can be achieved in time. The grill is ready when the coals are glowing red and they are nearly covered with gray ash. Pre-

---

*If you do not have Homemade Vegetable Stock on hand, make up a batch according to the directions on page 12, or dissolve ½ of a large, low-sodium vegetable broth cube in 2½ cups of hot water.

heat a gas grill for at least 10 minutes, or according to the manufacturer's specific instructions.) Drain the wood chips and place them on the coals just before grilling the squash.

Cut the squash in half lengthwise and lightly rub the skin side with ½ teaspoon of the canola oil. Place the squash on the grill, skin side down, close the lid of the grill, and cook for 20 minutes. Remove from the grill, brush cut side with the remaining oil, and place back on the grill, cut side down. Close the grill lid and cook for about 10 minutes longer, until soft. When cool enough to handle, remove the pulp from the skin and puree it in a food processor.

Wash the mushrooms, remove their stems, and cut them in half. Slice the halves into bite-size pieces. Place the sesame oil and mirin in a large skillet over medium heat. Add the garlic and cook for 1 minute, then stir in the mushrooms. Cook, stirring occasionally, about 5 minutes, until they are limp.

Combine the stock with the pureed squash, salt, pepper, and mushrooms in a stockpot over medium-high heat. When the mixture begins to simmer, stir in the pastina. Cook for 6 minutes, stirring frequently. Stir in the milk and cilantro and cook for about 4 more minutes, until the pastina is tender.

Each serving provides:

216	Calories	32 g	Carbohydrate
9 g	Protein	178 mg	Sodium
6 g	Fat	12 mg	Cholesterol
1 g	Dietary Fiber		

Linguine Verde with Spaghetti Squash and Fresh Sage

This readily available squash is often overlooked by cooks. It requires a different cooking technique than most winter squashes. This dish highlights its unique texture and flavor with sage and nutmeg. Linguine verde is available in most grocery stores and adds a nice color contrast. However, if it is not available, regular semolina pasta may be substituted. Despite the long cooking time, this recipe comes together very easily.

Yield: 6 main-course servings

Raw, unsalted pecans, chopped	⅓	cup
Spaghetti squash	3	pounds
Unsalted butter	2	tablespoons
Dry sherry	¼	cup
Garlic	3	cloves, minced
Fresh sage, minced	2	tablespoons
Lowfat milk	1	cup
Dried linguine	12	ounces
Parmesan cheese, finely grated	½	cup
Freshly grated nutmeg	¼	teaspoon

Toast the pecans in a dry, heavy-bottomed skillet over medium-high heat. Stir or shake the pan frequently until nuts are browning and emit a roasted aroma. Remove immediately from the pan and set aside.

Preheat the oven to 350 degrees F. Cut the squash in half lengthwise and scrape out the seeds. Lay each half cut side down in a glass baking dish and add water to measure 1 inch. Bake, uncovered, 45 to 50 minutes, until fork tender. Remove the squash from the pan and allow it to cool slightly. Scrape the "spaghetti" from the shell and set it aside.

Melt the butter in a large skillet over medium heat. Add the sherry, garlic, and sage. Sauté for a minute or two, then stir in the spaghetti squash and milk. Cook, covered, for 30 minutes, strirring occasionally. Add the cheese and nutmeg to the squash during the last few minutes of cooking time and stir to combine.

Meanwhile, bring several quarts of water to a boil in a stockpot and cook the pasta until al dente. Drain the pasta well and place it in a warmed serving bowl. Top with the squash and sprinkle with the toasted pecans. Serve immediately.

Each serving provides:

406	Calories	59 g	Carbohydrate
13 g	Protein	178 mg	Sodium
12 g	Fat	19 mg	Cholesterol
2 g	Dietary Fiber		

Acorn Squash Stuffed with Curried Couscous and Chilies

This is a departure from the routine seasonings used with winter squashes. The curry and chilies pair well with the sweetness of the tender, baked squash.

Yield: 4 main-course servings

Ground turmeric	1	teaspoon
Ground cumin	1	teaspoon
Fresh ginger, grated	1	teaspoon
Ground coriander	½	teaspoon
Granulated garlic	½	teaspoon
Cayenne	¼	teaspoon
Dried couscous	½	cup
Green onion	2,	minced
Acorn squash	2½	pounds (2 medium)
Canned diced green chilies	1	4-ounce can
Plain nonfat yogurt	½	cup
Unsweetened coconut milk	½	cup
Fresh-squeezed lemon juice	2	tablespoons

Put 1½ cups of water in a small saucepan and add the turmeric, cumin, ginger, coriander, garlic, and cayenne. Bring to a boil and stir in the couscous and green onion. Cover, remove from the heat, and let stand 5 minutes.

Meanwhile, preheat the oven to 375 degrees F. Cut the squashes in half and scoop out the seeds. Stir the chilies, yogurt, coconut milk, and lemon juice into the cooked couscous. Stuff the cavity of each squash with ¼ of the mixture and place the stuffed squash halves in a glass baking dish. Add hot water to a depth of 1 inch, then bake, covered, for 50 minutes. Serve immediately.

Each serving provides:

247	Calories	44 g	Carbohydrate
7 g	Protein	55 mg	Sodium
7 g	Fat	1 mg	Cholesterol
6 g	Dietary Fiber		

Stewed Winter Squash with Tomatoes, Chard, and Pine Nuts

VEGAN

Mediterranean seasonings with winter squash is an unusual combination in this country, but we guarantee you will enjoy this succulent dish. As a bonus, it is packed with health-enhancing nutrients. Its beta carotene level alone is enough to make it worth eating often.

Yield: 6 side-dish servings

Pine nuts	2	tablespoons
Acorn squash	1¼	pounds (1 medium)
Red onion	1	large
Swiss chard	1	pound
Olive oil	1	tablespoon
Garlic	3	cloves, minced
Dried oregano	2	teaspoons
Dried red chili flakes	¼	teaspoon
Salt	½	teaspoon
Homemade Vegetable Stock°	1¼	cups
Fresh pear tomatoes	½	pound, diced
Balsamic vinegar	2	tablespoons

Toast the pine nuts in a dry, heavy skillet over medium-high heat. Stir or shake the pan frequently to prevent scorching. Nuts are done when they are lightly browned and emit a roasted aroma. Immediately remove from the pan, mince them, and set aside.

°If you do not have Homemade Vegetable Stock on hand, make some according to the directions on page 12, or dissolve ½ of a large, low-sodium vegetable broth cube in 1¼ cups of hot water.

Cut the acorn squash in half and scoop out and discard the seeds. Slice off and discard the tough rind portion, and coarsely chop the squash. Coarsely chop the red onion. Carefully wash the chard and slice the stem portion. Do not dry the chard leaves; tear them into large pieces and set aside in a colander.

Heat the olive oil in a large, heavy-bottomed skillet with a tight-fitting lid over medium heat and sauté the garlic, oregano, and chili flakes for 1 minute. Add the squash, onion, chard stems, and salt, and sauté, stirring frequently, 5 minutes. Add the vegetable stock, cover, and cook 7 minutes. Remove the lid and stir in the tomatoes. Continue to cook, stirring frequently, 5 minutes.

Meanwhile, place the wet chard leaves in a saucepan over medium-low heat, cover, and cook 5 minutes, until they wilt. Make a bed of the chard on a warmed platter. Add the vinegar to the squash mixture and gently stir. Spoon the squash evenly over the chard and sprinkle with the pine nuts. Serve hot.

Each serving provides:

120	Calories	19 g	Carbohydrate
4 g	Protein	378 mg	Sodium
5 g	Fat	0 mg	Cholesterol
4 g	Dietary Fiber		

Simple Sauces and Vegetable Medleys

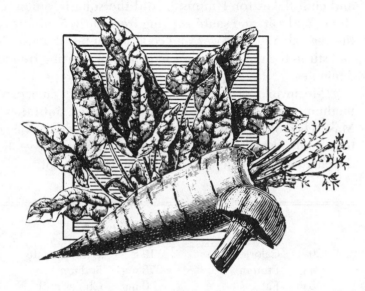

Vegetable side dishes appear on our tables daily. Sometimes we choose more elaborate preparations like those showcased in this book. Other times, however, we opt for ultra-simple steamed vegetables—one type alone or in colorful medleys.

These are delicious unsauced or seasoned simply with a squeeze of lemon, fresh or dried herbs, and a pinch of salt. Often, however, while the vegetables are steaming, we prepare an Almost Instant sauce as a topping. Some medley suggestions are provided here, along with recipes for our favorite sauces.

Curry Sauce with Mango Chutney

ALMOST INSTANT

Here is a sweet/hot sauce for any type of steamed vegetable to accompany other Middle Eastern dishes. You may make up a double batch and keep it in the refrigerator for up to a week.

Yield: ⅔ cup (about 10 servings)

Plain nonfat yogurt	½	**cup**
Curry powder	1	**teaspoon**
Mango Chutney (see page 18)	2	**tablespoons**

Whisk together the yogurt and curry powder, then stir in the chutney until well distributed. Prepare the sauce ahead of time, if possible, and set aside in the refrigerator so the flavors can blend. Remove from the refrigerator at least 15 minutes before serving to take the chill off. Spoon about 1 tablespoon over each side-dish vegetable serving.

Each tablespoon provides:

14	Calories	3 g	Carbohydrate
1 g	Protein	9 mg	Sodium
0 g	Fat	0 mg	Cholesterol
0 g	Dietary Fiber		

Dill Dijon Sauce

ALMOST INSTANT

This sauce is an excellent dip for artichokes, making enough for 8 servings, or about 20 servings when drizzled over other vegetables. We particularly enjoy it with steamed broccoli or asparagus. Leftover sauce will keep for at least a week in the refrigerator.

Yield: 1¼ cups (about 20 servings)

Plain nonfat yogurt	½	**cup**
Reduced-calorie mayonnaise	½	**cup**
Dijon mustard	1	**tablespoon**
Fresh-squeezed lemon juice	3	**tablespoons**
Fresh dill, minced	2	**tablespoons**
Granulated garlic	½	**teaspoon**

Place all of the ingredients in a bowl and whisk together until smooth. Serve the sauce in small ramekins with artichokes, or spoon about 1 tablespoon over each side-dish vegetable serving. Serve immediately, or refrigerate for up to a week.

Each tablespoon provides:

21	Calories	1 g	Carbohydrate
0 g	Protein	59 mg	Sodium
2 g	Fat	2 mg	Cholesterol
0 g	Dietary Fiber		

Tarragon Sauce with Mustard and Capers

ALMOST INSTANT, VEGAN

This is a lovely, slightly sweet Niçoise sauce. It is an especially good choice for cauliflower or green beans.

Yield: ½ cup (about 8 servings)

Dijon mustard	¼	cup
Honey	1	tablespoon
Tarragon white wine vinegar	1	tablespoon
Olive oil	2	tablespoons
Fresh tarragon leaves, minced	2	tablespoons
Capers	2	teaspoons, minced

Combine the mustard, honey, and vinegar in a bowl. Whisk in the oil, then stir in the tarragon and capers. Serve immediately, or refrigerate until needed. It will stay fresh for up to two weeks in the refrigerator. Spoon about 1 tablespoon over each side-dish vegetable serving.

Each tablespoon provides:

48	Calories	3 g	Carbohydrate
0 g	Protein	244 mg	Sodium
4 g	Fat	0 mg	Cholesterol
0 g	Dietary Fiber		

Simple Sauces and Vegetable Medleys

Horseradish Yogurt Sauce

ALMOST INSTANT

This tangy sauce combines some classic Eastern European flavors. It is delicious with the cruciferous vegetables; try it with steamed or braised cabbage.

Yield: ⅔ cup (about 10 servings)

Plain nonfat yogurt	½	**cup**
Fresh-squeezed lemon juice	2	**tablespoons**
Prepared horseradish	1	**teaspoon**
Paprika	½	**teaspoon**
Granulated sugar	½	**teaspoon**
Granulated garlic	¼	**teaspoon**
Green onions, diced	2	**tablespoons**

Whisk all ingredients together. Allow the flavors to combine in the refrigerator for about ½ hour, or heat slightly just before serving. This sauce can be made ahead of time, and will keep for up to a week in the refrigerator. Spoon about 1 tablespoon over each side-dish vegetable serving.

Each tablespoon provides:

9	Calories	2 g	Carbohydrate
1 g	Protein	9 mg	Sodium
0 g	Fat	0 mg	Cholesterol
0 g	Dietary Fiber		

The Best 125 Vegetable Dishes

Roasted Red Bell Pepper Sauce with Apple Juice and Brandy

ALMOST INSTANT, VEGAN

This is a terrific sauce for summer vegetables since it requires no cooking. You may use commercially roasted red bell peppers, which are packed in glass jars. The sauce will keep in the refrigerator for several weeks, so do not be intimidated by the quantity that this recipe makes.

Yield: 1½ cups (about 24 servings)

Roasted red bell pepper pulp	1	cup
Red onion, minced	¼	cup
Unsweetened apple juice	2	tablespoons
Brandy	1½	tablespoons
Fresh dill, minced	1	tablespoon
Garlic	1	clove, minced
Dried red chili flakes	¼	teaspoon
Ground cloves	⅛	teaspoon
Salt	⅛	teaspoon

Combine everything in a food processor and puree to a smooth sauce consistency. Make a few hours ahead of time and set aside in the refrigerator so the flavors can blend and return to room temperature before serving, or set aside at room temperature for up to 30 minutes while you prepare the rest of the meal. Spoon about 1 tablespoon over each side-dish vegetable serving.

Each tablespoon provides:

5	Calories	1 g	Carbohydrate
0 g	Protein	12 mg	Sodium
0 g	Fat	0 mg	Cholesterol
0 g	Dietary Fiber		

English Mint Sauce

VEGAN

This traditional British condiment, more liquid than thick, is especially good served over boiled new potatoes or shelled peas.

Yield: ½ cup (about 8 servings)

White distilled vinegar	½	**cup**
Honey	2	**tablespoons**
Salt		**A pinch**
Fresh mint leaves, minced	½	**cup**

Combine the vinegar, honey, and salt with ¼ cup water in a small saucepan. Bring just to a boil, reduce heat, and simmer uncovered for 5 minutes. Pour over the mint leaves in a glass bowl and allow to steep for 30 minutes. Strain the liquid, discarding most of the mint. Serve hot or cold, spooning about 1 tablespoon over each side-dish vegetable serving. Leftover sauce may be refrigerated for 2 to 3 weeks.

Each tablespoon provides:

19	Calories	5 g	Carbohydrate
0 g	Protein	17 mg	Sodium
0 g	Fat	0 mg	Cholesterol
0 g	Dietary Fiber		

The Best 125 Vegetable Dishes

Tofu Sesame Sauce

ALMOST INSTANT, VEGAN

This pureed tofu sauce has a velvety consistency and its flavor is Middle Eastern in character. It is especially good with steamed broccoli and cooked bulgur.

Yield: 1 cup (about 16 servings)

Soft-style silken tofu	**5**	**ounces**
Toasted sesame tahini	**2**	**teaspoons**
Low-sodium soy sauce	**2**	**teaspoons**
Honey	**1**	**teaspoon**
Cider vinegar	**2**	**tablespoons**
Granulated garlic	**½**	**teaspoon**

Combine all ingredients in a blender or food processor along with 1 tablespoon of water and puree to a smooth consistency. Serve immediately or keep in the refrigerator for several days. Spoon about 1 tablespoon over each side-dish vegetable serving.

Each tablespoon provides:

11	Calories	1 g	Carbohydrate
1 g	Protein	26 mg	Sodium
1 g	Fat	0 mg	Cholesterol
0 g	Dietary Fiber		

Spicy Far East Vinaigrette

ALMOST INSTANT, VEGAN

Originally developed as a dipping sauce for shrimp dumplings, this thin, intensely seasoned concoction is also delicious drizzled over cooked vegetables as part of a Far East feast.

Yield: ½ cup (about 8 servings)

Sake	3	tablespoons
Mirin	2	tablespoons
Rice wine vinegar	2	tablespoons
Low-sodium soy sauce	1	tablespoon
Dark sesame oil	1	teaspoon
Chili oil	½	teaspoon
Garlic	1	clove, minced

Whisk the ingredients together and set aside at room temperature so the flavors can blend. This sauce can be held in the refrigerator for up to 2 weeks—its flavor will intensify as it ages. For best results, return it to room temperature before serving. Spoon about 1 tablespoon over each side-dish vegetable serving.

Each tablespoon provides:

28	Calories	2 g	Carbohydrate
0 g	Protein	76 mg	Sodium
1 g	Fat	0 mg	Cholesterol
0 g	Dietary Fiber		

The Best 125 Vegetable Dishes

Creamy Oil and Vinegar with Fresh Basil

ALMOST INSTANT, VEGAN

We frequently make our own flavored oils and vinegars. If you have garlic-basil olive oil and vinegar, use them and omit the minced fresh basil for a subtle, but perfect sauce or dressing. Use a good, fruity olive oil to maximize the flavor. Serve over fresh tomatoes, grilled peppers, or your favorite salad greens.

Yield: ½ cup (about 8 servings)

Olive oil	¼	cup
White wine vinegar	2	tablespoons
Half-and-half	1	tablespoon
Granulated sugar	¼	teaspoon
Granulated garlic		Scant ⅛ teaspoon
Fresh basil leaves, minced	½	teaspoon

Whisk together the oil and vinegar. Add the half-and-half and whisk to combine, then whisk in the sugar, garlic, and basil. Any leftovers will keep in the refrigerator for several days. Bring back to room temperature before serving. Spoon about 1 tablespoon over each side-dish vegetable serving.

Each tablespoon provides:

63	Calories	0 g	Carbohydrate
0 g	Protein	1 mg	Sodium
7 g	Fat	1 mg	Cholesterol
0 g	Dietary Fiber		

Lemon Garlic Sauce

ALMOST INSTANT

This delicious sauce brings the flavors of Southern Italy to the dinner table. It combines wonderfully with green beans or Brussels sprouts.

Yield: ⅓ cup (about 12 servings)

Olive oil	3	**tablespoons**
Fresh-squeezed lemon juice	2	**tablespoons**
Garlic	2	**cloves, minced**
Salt		**A pinch**
Parmesan cheese, finely grated	3	**tablespoons**
Pepper		**Several grinds**

Whisk together the olive oil, lemon juice, garlic, and salt. Toss with cooked vegetables in the following ratio: 1 tablespoon of the sauce and 2 teaspoons of Parmesan cheese per 2 side-dish servings. Pass the pepper grinder.

Each serving provides:

37	Calories	0 g	Carbohydrate
1 g	Protein	34 mg	Sodium
4 g	Fat	1 mg	Cholesterol
0 g	Dietary Fiber		

Tex-Mex Vinaigrette with Orange Juice and Cilantro

ALMOST INSTANT, VEGAN

This fresh-tasting vinaigrette is delightful over steamed cauliflower, but it could be enjoyed over any vegetable accompanying a south-of-the-border meal. Also try this sauce as a salad dressing or marinade for cold vegetables.

Yield: ½ cup (about 8 servings)

Fresh-squeezed orange juice	¼	cup
Canola oil	2	tablespoons
Fresh-squeezed lime juice	1	tablespoon
Ground cumin	½	teaspoon
Chili powder	¼	teaspoon
Salt	⅛	teaspoon
Pepper		Several grinds
Fresh cilantro, minced	2	tablespoons
Red onion, grated	1	tablespoon

Whisk together the orange juice, oil, lime juice, cumin, chili powder, salt, and pepper. Stir in the cilantro and red onion. Toss with a bowl of steamed vegetables for 8, or spoon about 1 tablespoon over each side-dish vegetable serving. This sauce will keep for a week or longer in the refrigerator.

Each tablespoon provides:

35	Calories	1 g	Carbohydrate
0 g	Protein	36 mg	Sodium
3 g	Fat	0 mg	Cholesterol
0 g	Dietary Fiber		

Basic White Sauce

ALMOST INSTANT

*White sauce is a tried-and-true vegetable topping. It is simple to pre-
pare and can be seasoned any number of ways (some suggestions are
included below). Serving size will range between one and two tablespoons, depending on what vegetable is being served, in what quantity, and the composition of the rest of the meal. Experiment with
different combinations of seasonings to create your own favorites.*

Yield: ⅔ cup (about 6 servings)

Nonfat milk	**¾ cup**
Unsalted butter	**1 tablespoon**
Unbleached flour	**1 tablespoon**
Salt	**A pinch**
Pepper	**Several grinds**

Heat the milk in a small saucepan until steaming—do not simmer. Melt the butter in a saucepan over medium-low heat, then
stir in the flour and cook for about a minute, but do not let the
flour scorch. Add the hot milk in a slow, steady stream, whisking constantly until smoothly incorporated. Add salt and pepper.
Increase the heat to medium and cook for about 5 minutes,
until sauce has thickened up. Serve as is, or season as suggested
below.

Variations
- Season the roux by cooking about a teaspoon paprika, dry
  mustard, curry powder, or another favorite spice in the
  butter for a moment before adding the flour.
- Add a tablespoon of minced fresh tarragon, basil, dill, or
  another fresh herb toward the end of the cooking time.
  Consult the following chart for our preferred vegetable-
  herb combinations.

- For cheese sauce: When sauce has thickened, stir in ½ cup of grated cheese until melted and incorporated.
- For wine sauce: Just before serving, whisk in a tablespoon or two of dry white or red wine, sherry, port, or brandy.
- For mustard sauce: Whisk a tablespoon of Dijon mustard into the finished sauce.
- Try combinations of the above: For instance, wine sauce with fresh tarragon.

Each serving provides:

32	Calories	2 g	Carbohydrate
1 g	Protein	38 mg	Sodium
2 g	Fat	6 mg	Cholesterol
0 g	Dietary Fiber		

Herb and Spice Companions for Vegetables

Over time, you can explore different vegetable seasonings to find out what you like. Below, we present some of our preferences. You may use any of the recommended seasonings alone, or try combining two herbs in a dish, keeping in mind that intense flavors can overpower more subtle ones.

Artichokes: dill, curry powder, or mustard

Asparagus: dill or nutmeg

Avocado: chili powder, cilantro, or mustard

Beets: mustard, ginger, or caraway

Broccoli: nutmeg, oregano, or paprika

Brussels sprouts: dill, mustard, or celery seed

Cabbage: curry powder, dill, or celery seed

Carrots: anise, chives, or dill

Cauliflower: tarragon, cilantro, rosemary, or cumin

Corn: cumin, sage, or chili powder

Cucumber: dill, basil, mint, or chives

Eggplant: curry powder, basil, or oregano

Green beans: tarragon, ginger, or dill

Leeks: rosemary, mustard, or tarragon

Mushrooms: thyme, paprika, or nutmeg

Onions: sorrel, fennel seed, or curry powder

Peas: mint, tarragon, or ginger

Peppers: thyme, oregano, or cumin

Potatoes: dill, parsley, caraway, or chives

Spinach: nutmeg, mustard, or oregano

Summer squash: basil, cilantro, or anise seed

Sweet potatoes: cinnamon, cloves, nutmeg, or ginger

Tomatoes: dill, basil, chives, or oregano

Winter squash: sage, curry powder, or ginger

Steamed Vegetables

Time the steaming of vegetables to coincide with the completion of the rest of the meal. Place the vegetables on a steaming tray over a couple of inches of *cold* water in a lidded pot. At the appropriate time, turn on the burner to medium-high heat. We have provided in the table below a range of estimated steaming times. Set your timer for the beginning of the range, test the vegetables with a fork when the timer goes off, and continue to cook if you prefer a more tender consistency, testing again every minute or so.

Most vegetables taste best when cooked to the al dente stage, retaining some firmness, but easy to pierce with a fork. Overcooking makes some vegetables bitter or mushy, and can seriously deplete important nutrients.

Vegetable Steaming Times

Artichokes, whole	25–45 minutes
Asparagus	7–10 minutes
Beans, green	10–12 minutes
Beets, small, whole	12–18 minutes
Beets, medium, whole	20–30 minutes
Broccoli spears	8–12 minutes
Brussels sprouts, whole	12–18 minutes
Cabbage, 2-inch wedges	7–10 minutes
Carrots, ¼-inch slices	8–12 minutes
Cauliflower, medium, whole	16–20 minutes

Cauliflower, flowerets	8–12 minutes
Corn on the cob	8–10 minutes
Corn, fresh kernels	12–18 minutes
Onions, pearl	18–25 minutes
Peas, edible pod or fresh shelled	7–10 minutes
Potatoes, cubes	12–14 minutes
Rutabagas, cubed	15–20 minutes
Spinach and other greens	4–6 minutes
Summer squash, ¼-inch slices	7–10 minutes
Yams or sweet potatoes, 1-inch slices	15–20 minutes
Winter squash, cubed	20–30 minutes

Vegetable Medleys

Vegetables can be cooked together in innumerable combinations. Some of our favorites are listed below. Color, texture, and flavor are all important components of a successful medley. Experiment to discover favorites of your own.

When cooking medleys, start any vegetables that require a longer cooking time first and add the quicker-cooking ones as the clock counts down. As a general guideline, dense root vegetables require the most cooking, flower and seed pod vegetables like broccoli and green beans require a moderate cooking time, and leafy vegetables take the least time.

Classic Vegetable Medleys

- Broccoli and red bell peppers
- Cauliflower and carrots
- Green beans and mushrooms
- Peas and pearl onions
- Summer squash and bell peppers
- Potatoes and cabbage
- Corn and Swiss chard
- Eggplant and tomatoes
- Spinach and red onion

Index

Recipe titles appear in italic.

Index

Index

Photograph by Hope Harris.

Susann Geiskopf-Hadler and Mindy Toomay have been friends
and feasting companions since 1971. They reside with their husbands in Sacramento, California, where an abundance of fresh
vegetables, fruits, and seafood inspires their culinary efforts.

More **The Best 125** Cookbooks
by Mindy Toomay and Susann Geiskopf-Hadler

The Best 125 Meatless Pasta Dishes $12.95

Drawing on the cuisines of many nations, as well as the authors' seasoned imaginations, this book expands your sense of pasta's possibilities. With its emphasis on fresh ingredients and tantalizing flavors, this book proves we can eat less meat without sacrificing enjoyment. Recipes include Dried-Tomato Pesto with Mint, Savory Pumpkin and Pasta Soup, Spinach Lasagna with Port, and Tortellini Salad with Roasted Walnuts.

The Best 125 Meatless Main Dishes $12.95

A follow-up book to their instantly successful first book, Toomay and Geiskopf-Hadler once again team up to bring you another collection of tantalizing and healthful meatless meals. Their inventive dishes include Asparagus, Chevre, and Fresh Dill Baked in Filo Pastry; Risotto with Porcini, Fresh Basil, and Pine Nuts; Roasted Garlic, Red Pepper, and Ricotta Calzone with Fresh Basil; and much more!

The Best 125 Lowfat Fish and Seafood Dishes $14.95

Healthful and innovative, this cookbook offers intriguing new ways to enjoy fish and seafood at a time when their popularity as prime sources of delicious, lowfat protein is at an all-time high. Includes chapters on Fish and Seafood en Papillote, Seafood Pastas, Risotto and Rice dishes, and Main Course Salads, among others. Many of the recipes are "Almost Instant," requiring no more than 30 minutes to prepare.

FILL IN AND MAIL TODAY

Prima Publishing
P.O. BOX 1260BK
ROCKLIN, CA 95677

USE YOUR VISA/MC AND ORDER BY PHONE:
(916) 786-0426 (Mon.–Fri. 9–4 p.m. PST)

Dear People at Prima,
Please send me the following titles:

Quantity	Title	Amount
_____	_____	_____
_____	_____	_____
_____	_____	_____
_____	_____	_____
_____		

Subtotal	$	_____
Postage & Handling	$	3.95
7.25% Sales Tax (California only)	$	_____
TOTAL (U.S. funds only)	$	_____

☐ Check enclosed for $_____ (payable to Prima Publishing)

Charge my ☐ MasterCard ☐ Visa

Account No._____ Exp. Date _____

Signature _____

Your Name _____

Address _____

City/State/Zip _____

Daytime Telephone(   ) _____

SATISFACTION GUARANTEED!
Thank You for Your Order